TELEBOMB

The Truth Behind the $500-Billion Telecom Bust
and What the Industry Must Do to Recover

JOHN HANDLEY

AMACOM

AMERICAN MANAGEMENT ASSOCIATION

New York • Atlanta • Brussels • Chicago • Mexico City • San Francisco
Shanghai • Tokyo • Toronto • Washington, D.C.

This publication is designed to provide accurate and authoritative information in regard to the subject matter covered. It is sold with the understanding that the publisher is not engaged in rendering legal, accounting, or other professional service. If legal advice or other expert assistance is required, the services of a competent professional person should be sought.

Various names used by companies to distinguish their software and other products can be claimed as trademarks. AMACOM uses such names throughout this book for editorial purposes only, with no intention of trademark violation. All such software or product names are in initial capital letters or ALL CAPITAL letters. Individual companies should be contacted for complete information regarding trademarks and registration.

Library of Congress Cataloging-in-Publication Data

Handley, John, 1961–
    Telebomb : the truth behind the $500-billion telecom bust and what the industry must do to recover / John Handley.
        p.   cm.
    Includes index.
    ISBN 0-8144-0833-8 (hardcover)
    1. Telecommunication—United States.   2. Telecommunication—Deregulation—United States.   3. Telecommunication policy—United States.   4. United States. Telecommunications Act of 1996.   I. Title.

HE7775.H33   2005
384'.0973—dc22   2005005682

Printing number

10   9   8   7   6   5   4   3   2   1

To Elena, my life and my love.

CONTENTS

ACKNOWLEDGMENTS

The first ideas of what would become *Telebomb* began during a series of conversations I had with my friend and mentor Don Rippert during the summer of 2002. Even the title came from one of those conversations, although the idea came many gin-and-tonics into the evening, so my memory of which one of us coined the term is a bit fuzzy.

Don not only encouraged the ideas behind the book but he was the greatest of my mentors at Accenture, the technology and management consultancy. During the ten years I worked for him, he had the faith to send me, on my own, into new areas to make things happen. He let me have the freedom to find my own way, to make and fix my own mistakes, and to let me decide what route my career should take. He let me find a genuine definition of success that I believed in and used to the maximum benefit of Accenture and myself. Later generations of Accenture management may not have shared the same vision, but I feel that the ability to define my own path within the company built the most value for all.

When I thought it was time for me to leave Accenture, Don also had the courage to tell me in a straightforward manner that it was the right decision.

For that and so many other little things: Thanks, Don.

Special thanks are deserved by the crew at AMACOM Books for leading me through the publication process. Thanks especially to Jacquie Flynn and Barry Richardson for their big roles in making this project happen.

During the writing of this book, my wife, Elena Handley, was my firmest supporter. Even as the project wore on, she was at my side the whole time. She faithfully read every draft of every chapter, including each of the many rewrites. In addition to her support of the project in general, she lent me her perspective as a telecommunications novice, although she knows more about the subject than she thinks. After years of pretending to care about what I was looking at on the tops of the telephone poles around our neighborhood, I think she finally got a little perspective on what I did during my fifteen years at Accenture. My children still think I used to fly on airplanes for a living.

My sister, language person and news editor Beth Handley, also read early drafts of each chapter as they reached completion. Her perspective as an experienced copy editor and newspaper person gave me valuable insight into the reader's perspective. I am quite grateful to her and the experience she has gained during her career at the *Roanoke Times*.

Eddy Yager, my friend and former business partner, also rates special kudos for reading the entire manuscript under deadline. He trudged through the snow to meet me on more than one occasion. I thank him for giving me his time and for lending me his accumulated telecommunications industry experience.

The research and writing of this book were made much simpler and easier because of my Digital Filing Cabinet (DFC). I gathered thousands of pages of research material for *Telebomb,* all of which are safely indexed and stored away. The search and organization capability of the DFC covers all the research material, no matter what format or source. Where else could I find a tool that doesn't care where I am or whether it is searching though Word files, Excel spreadsheets, PowerPoint presentations, PDFs, images, faxed pages, or personal notes? Thanks to the crew at New Mexico Software and, in particular, NMXS's chief executive officer, Dick Govatski.

I have leaned on many of my former partners at Accenture for content reviews throughout the process. Rob Martin, Jack Sepple, Jim Arrison, and Annette Peterson have come through with their comments and support for the project.

Several people helped with the early research and visualization of this book. For their time and input, I would like to thank Vijay Venkateswaran and Wilson Randolph. Thanks also to my research assistant, Robert Ratcliffe.

To my many clients and colleagues from my time at Accenture, thanks for the interesting work, conversations, and support.

To my children, Laura, Alex, James, and Joe: I love you. Now go to bed.

Last and certainly not least, I would like to recognize Alex Dean for the fundamental role he had in making my career at Accenture a success. He opened many doors that I would later pass through on my way to the partnership. He embodied the concepts of client service and stewardship within the Accenture partnership that made it a great place to be for so many years.

While many have contributed to this work, and the completed work would be of lower quality without them, any mistakes or errors in the book remain mine.

INTRODUCTION

The notorious dot-com crash was heavily covered by the press, but a larger revolution was going on at the same time in the telecommunications industry and it received comparatively little attention. The telecommunications revolution followed a similar trajectory to the dot-com boom and bust, but it wasted more investor dollars and created much more havoc in the economy than the dot-coms. In fact, the "telebomb" likely wasted more real investor dollars than any—and possibly all—of the previous stock manias in the U.S. equity markets.

The dot-com wave broke and washed away the pretenders, leaving an industry populated by only a few strong companies. However, the telecommunications revolution has, through its ups and downs, touched most citizens in the United States. All are customers and many are investors in and/or employees of the industry. Even those who have not yet felt the changes brought on by the Internet revolution will do so in the next few years.

The overall cost of the crash in the telecommunications industry was staggering. More than $500 billion was lost because of overinvestment and ill-advised mergers. The network construction boom in the industry led to a spending bubble that consumed $220 billion above a steady-state investment rate within the industry that already approached $50 billion per year. The result of merger mania also brought losses to the industry. High-profile failed mergers such as AOL/Time Warner, Qwest/USWest, and AT&T's many cable acquisitions resulted in asset write-offs of nearly $300 billion.

WHAT CAUSED THE TELEBOMB?

How could so much money be wasted? Perhaps the first question should be: "How could so much money be raised in the first place?" Leading up to the telebomb, a unique combination of events occurred that have not been seen in telecommunications or any related industry in modern business history. The dot-com phenomenon was only one factor. It spawned both hype about the Internet and a resulting fascination in anything that had to do with the Internet. A related factor was the ease of obtaining capital to finance the foolish investments that many telecommunications carriers made. The ease of obtaining money not only was related to the dot-com euphoria sweeping the economy at the time but was also reflective of broader societal trends, most notably an economic expansion longer than any seen in recent memory.

Completing the predisaster trifecta, the U.S. Congress passed the Telecommunications Act of 1996, rewriting more than sixty years of federal regulation of the industry, destroying regulations that were admittedly unduly constraining, but not replacing them with any meaningful or consistent regulatory structures. The Federal Communications Commission—the arm of Congress that interprets, enacts, and enforces the Telecommunications Act—spent the next eight years stumbling in the dark trying to figure out just what the hell Congress meant. The many successful judicial challenges to the Federal Communications Commission's (FCC's) interpretation of the Telecommunications Act of 1996 created an ambiguity in the market that was, in many ways, worse than the regulations blown up by the act. Thus, the regulatory balance was ruled more by the lack of any specific new equilibrium point than by the creation of any new, procompetitive regulatory regime. From there the Law of Unintended Consequences took over. Loopholes were found and exploited by many overenthusiastic or unscrupulous entrepreneurs who used the lack of structure in the industry to fund business plans that had little chance of success, regardless of how many billions of dollars were spent on them.

Thus, the combination of the Internet, uncontrolled deregulation, and the easy money that the dot-com era brought with it created an environment in which billions of dollars could be thrown away. Investors gave money to corporate executives who chased the promise of the riches that the Internet age would bring. The Internet eventually would deliver on its promise, but not until well after many of these investments were written off.

While the pure dot-coms blew through the economy barely leaving a trace, many of the bankrupt telecommunications carriers were billion-dollar ventures. The telecom carriers were real companies with thousands of employees, 401(k)s, and retiree health plans. These carriers spent far more money than the nontelecommunications dot-coms that were chasing the dream of a new Internet-enabled world. In terms of money taken directly from investors and spent developing businesses that eventually failed, the telecommunications industry wasted far more investor dollars than the noncarrier dot-coms. In comparison, contrast the dollars actually spent and lost by pure dot-com companies with the losses of the carriers:

- Largest dot-com failure (Webvan)—$1.2 billion

- Small carrier failure (CoreExpress)—$0.6 billion

- Midsize carrier failure (Williams Communications)—$7 billion

- Large carrier failure (WorldCom)—more than $30 billion

COULD IT HAPPEN AGAIN?

An initial recovery was under way in 2003, but ominous clouds still hang over the telecommunications industry today. Broad shifts in consumer habits continue to wash away at the shores of the industry, changing the landscape in ways that have profound implications for how the industry, its customers, and its investors will perceive the industry for many years to come. These consumer trends resulted in multibillion-dollar asset writedowns in 2004 by the former Big 3 long-distance companies (AT&T, MCI, and Sprint). The sudden disappearance of financial assets marks an industry that is still in transition.

The write-off of obsolete assets in 2004 repeated a pattern last seen in the 1980s and early 1990s. The Big 3 long-distance carriers took huge writeoffs in the late 1980s when their older technology (analog transmission equipment in the 1980s) became obsolete. The Big 3's write-offs were followed by a similar devaluation of older assets by local telephone companies in the early 1990s. In 2004, the former Big 3 took the same steps to write down assets that could no longer produce revenue because of the significant changes in the business model of the industry. The local companies, particularly the former Bell companies, face the same challenge over the next five to ten years.

The continued uncertain and inconsistent regulation of the U.S. telecommunications industry, coupled with the increasing insinuation of the Internet into daily life in America, makes for an unpredictable future and another potential telebomb if not dealt with soon. The changes brought about by the Internet, although unsettling to those who do not like change, are for the most part desirable (although still in need of refinement). The regulatory picture, however, is a huge black cloud over the industry.

It is not only the inconsistency of how various regulations affect different segments of the market but also the fact that the FCC can't seem to find positions that can be defended once put under judicial scrutiny. Admittedly, the FCC was dealt a poor hand in the Telecommunication Act of 1996. However, the FCC's continued inability to exert control over the broad strokes of regulation of the telecommunications marketplace has the potential to relegate the FCC to the sidelines as a low-level administrative function during any future industry downturns, thereby taking a critical balancing agent off the field. The ineffectiveness of the FCC has continued through three different chairpersons appointed by both Democratic and Republican presidents.

WHAT THIS BOOK IS ABOUT

Telebomb tells the story of the telecommunications industry and how it moved from being a sleepy utility to a boom industry and Internet darling. This book is arranged in approximate chronological order, following each of the key trends that developed around the time of the passage of the Telecommunications Act of 1996 through to the crash. The winners and losers, both present and future, are analyzed and long-range prescriptions for the industry are explained.

The first tremors of the telebomb were felt around the time of AT&T's first divestiture in 1984. The industry recovered reasonably well from the disaggregation of the largest corporation in the United States and the move to a competitive long-distance market (unlike the airline industry, which was deregulated about the same time). However, several long-term changes that contributed to the telebomb began in the aftermath of divestiture.

The industry settled into a set of oligopolies in the local, long-distance, and cable segments of the industry in the late 1980s. However, as the 1990s dawned, influences from outside the industry presaged that the post-divestiture stasis was over. The stage was set for a new telecommunications environment by societal and economic changes, many of which drove demand for telecommunications services. For example, the North American Free Trade Agreement (NAFTA) eased the movement of goods (and jobs) between countries in North America. With these movements came an increased need for telecommunications.

Many executives outside the telecommunications industry were also honing their skills for the coming telecommunications boom in the 1980s and early 1990s. Gary Winnick, later to run international carrier Global Crossing before its date in bankruptcy court, was busy helping Michael Milken build his junk bond empire. Philip Anschutz, later chair of Qwest, was running the Southern Pacific railroad.

The most disruptive force of all in the early and mid-1990s, though, was the commercialization of the Internet. The culture of change catalyzed by the Internet is still at work and will cause many more changes, both in the telecommunications industry and in society as a whole. Although the dot-coms got most of the spotlight, the telecommunications industry was steadily plowing ahead into the brave, new Internet world. The changes in the telecommunications industry wouldn't (and, in fact, couldn't) happen fast enough to satisfy the hyperactive business plans of the many dot-com pretenders, but the failure of these companies is more a testament to the dot-coms' ignorance of the Internet's infrastructure than a failure of the carriers to support them.

Yet, the promise of the Internet, particularly in the mid-1990s, was too much for even the strongest companies to ignore. In this environment, the telecommunications industry's voracious need for capital met the easy money of the dot-com era. The industry was in for a major overhaul, whether it was ready or not.

The Telecommunications Act of 1996 loosened or destroyed many regulatory mechanisms, but it created few and left most of the hard work required to re-regulate the industry to the Federal Communications Commission. The FCC wasn't able to exert any new power, thereby opening the regulatory process to chaos. The weakness of the act was obvious to anyone who read it carefully (few did). The act contains little substantive mention of the Internet. The only section that dealt directly with the Internet was a section that dealt with online pornography. And that section was later struck down in court.

The act was the final catalyst required to trigger the chaotic environment that produced the telebomb over the next eight years. With the act came a significant reduction in the adult supervision over an industry that was about to inherit more money than it knew what to do with. It is no wonder that so many industry scions ran amok.

Against this backdrop of the Internet, easy money, and uncontrolled deregulation, five long-term trends swept the industry. All but one of the trends began in one of the neat industry subsegments that existed before deregulation. But as the industry coalesced across the old, artificial boundaries, the competitive rules were not what anyone expected.

Trend #1—The Second Race to Cover the United States in Optical Fiber

Beginning in 1997, various parties interested in seeing the Internet grow began to use the sound bite that "Internet traffic doubles every ninety days." Although this was probably true during the early commercialization of the Internet in 1995 and 1996, it should have been obvious that growth on that scale could not be sustained. The investment of more than $50 billion in intercity fiber-optic capacity by the so-called second racers during the late 1990s was premised on little more than this fundamental fallacy.

Trend #2—The Big Get Bigger: The Entry of the RBOCs into the Long-Distance Market

At the first divestiture of AT&T in 1984, each of the regional Bell operating companies (RBOCs) took away approximately 10 percent of the Bell system's assets. Ten years after divestiture on January 1, 1994, the seven RBOCs still had roughly the same assets relative to AT&T, holding 75 percent of the total ex-Bell assets. By the end of 2003, however, SBC Communications was double the size of AT&T based on total assets, and Verizon Communications was three times AT&T's size. BellSouth was about the same size as AT&T. Qwest Communications International, having written off all the assets from the "classic Qwest" overbuild, was the smallest of the companies but was still larger relative to AT&T than it was at divestiture.

Trend #3—The Last Stand of the Long-Distance Companies

By the time the Telecommunications Act of 1996 was debated in Congress, the long-distance companies certainly knew that the RBOCs were coming after the long-distance market. In the face of the RBOCs' onslaught, the long-distance providers invested in the RBOCs' bastion of local services as well as complementary services such as wireless. Each one of the Big 3 took a different route toward developing an ability to offer local service on its own network. Each strategy failed, although some more spectacularly than others.

Trend #4—The Rise and Fall of the Start-Up CLECs

The Telecommunications Act of 1996 required the RBOCs to support competitors in the local markets as a condition for gaining approval to offer long-distance service. (AT&T had been required to do the same for its new long-distance competitors in the 1980s.) This regulatory wrinkle propelled many dot-com-style business plans, most of which failed. This new generation of dot-com-style phone companies, called competitive local exchange carriers (CLECs), sprang up across the country in the late 1990s and disappeared at roughly the same rate as the dot-coms. From a peak of more than three hundred competitive carriers in 2000, the industry shrunk its way down to about eighty carriers by the end of 2003.

Trend #5—Lost Opportunities by the Cable Companies

The only other companies (besides the RBOCs) that had physical access to homes across the United States were the cable companies. Cable networks offer more bandwidth than telephone networks. Fully digitized, a cable network can deliver over ten times more bandwidth than the RBOCs' digital subscriber line (DSL) service. The cable companies had the ability to offer more services earlier than any other network carrier in the industry but spent more time focused on ill-advised merger-and-acquisition transactions during the 1990s than on upgrading their networks to offer advanced services. In doing so, they squandered their most basic advantage.

The Aftershock of the Telebomb

Each of the five trends involved companies entering new, uncharted waters. All involved the investment of immense amounts of cash designed to attract customers with new services. The number of customers remained static, however, and the existing customers gave away new dollars only grudgingly. The logical result of this much capital hitting the market at once was that many of the companies trying to shoehorn themselves into an increasingly crowded market space couldn't make it. Most of the new players in the industry and a few of the established players went out of business. Before the Telecommunications Act of 1996 was passed, from 1988 to 1996, only two telecommunications carriers declared bankruptcy. Between 1997 and 2003, 104 carriers declared bankruptcy.

The Darwinist creative destruction began with companies that were already marginalized in the new communications landscape—the long-distance resellers, paging and fixed wireless businesses. The pay phone business also began its long slide into oblivion in the late 1990s. Next to go were the most fanciful of the new technology plays—low-earth orbit (LEO) satellites and the facilities-based CLECs that followed the second racers into local markets. The last broad category of bankruptcies were the companies that stayed afloat through some regulatory or market wrinkle that allowed them to generate enough revenue to stave off the breaking of the initial blast wave of the telebomb. But these companies, including Internet service providers (ISPs), integrated carriers, and the international long-distance carriers, weren't able to recover well enough to sustain their earlier investments.

Many companies barely survived the telebomb. For example, one company that came out barely holding on was Level 3 Communications. It signed up a marquee investor, Warren Buffet, to invest $100 million as part of a $500 million financing tranche in 2002. Signing Buffett was more of a backroom deal than a show of support. In 2003, Buffett's investment company, Berkshire Hathaway, converted its bonds into more than 160 million shares of Level 3 common stock and immediately sold them, contributing to a one-third drop in Level 3's stock price. Level 3 spent more to build its network than any other new carrier during the boom, yet it has not found the formula to make that investment a success.

LONG-TERM PRESCRIPTIONS FOR THE INDUSTRY

The final chapter of *Telebomb* explores three long-term changes that must be made within the industry. These ideas are based on the author's attempt to learn the lessons of history and apply them to likely future scenarios with an accent on what is needed to prevent a reoccurrence of the telebomb. The prescriptions are as follows:

- *Content vs. Pipes.* Telecommunications carriers should focus on their networks and let the content providers develop the services that ride over the network.

- *Efficient Wholesaler.* Cheap, general-purpose networks will be required to compete with all the leftover fiber from the second race.

- *Regulatory Reform.* Regulatory reform is needed to address specific problems within the industry. The Telecommunications Act of 1996 needs sweeping revisions to clean up the mess that was handed to the FCC. The industry structure assumed to exist within the existing regulatory framework no longer exists.

These issues must be addressed to ensure that the United States remains the leader in network connectivity. In an increasingly global economy, being more connected can only help the United States remain competitive.

CHAPTER 1

BEFORE AND AFTER THE BREAKUP OF AT&T

"The two words 'information' and 'communication' are often used interchangeably, but they signify quite different things. Information is giving out; communication is getting through."

—SYDNEY J. HARRIS, AMERICAN NEWSPAPER COLUMNIST

You can still see the remnants of the first long-distance networks on telephone poles across the United States. These original copper wire systems were placed beginning around the turn of the twentieth century. They were given up in favor of advanced coaxial carrier systems in the 1950s and fiber-optic circuits in the 1980s. The original copper systems, however, often were not physically removed. For example, Interstate 70 between Hagerstown and Hancock in Maryland closely follows the path of the Chesapeake & Ohio Canal that links Cumberland, Maryland, with Georgetown, D.C. Between the road and the retired canal (now a national park) are several mile-long stretches of telephone poles with open (noninsulated) copper wire strung between glass insulators that are now found more often in flea markets than in the telephone network.

The canal in turn lies beside the Potomac River. The path of I-70 at this point once carried the National Road, later U.S. Route 40, which crossed the country in the early days of the automobile. There is also a rail bed between I-70 and the Potomac River, originally owned by the Baltimore & Ohio Railroad, now the CSX Corporation. Parts of that unused rail bed have become a rails-to-trails project called the Western Maryland Rail Trail. To complete the picture, Level 3 Com-

1880
1890
1900
1910
1920
1930
1940
1950
1960
1970
1980
1981
1982
1983
1984
1985
1986
1987
1988
1989
1990
1991
1992
1993
1994
1995
1996
1997
1998
1999
2000
2001
2002
2003
2004
2005
FUTURE

MONOPOLY

DIVESTITURE

STABILITY

BOOM

BOMB

RECOVERY?

munications ran fiber-optic lines between the lanes of I-70 in the late 1990s. Figure 1-1 shows the aerial photography of the area.

So within a few hundred yards lie seven generations of communications technology: river, canal, rail, copper telephone network, the original National Road, I-70, and fiber-optic transmission lines. Remember that before the advent of electronic communications, all messages were carried by whatever physical conveyance was available including river and canal boats and trains. One can imagine the struggle of four thousand immigrants laboring to build the canal and the large holding ponds in this area in the first half of the nineteenth century and compare it with the labor of a handful of workers with backhoes and spools of fiber-optic cable in the late 1990s.

These seven generations of technology were developed over nearly two

FIGURE 1-1.
SEVEN GENERATIONS OF COMMUNICATIONS TECHNOLOGY.

Former Baltimore and Ohio Railroad
(Open copper wire is on poles between rail bed and I-70)

U.S. Route 40
(National Road)

Potomac River

Chesapeake and Ohio
Canal towpath
(as it crosses Licking Creek)

Interstate 70
(Level 3 fiber buried between the lanes)

0 ⊢——⊥——⊥——⊣ 100yd

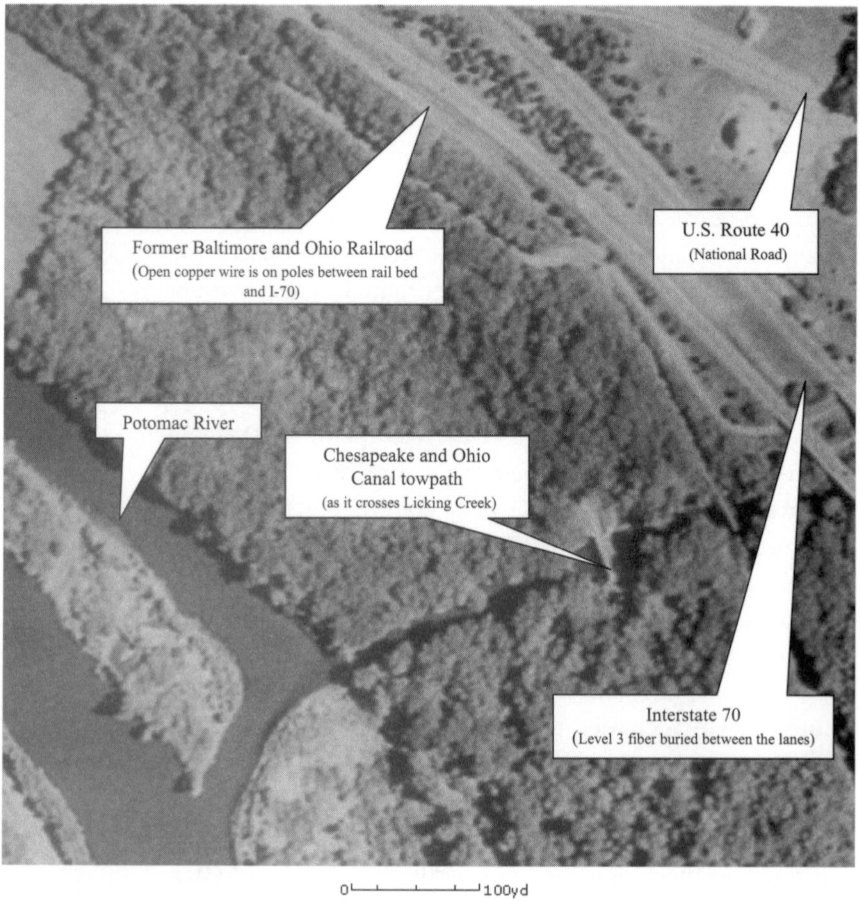

SOURCE: Image courtesy of the U.S. Geological Survey.

hundred years. During that time, there was a natural ebb and flow of new ideas and investments to provide successively better communications services to the nation.

Three of these transport paths were developments of the nineteenth century—canal, rail, and copper telephone networks. The National Road, I-70, and the fiber-optic transmission lines were creations of the twentieth century. (The Potomac River, of course, has been there as long as recorded history.) The canal and rail lines were both initially developed in the first half of the nineteenth century. They competed with each other for investment dollars, with the rails eventually winning. The competition between the two industries caused more than one young company (on either side) to fail. The business failures that accompanied the competition soured many businesspeople and entrepreneurs on infrastructure investments, preferring to leave those to the government.

It took another fifty years to convince the investing public to supply capital for the construction of the other nineteenth-century communications technology investment, the telephone. Other communications systems were established in the intervening years, such as the Pony Express, but none garnered the investment cash required to bring them to general use among the population. The national telephone network was different from the rail and canal lines in that whereas the telephone network was built with private investments, those investments were protected by two government-sponsored institutions.

First, Alexander Graham Bell was granted patents on the telephone in 1876 that gave him a virtual monopoly on the electronic voice communications market throughout the late nineteenth century. Once those patents expired, competitors arose to threaten the American Bell Telephone Company. The Bell system had a potent competitive weapon in that although competitors were able to build local telephone networks, they were not able to connect those systems from city to city because of the expense. Thus, they relied on the Bell system to provide that connectivity. The Bell system began buying up the independent telephone companies using leverage that only it had—its ability to cut the local systems off from the long-distance network.

The second protection that the Bell System received was in the form of a 1913 agreement between the U.S. Department of Justice and American Telephone & Telegraph, as the American Bell Telephone Company had been renamed. This agreement was known as the Kingsbury Commitment because it came in the form of a letter from AT&T vice president Nathan Kingsbury to the U.S. attorney general. In the letter, AT&T agreed to provide long-distance services to all independent phone companies and, in essence, not to buy any more local companies. In return, AT&T became a protected monopoly. The net result was that although the investments in the original telephone networks were private, they were protected from competition. The investments were safe and provided slow and predictable returns.

The next two generations of communications technology, the U.S. Route system and the interstate highways, were publicly funded projects. The U.S. Route system was conceived before the Great Depression, but the initial construction was largely funded as make-work projects in the 1930s. The Interstate Highway System was an improvement on the U.S. Route system and replaced it in many areas. Construction of the Interstate Highway System began in the late 1950s and continues today, although the bulk of construction was completed in the 1970s.

The fiber-optic network deployments of the 1990s resembled the canal-versus-railroad investments of the early nineteenth century more than any of the other periods of major communications change. Not only was the money privately raised but there were also many companies competing for investment dollars. This construction boom stood in contrast to an increasing reliance through history on public funding for transport infrastructure projects. None of the projects in the intervening years was completed with private funding and all had some kind of government protection. The results were similar to those of the canal-versus-railroad races: poorly served and unserved customers, lost investor dollars, laid-off employees, and stranded assets.

The telecommunications industry has been through a period of explosive growth and a precipitous crash—the telebomb—and has begun rebuilding itself into a reasonably healthy industry. How did the boom-and-bust cycle come about in the telecommunications industry? Who were the personalities that made it happen? And more important, now that industry equilibrium is emerging, how will the changed network business affect our lives?

DIVESTITURE: NO NEED FOR PANIC

The first preshock of the telebomb was the divestiture of the RBOCs from AT&T in 1984. This separation of AT&T into eight separate companies (with the RBOCs, affectionately known as the "Baby Bells") was heralded as a way to open the long-distance market to competition by separating the bottleneck local networks from the parent AT&T Long Lines service and forcing the local companies to open their networks to all long-distance companies on essentially equal terms. At the time, it was assumed that the local companies were a natural monopoly because of the huge investment required to build a telephone network and the uncertain benefits of competition.

Similar arguments were used only six years earlier, in 1978, to deregulate the airline business. Airline deregulation brought disruption to travelers, investors, and airline employees alike. Many of the well-known names in the business—Eastern Air Lines, Braniff International Airways, Pan American World Airways, and others—disappeared in the aftermath. They had been formidable competitors and large corporations only a few years earlier. Other than the fact that the airline industry didn't have a definable boundary between local and long distance, the two industries had many similarities. Many assumed that a similar fate awaited companies and customers in a competitive long-distance business.

The telecommunications industry experienced some turbulence because of divestiture, but not the sea change that befell the airline industry. In 1982, as the first plans were being formulated to send the then–Baby Bells out into the world on their own, industry employment stood at 1.07 million. The structural changes brought about by a competitive long-distance industry and restructured RBOCs caused 188,400 jobs (2 out of every 11) to leave the industry between 1982 and 1986. From that point, employment in the industry stabilized at about 900,000 jobs until hiring picked up because of the Telecommunications Act of 1996.

Divestiture succeeded in opening the long-distance market to competition. Thousands of new companies flooded the market, but their numbers dwindled as competition heated up. Long-distance pricing fell dramatically at first but quickly went into a pattern of regular, yet modest, price decreases. While numerous niche players remained after the late 1980s, the consolidation of the industry at that time was dramatic.

By 1990, the long-distance market became a cartel of three main players. AT&T, MCI Communications, and Sprint—the Big 3—effectively had the market to themselves. The local market remained a monopoly until the Telecommunications Act of 1996 declared that monopoly over.

A look at the first competitive wave in the telecommunications industry provides a foreshadowing of what the competitive market would look like in the late 1990s.

THE FIRST SHAKEOUT

Many long-distance companies were created in the wake of divestiture and the regulatory work done by MCI and other potential competitors of AT&T.

They were all looking to feast at a trough of cheap network access created by regulators to promote competition. Most of these carriers never became large companies. The Holy Grail for most of them was to be bought by a larger company.

The long-distance companies established at this time followed one of two paths. Builders invested in their own national networks. They became network operators, constructing their own fiber-optic capacity. The three carriers that became the oligopoly of the early 1990s, AT&T, MCI, and Sprint, all chose this route. Resellers were content to simply resell the network services of others.

The Resellers

The resellers sold identical products. They couldn't differentiate among themselves because they were all selling the services of AT&T or another member of the oligopoly. They resorted to gimmicks to get people to buy their services. Many multilevel marketing schemes grew up around these long-distance services. Some survive to this day.

I DON'T KNOW AND I DON'T CARE

Once Equal Access was implemented (between 1984 and 1988), consumers faced many nearly identical choices in long-distance service. For the first time, they were required to pick a long-distance service instead of relying on the service provided by AT&T. (Equal Access was the name given to the process of opening the local networks so that all long-distance services could be used by any consumer in the same manner as AT&T's long-distance service was used in the past. Under Equal Access, all subscribers are allowed to access their choice of long-distance company using 1 + dialing as they had with AT&T.)

A complicating factor in the selection process was that the phone company providing local service was required to remain neutral in the choice of long-distance providers. In many cases, the local service providers were recently part of AT&T, so regulatory restrictions were put in place to enforce their neutrality. The local phone companies' sales representatives could not answer any questions about the choice of long-distance carrier. Also, the list of potential long-distance companies was too long to be read over the phone, so confused consumers had no clue how to respond unless they already knew the name of a long-distance company. In 1995, entrepreneur Dennis Dees cashed in on the confusion, registering his reseller operation under the names "I Don't Know," "Who Cares," "Who Ever," "Anyone Is Okay," and "It Doesn't Matter." Any consumer who responded to the local service rep with the phrase "I don't know" became a customer of the I

Don't Know long-distance service. In 1997, Dees was joined by another entrepreneur who started an "I Don't Care" long-distance service.

The resellers began shrinking in the mid-1980s. Their share of industry revenue receded as the Big 3 became the oligopoly carriers. The resellers either went out of business or were purchased by one of the larger companies. An example of this activity was the merger of SoutherNet and Teleconnect into TelecomUSA, which was in turn purchased by MCI. SoutherNet built some of its own facilities but could not compete with the members of the oligopoly.

Case in Point: The Growth of LDDS

The Long Distance Discount Service (LDDS), with the infamous Bernie Ebbers as its CEO, was a reseller that understood it must achieve a certain operational scale to survive. Because there were many undifferentiated players in the market and competition was fierce, the best way to achieve scale was to buy other long-distance companies. In other words, LDDS had to get bigger. And so it did, buying other resellers, many of which were the walking wounded of the business.

But the resale opportunity was shrinking. As the regulators intended, eventually the preferential interconnection rates and guaranteed access to the old AT&T Long Lines network disappeared, leaving the upstarts to find other ways to compete. Many raised their rates and depended on telemarketing or affinity programs (similar to the airlines' frequent flyer mileage or other give-away programs) to keep the steady flow of new customers coming. But, for a determined entrepreneur, shrinking was not an option. LDDS had already begun what would become at least twenty major corporate merger-and-acquisition transactions, including the grandly named World Communications, Inc. That name suited Ebbers's ambitions just fine, so LDDS was renamed WorldCom. Ebbers also figured out that WorldCom must own some of the assets that supported the business if it was going to be successful in the long run.

To get a network of its own and become a "facilities-based carrier" (as the telecom geeks call it) or "vertically integrated" (as the business profs call it), WorldCom made one of the first big bets that would lead it to become a company smaller than AT&T with twice the debt load. In 1994, it paid $2.5 billion to the Williams Companies for Williams Telecommunications Group (WilTel), a carrier with a fiber-optic network that was literally blown through unused gas pipelines.

The Williams Companies owned and operated a network of gas and petroleum pipelines throughout the United States. Over the years, the company replaced many of its pipelines because of the normal obsolescence of older pipeline material. The old and new pipelines sat on the same rights of way; the old pipelines were simply abandoned in place.

Someone at Williams eventually figured out that the pipelines, while no longer capable of carrying petroleum products, were suitable for housing fiber-optic cable. The engineers at WilTel even rigged a system for installing the cable. One end of a fiber-optic cable was attached to a device that looked like a shuttlecock (birdie) used to play badminton. The rounded end of the shuttlecock was then placed in the pipe with the part that looked like the feathers of the shuttlecock toward the open end. When air was blown against the "feathers," they expanded to fill the empty pipe and the shuttlecock was blown down the line.

WilTel owned national rights of way and built quickly. It had more fiber in its network than MCI as late as 1986. In 1994, its network contained thirteen times the number of strand miles of fiber as LDDS. But the assets were underutilized, producing less than $400 million in revenue in 1994. Wiltel had a network and few customers. WorldCom had customers but little network of its own. The two companies were a good match.

The WilTel deal bought Bernie Ebbers some legitimacy in the long-distance business. Up until the WilTel deal, he was considered by the other executives in the industry to be "all hat and no cattle." True to its Midwestern roots, WilTel was "cattle" to Ebbers.

Williams resisted WorldCom's first offer of $2 billion, understanding that it had achieved a low-cost position and was sitting on a potential cash cow. But when WorldCom came back with a $2.5 billion offer, the company feared a shareholder revolt if it didn't take the money. Williams was so confident of its own network-building skills that as soon as the noncompete clauses in the sale agreement with WorldCom expired, Williams built another network. It wasn't as successful the second time.

The major problem with WorldCom's pending purchase of WilTel was that WorldCom didn't have $2.5 billion. So Bernie Ebbers and WorldCom discovered the magic of debt financing and borrowed the money. Beginning about this time, the company also benefited from the fact that no one could track its historic financial performance. The acquisitions were laid in so thick that any comparison of its financial statements to prior periods yielded no real information.

By the time WorldCom's merger activity peaked with the 1998 purchase of MCI, the deception was so heavy that the MCI deal was touted as a deal involving only trading common stock (MCI's for WorldCom's) when, in fact, WorldCom borrowed $6 billion to pay off MCI's largest shareholder, British Telecom. The $6 billion junk bond offering represented more than 15 percent of the debt on WorldCom's balance sheet when it filed for Chapter 11 bankruptcy protection in 2002.

The watchers in the financial markets should have viewed WorldCom's high debt level with suspicion, but they were too busy queuing up to underwrite WorldCom's next deal. Part of Ebbers's self-deceit was the fact that virtually all the people he came in contact with on business matters considered him to be a genius. Investors who made money on his stock didn't know or care what Ebbers knew; they only cared that they got rich in the process. Investment professionals, bankers, and his own financial team at WorldCom may have known better, but no one dared tell the emperor that he was naked.

What began as a series of small company mergers grew at ever-faster rates, fueled by the speed with which business seemed to move in the late 1990s. Like a driver at night who is driving so fast that he needs to see beyond the area that headlights can illuminate, no one really knew what was coming next. In this situation, the eventual unraveling of the company seemed almost inevitable.

The Builders

The first national network was built and owned by AT&T. It was built with money collected from subscribers to AT&T's regulated telephone service. AT&T's competitors argued that the network was thus a public asset. This argument largely stuck, although AT&T retained ownership and leased capacity on the network to new entrants once AT&T's monopoly was over.

Beginning in the late 1960s, one of AT&T's first serious competitors began building a national network using microwave transmission systems. The company, Microwave Communications Incorporated, drove the judicial and regulatory agenda that forced many procompetitive changes into the industry. By the late 1970s, technical developments were making the traditional copper long-haul circuits obsolete. Fiber-optic systems (pioneered at AT&T's Bell Laboratories, of course) were set to replace copper in all long-haul routes.

By the late 1980s, stand-alone fiber-optic systems carried most long-distance telephone traffic in the United States. With the development in the early 1990s of standards-based, integrated fiber-optic systems—meaning that they were compliant with either the SONET or SDH standards—the use of fiber optics became the only option for the vast majority of long-haul network construction. (Synchronous Optical NETworking [SONET] was devised by Bellcore, the research-and-development [R&D] arm of the RBOCs, as the fiber-optic transmission standard for the North American telecommunications network. Synchronous Digital Hierarchy [SDH] is the international fiber-optic transmission standard used in most other countries.)

Like AT&T replacing its copper transmission systems, Microwave Communications also replaced its microwave systems in the late 1980s and early 1990s with fiber optics and shortened its name to simply MCI. Copper and microwave transmission systems all but disappeared from the active long-haul networks. Both AT&T and MCI wrote off the last of their analog and copper transmission networks in the mid-1990s.

So for the few companies that took the judicial and regulatory intent of the events around AT&T's divestiture seriously, there was a new technology that could allow them to easily meet or, in some cases, surpass the quality provided by the AT&T network. The race to build competing networks began.

THE FIRST RACE TO COVER THE UNITED STATES IN FIBER

Beginning in the early 1980s Sprint, the last of the Big 3 builders, took on the ambitious plan of building a nationwide fiber network. As a subsidiary of the Southern Pacific Railroad, it had the advantage of being able to lay fiber on Southern Pacific's extensive rail routes. In fact, SPRint got its name in part from the railroad. Sprint was sold to GTE in 1983 and to United Telecommunications over several years in the late 1980s and early 1990s. Eventually, United Telecom took the Sprint name for the entire corporation.[1]

Like Wiltel, Sprint's initial advantage lay in the fact that it didn't need to buy or negotiate many right-of-way agreements and that the Southern Pacific owned one of the largest rail networks in the country.

To lay the network, Sprint developed the fiber train. It was a self-contained trenching unit on rails that could lay fiber at the speed of 5 to 10 miles per hour, better than walking speed, when fully operational. It contained a locomotive, a trenching car (essentially a large Ditch Witch on an arm), fiber spools to place the fiber in the new trench, a car to fill in the trench, and cars with extra spools of fiber.

With the fiber train, Sprint was able to lay cable quickly and economically. It built a national network and carried essentially all its long-haul traffic on fiber by 1985. Thus, it won the first race to cover the United States in fiber. MCI didn't surpass Sprint's fiber route miles until 1997. As a result of its lead in the deployment of fiber optics, Sprint began to base its ad campaigns on its higher quality, boasting that Sprint users could hear a pin drop over its network.

The lesson to be learned from the first race was that an innovator with new, better technology and no ties to any legacy technology (copper or microwave, for example) is more willing to take the risks necessary to gain an advantage on more complacent competition.

In 1986, Sprint's network contained more route miles of fiber than AT&T's. AT&T still had more capacity because most of its traffic was carried on copper carrier systems. AT&T's network was built on older rights of way including many now-defunct rail beds. AT&T's routes were stable because they tended to be less active, or even abandoned. And in some cases, they were so old that nobody knew precisely where they were. So, the effort required to cover them in fiber was significant. On top of that, AT&T still had the monopoly mind-set that a useful technology shouldn't be replaced until it was fully depreciated. Its competitors never substituted accounting rules for market-based decision-making processes. If they had a better technology and could make the business case to implement it, they would write off the older, inefficient technology. And, as we later found out, they sometimes wrote off the accounting rules themselves.

Sprint won the initial race but continually lost in the marketplace. It was mired in third place behind AT&T, the former monopoly, and MCI, which began to collect customers much earlier. It didn't seriously challenge that status quo in the market until it stopped dropping pins and started dropping dimes, by cutting prices to meet the market in the 1990s. Successive rounds of price cuts increased customer demand throughout the 1980s and 1990s.

MCI BUILDS A NETWORK

MCI's first chief executive, Bill McGowan, was reputed to brag that while AT&T did its research with scientists, MCI did its research with lawyers. In the 1980s, this was often used to label MCI as a leech on the national network owned by AT&T. It was true that MCI did not spend billions on basic research and that it had a large hodgepodge of technology in its network. This assortment of technology compared unfavorably to AT&T and Sprint, but MCI was serious about building its own network to compete on a national scale.

In the early days of MCI, McGowan and founder Jack Goeken took on AT&T's monopoly power by chipping away at it bit by bit. McGowan maintained the vision of MCI eventually becoming an equal competitor with AT&T and kept the dream alive by prodding MCI's employees and investors to stick with the company long enough to see it through "the next quarter." His uncanny ability to raise money on a just-in-time basis kept the company afloat, as did his ability to convince the employees that the stock he paid them with would someday be worth something. McGowan's spirit kept MCI together during the fifteen years it took for the company to make it to AT&T's divestiture. He stayed with the company through an additional eight years and two hearts (he had a heart transplant operation in 1987), passing away in 1992.

MCI's history most closely parallels the entire industry. It came to national visibility around the time of divestiture and grew rapidly through the boom times. At the hands of a later generation of leadership that was unprepared to cope with anything less than brilliant success, it sank into bankruptcy as the boom turned to bust. And yet it emerged from bankruptcy as a financially viable service provider and employer as the clouds over the industry began to part in 2004.

As divestiture and the resulting industry changes emerged in the early 1980s, MCI undertook to expand its reach across the country. Unlike Sprint, which was handed national rights of way, and AT&T, which built them over the past one hundred years as a regulated monopoly, MCI did the hard work of negotiating its own rights of way, one at a time. MCI tended to follow highways, particularly interstate highways and major U.S. routes.

Unfortunately, these highway roadbeds tend to be areas of frequent construction activity as roads are expanded, interchanges are built, or normal repaving activities are performed every few years. This led to service disruptions that tended to give MCI less than stellar reliability. (One of MCI's network managers once remarked that fiber-optic lines were an excellent tool for finding backhoes. They referred to such network outages as FSBEs, or fiber-seeking backhoe events.)

But the fiber-optic networks were still much more reliable and cheaper to maintain than copper circuits. The introduction of modern fiber optics made competing with AT&T possible, an occurrence timed fortuitously with the regulatory intent of divestiture. One wonders how readily MCI and Sprint would have been able to pry customers from AT&T if they didn't have the advantage of new technology.

THE RISE OF THE DEAL MAKERS

Both the resellers and the builders engaged in significant merger-and-acquisition activity. Particularly for the resellers, these deals were the best way to grow given the high number of long-distance companies. Like adding "dot-com" to a company name in the late 1990s, the best way to grow in the telecommunications industry of the late 1980s was to buy competitors.

The MCI that emerged from bankruptcy in 2004 was built as the product of mergers among more than fifty companies. Figure 1-2 shows the chain of mergers from 1991 forward. The long list of who bought whom has the ring of an Old Testament line of heredity.

In late 2003, the combined WorldCom and MCI still maintained sixty-six separate carrier identification codes as registered with Neustar, the North American numbering plan administrator. Many of the company names and abbreviations are legacies of the acquired companies:

- Brooks Fiber Communications

- Satellite Business Systems (SBS)

- Western Union International

- RCA Globecom

- New Century Communications

- TelecomUSA (twelve different codes)

- Metropolitan Fiber Systems

- LDDS

SWAPPING CAPACITY AMONG NETWORKS

As the builders turned up their own national fiber-optic networks, they began claiming the advantages of fiber: call clarity, fewer dropped calls, and so forth, in national advertising. This happened before any of them actually owned truly national fiber capacity. To gain fiber-based access to most cities in the United States, the builders began the practice of swapping capacity on each others' routes. In these swaps, carrier A would lease capacity on its Chicago–to–New York route (for example) to carrier B in exchange for equivalent capacity connecting two cities not directly connected on its own network, say on carrier B's Chicago-to-Denver route. Swapping capacity on each other's networks was an accepted practice; in fact, it was necessary at the time to achieve a national network at a reasonable cost before each company obtained sufficient resources to build its own complete, national network.

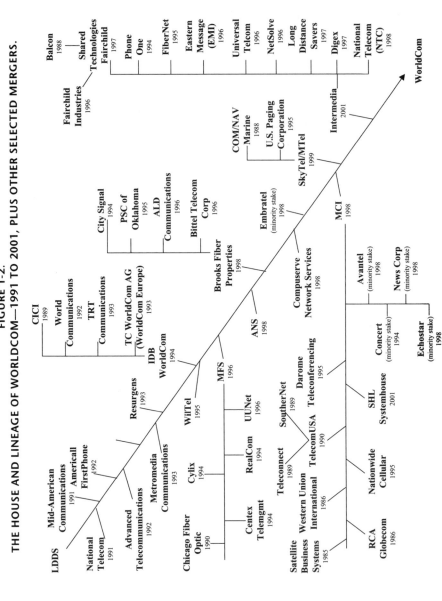

The accounting treatment for the swaps was, in many cases, aggressive. However, because the aggregate dollar amounts of the transactions were only a small percentage of the companies' revenue, the transactions were not considered material to the overall financial health of the companies. "Materiality" is an accounting concept. If the effect of a given financial item is not significant, or material, to the company's overall financial picture as painted by the financial statements of the company, it can be essentially ignored by an auditor.

The fact that these types of transactions and the related accounting were routine in nature was relied on by companies participating in the second national fiber build in the late 1990s to such an extreme that the transactions represented up to 25 percent of the sales at some of these companies. At this point, they became "material" and warranted further scrutiny. Thus began the downfall of Global Crossing and Qwest in 2001.

The swapping of capacity also had the unintended effect of limiting network diversity. The principle of diversity in network design is used to lower the risk of a network outage by providing multiple network paths into a given area. When the carriers began swapping capacity, they often didn't share with each other the physical topology of each route that was purchased. The only thing that the purchasing carrier knew was that the circuit started in, say, Denver and ended in Sacramento.

The diversity problem was more acute in the western United States. The routes over the Rocky Mountains were the last to be built due to the expense of crossing the difficult terrain. In the early 1990s, there was a flood in the Pacific Northwest that took out a bridge that had also served as a fiber-optic crossing. That single event took out much of the network traffic to and from Seattle because, as it turned out, all of the major carriers had traffic running through fiber attached to that bridge.

After the Modified Final Judgment (MFJ) and the oligopoly in the long-distance business, the industry structure was stable from the mid-1980s until the Telecom Act was passed in 1996. Since the competitive boundaries had been staked out and were being defended by strong companies, small gains in market share were hotly contested.

Far from the predictions of chaos in the phone network that were common at the divestiture of the RBOCs from AT&T in 1984, the long-distance business was becoming as sleepy as the local phone business that AT&T ditched because it wasn't exciting enough. From the consumer's point of view, the main difference between the two was that with long-distance services, changing carriers was as easy as saying yes to a telemarketer or cashing one of the many bounty checks that showed up in the mail. To change local service providers, a customer had to move to a different area of the country.

The only way for AT&T, MCI, and Sprint to differentiate themselves from each other was with marketing, and in some cases, just plain luck. In the meantime, the overly enthusiastic capital markets of the 1990s would give entrepreneurs $40 billion to build competing networks.

WHAT GOES AROUND COMES AROUND

In the mid-1990s, dial-around long-distance services became popular. The dial-around services, better known as "10-10" services because of slogans used in the continual television advertising required to keep the services alive, became counterculture options to the big phone companies. To use them, a caller has to dial 1-0-1 and a four-digit number that usually begins with a zero. Hence 1-0-1 plus 0, or 10-10.

Not to miss the party, the big companies started their own (in some cases, several) dial-around services and ran the advertising without mention of the parent company. AT&T operated the Lucky Dog Telephone Company as a dial-around service, for example. One of the dial-around services that sprang up in 1998 was TelecomUSA. A potential caller who looked hard enough could find out that TelecomUSA was actually MCI. The amusing thing about the name TelecomUSA is that it was the name of a phone company that merged with MCI in 1990. The first TelecomUSA was the product of the merger of SoutherNet and Teleconnect in 1989. (It was the first communications company run by Clark McLeod. McLeod's next venture, McLeodUSA, is profiled in Chapter 7.) The name TelecomUSA had been used for only about a year before MCI bought the company. All of TelecomUSA's customers were converted to MCI products, and the name disappeared by 1992. With the dial-around service, the name was used again, but for a completely different phone service.

NOTE

1. Michael K. Kellogg, John Thorne, and Peter W. Huber, *Federal Telecommunications Law* (Boston: Little, Brown and Co., 1992), p. 403.

1880
1890
1900
1910
1920
1930
1940
1950
1960
1970
1980
1981
1982
1983
1984
1985
1986
1987
1988
1989
1990
1991
1992
1993
1994
1995
1996
1997
1998
1999
2000
2001
2002
2003
2004
2005
FUTURE

CHAPTER 2

STABILITY AS THE WORLD CHANGED

"When you're finished changing, you're finished."
—BENJAMIN FRANKLIN, AMERICAN STATESMAN AND
PHILOSOPHER

One of the arguments used when courting investors for the hundreds of new, competing carriers in the 1990s was that the existing carriers were too set in their ways and therefore ripe for a new company to come in and knock them off. The markets were, in fact, in a competitive stasis. Where competitive offerings were available, there was little to differentiate among the carriers' products. But to take this stasis as a weakness was too simple a reading of the situation. Although the competitive lines were brightly drawn, the largest carriers were also firmly entrenched. They had financial strength, solid technology, and large customer bases.

The world was going to change for everyone associated with the communications and media business, but most of the upstarts, after a brief moment of glory during the dot-com stock bubble, would fade. The real question was, which of the solidly entrenched large companies would be able to cross over and compete in the other market segments?

OPERAT-OR! OPERAT-ER!

In the early 1990s, AT&T decided to rejuvenate its operator-assisted calling services, always profitable for long-distance companies because of the high per-minute rates charged for calls completed through a live operator. AT&T decided to base the marketing messages on the toll-free number to be dialed for operator assistance by AT&T,

1-800-Operator. When callers dial 1-800-Operator, they are really dialing:

```
1 - 8 0 0 - O P E R A T O R
1 - 8 0 0 - 6 7 3 7 2 8 6
```
(The second "R" is extraneous and ignored by the telephone network.)

In the 800-number database shared by the phone companies in the North American Number Planning Area, 800-673-7286, was noted as requiring routing to AT&T. Any local phone company receiving that dialed number routed the call to AT&T; AT&T's network handled the call from there.

What AT&T didn't figure on was the spelling skills of the American public. Instead of dialing 1-800-Operator, many (tens of thousands) dialed 1-800-Operater. 1-800-Operater translates differently:

```
1 - 8 0 0 - O P E R A T E R
1 - 8 0 0 - 6 7 3 7 2 8 3
```

In the 800-number database, 800-673-7283 was noted as requiring routing to the network of MCI Communications. MCI, however, did not have anywhere to route those calls. The number was unused so when the calls hit the MCI network, they would "dead end."

One of the bright engineers at MCI recognized the high number of dead-end hits on its internal routing database. In a moment of inspiration, someone guessed what was going on and rerouted the number to MCI's own operator-assisted service, 1-800-Collect.

The result was millions of dollars being spent by AT&T customers on a service provided by MCI. It took AT&T several months to figure out what had happened. Once it did, 1-800-Operator was replaced with 1-800-CALLATT.

From this type of marketing-focused and plain-luck event, the long-distance market of the early 1990s was defined.

REGULATED COMPETITION

The telecommunications industry in the United States has faced two periods of major upheaval. The first was caused by the divestiture of the RBOCs from AT&T in 1984. The second period of upheaval was not the consequence of a single event but began in the mid-1990s as a result of the perfect storm of easy dot-com money, uncontrolled deregulation, and merger mania.

The time between the two periods of upheaval, from roughly 1988 until

1996, represented the quiet before the storm. The regulatory boundaries changed significantly in the early 1980s but became well understood. Once those changes were digested, the telecommunications industry was almost sleepy. While the situation in broader society seemed ready for change, the industry settled down into a set of comfortable oligopolies in each of three separate and distinct landline telecommunications markets: local telephone service, long-distance telephone service, and cable television. (The mobile phone business did not begin developing into a mass-market service until the mid-1990s.)

Merriam-Webster defines oligopoly as "a market situation in which each of a few producers affects but does not control the market."[1] There were profitable companies (or at least stable ones in the case of the cable industry) in each of the three market segments. Other than AT&T (through its prior ownership of the RBOCs) and Sprint (the only truly integrated carrier at the time), none of the participants in any of these markets had any legitimate claim to experience in the other segments. The practical effect was that many of the companies that collided in the late 1990s had lived a somewhat protected life within their own walled gardens. Once the second major tide of change hit the industry, the carriers began playing for the first time in new sandboxes with unfamiliar rules.

The general economy was calm during this period, particularly by the standards of the dot-com era. The stock market, represented by the Dow Jones Industrial Average (DJIA), showed average annual growth of 7.2 percent for the five years from 1990 to 1994, on par with its historical averages. Contrast that to the boom-and-bust years to follow. The next five-year period (1995–1999) averaged a 24.7 percent annual gain. The three bust years (2000–2002) averaged a 10.0 percent annual decline. The technology sector, represented by the NASDAQ Composite Index, showed an even more spectacular rise and fall.

Toward the end of the period of stability, the free trade movement and the global economy began to spread rapidly across borders and time zones. For these trends to continue, telecommunications services needed to become much less expensive, more seamlessly integrated, and more widely available. Only tentative moves were made during this period of stability to breach the walls that defined the segments of the telecommunications market. Both from within the walled gardens and from the outside, only small-scale competition emerged in any segment with the exception of long distance.

It would take a consumer revolt—the popularity of the Internet—to flatten the walls between the neighboring markets. Unfortunately, the popularization of the Internet also brought to the communications industry one of the most destructive overinvestment cycles in the history of business. Key to understanding how the overinvestment happened is a description of the Balkanization present in the industry in the early 1990s.

LONG-DISTANCE MARKET DEVELOPMENT

The long-distance business in the early 1990s followed the textbook as far as market development was concerned. After divestiture and the opening of the long-distance market, start-up companies flooded the field. The new entrants of the 1980s brought creative ideas and fresh capital to the field. They developed innovative products and new ways of doing business along the way.

Once most of the technical developments were wrung out of the new market landscape, product innovation gave way to price competition. Technology innovations, such as SONET standardized the development of fiber-optic transmission systems and paved the way for more widespread deployment. But the gains were used, particularly by the long-distance network operators, to reduce costs for existing products rather than to offer significant new products.

The long-distance companies searched for new revenue. As the 1-800-Operator example shows, in this competitive market, it was hard to tell the difference between strokes of luck and genius. New products tended to be simply variants of prior products targeted at more specific segments of the market.

During this time, the companies that joined AT&T to form the oligopoly kept building their businesses. They finished most of their network build outs by 1992, but they were still building products, customer bases, and revenue on top of those assets. The long-distance business consolidated in the late 1980s. From 1990 through 1995, the Big 3 oligopoly carriers—AT&T, MCI, and Sprint—garnered 86 to 89 percent of the revenue of the long-distance industry every year. Even though those three companies commanded most of the revenue in the industry, the total number of long-distance providers in the industry actually increased during this time, from 253 at the end of 1988 to 583 at the end of 1995.[2]

Only a handful of the new providers built their own network. These new resellers' marketing schemes included variants on just about every sales technique allowable in a free-market economy including multilevel, network, and affinity marketing. Several illegal techniques were used as well. This era saw the coining of the term *slamming,* which occurs when a subscriber's choice of long-distance carrier is changed without the person's knowledge. Two other terms, *cramming* (adding unwanted features, like caller ID, to a phone line) and *spamming* (sending unwanted e-mail), were also added to the telecommunications lexicon over the next few years.

The big guys learned lessons from the guerilla marketers. An indicator of the shift from network technology development to marketing was MCI's Friends and Family plan. It was among the first offerings by the oligopoly carriers to use network marketing techniques. MCI's residential long-distance customers who subscribed to Friends and Family received significant discounts when they called long-distance numbers that they identified as their most-called numbers, presumably acquaintances and relatives. The catch was that those numbers also had to belong to MCI customers.

The telephone numbers of the friends and family members for whom the customer wanted to receive the discount were provided to MCI. Where the numbers were not those of MCI customers, MCI began marketing to them, extolling the virtues (read discounts) that could be attained if only the friend or family member were an MCI customer. The product was an instant hit and allowed MCI to gain market share.

AT&T coasted on its reputation. It was able to hold on to a large (though falling) portion of the long-distance customers in the United States, based on its reputation for quality and customer service. Sprint and MCI were able to compete by offering ostensibly the same service for a little bit less. Sprint's and MCI's tariff rates (think manufacturers suggested retail price, or MSRP) were frequently one cent per minute less than AT&T's.[3] (Throughout this book, and throughout the telecommunications industry, the term *tariff* is used to mean a published list of services offered and the prices that will be charged for those services—like a restaurant menu—not a tax. In this example, the tariff rates were the MSRP for per-minute charges that the companies charged their customers.)

THREE MEN WHO RENEWED COMPETITION IN LONG DISTANCE

As the era of stability was ending, competition began to develop within the long-distance industry. Three other entrepreneurs who became rich at least in part through selling carriers during the industry consolidation turned around and created new competitors.

Clark McLeod was a serial entrepreneur who excelled at being a big fish in a small pond. He started his working career as a middle-school teacher but was soon working side jobs selling radio advertising and telephone equipment. He then seized on the opportunities opened by the nascent competition in the long-distance market. The company he formed eventually became TelecomUSA. In 1992, Clark McLeod sold his long-distance business, TelecomUSA, to MCI. No sooner had he closed that deal than he began his self-named company to build a fiber-optic network for the State of Iowa. The new company, McLeodUSA, would later become a competitor in the local market. In the time between TelecomUSA's rise to prominence and McLeodUSA's bankruptcy filing, Clark McLeod was the most revered business figure in Cedar Rapids, Iowa.

Through 1996, Jim Crowe was CEO of MFS Communications, a carrier initially created by Peter Kiewit Sons' Inc. that built competing local networks in business districts of major cities in the United States. After selling MFS to WorldCom, Crowe returned to start Level 3, the last company to complete a national long-distance network build in the United States in the late 1990s. Level 3 was also a Kiewit project; in fact, Level 3 inhabited the same corporate shell that contained MFS in the early 1990s. Crowe was a promoter and deal maker first and an operations executive second. But once it became clear that Level 3 wasn't going to reach its potential, Crowe became much less visible outside the investor community.

In 1990, Philip Anschutz's main business interest was the Southern Pacific Railroad, the creator of Sprint. The memory of building the Sprint network sparked a gleam in his eye that would later become Qwest Communications International, his attempt to enter the long-distance business. Qwest wouldn't begin laying fiber across the country until 1995. Prior to Sprint and Qwest, Anschutz's other business interests were in the oil and gas industry. In those businesses, as with Qwest, Anschutz was primarily a financial investor, staying out of the industries' technology debates, in contrast with most of the other entrepreneurs who sought to use their vision for the industry as part of their public relations campaigns.

In general, there was an inverse relationship between the fame of each of these executives and the fortunes of the company. Each tried to replicate his initial success in an openly competitive market and either failed (McLeodUSA) or achieved only mediocrity (Qwest and Level 3). This pattern was repeated among many executives in the industry: Although they built successful companies during the time of the walled gardens, competition in the competitive world to come made future success much more difficult.

RBOC Development—The Grass Is Always Greener

The seven regional Bell operating companies created by the divestiture of AT&T continued as regulated monopolies. They stayed on the straight and narrow path that was set out for them in the MFJ, providing little more than basic telephone service. The Baby Bells benefited from a national telecommunications policy that called for universal service. To support universal telephone service the industry was structured, through a complex series of cross charges and rate structures, so that virtually every citizen in the United States who wanted phone service could afford it. These efforts were so successful that phone service could be found in more than 93 percent of all homes in the country by 1989.[4] Because the market for phone service was saturated, the only growth came from ancillary services and general population increases. Slow but steady growth was the norm for the local companies throughout their institutional memory.

One result of the slow-and-steady nature of the RBOCs was that they were not entrepreneurially led like MCI and the new entrants that would show up in the late 1990s. In fact, the RBOCs tended to march in lockstep, even a dozen years after divestiture. Part of this was due to the common upbringing of their executives in a Bell System culture that rewarded conformity. (Twenty years after divestiture, all four CEOs of the remaining RBOCs were veterans of the all-in-one Bell system. All four began their careers with AT&T in the 1960s.)

The Baby Bells correctly surmised that they were never going to get out of their slow-growth situation by selling plain old telephone service (known as POTS in the industry). They were barred by the MFJ from offering long-distance services, and the Internet wasn't yet on enough people's radar, so the only other local service market that had any proven attractiveness was video services. This meant going head-to-head with the cable companies by offering video services to their subscriber base.

Trying to Enter the Video Market

The Bells' attempt to compete in the video market was the first of what later would be a number of battles where a company from one of the walled gardens would cross over to compete in another one of the gardens. The fact that the Bell video efforts were unsuccessful was also a sign of things to come.

The video services market, as defined by the cable business at the time, was attractive to the Bell companies. But it was also a market they were barred from as a result of the Cable Communications Policy Act of 1984. Bell Atlantic led a successful effort to overturn those provisions of the law on First Amendment grounds in 1994. Thus allowed into the video services business, the Bells embarked on a search for the perfect video technology. This flavor-of-the-month approach burned hundreds of millions of dollars but lacked enough focus to get any of the new technologies deployed to a critical mass of subscribers.

The key technology "flavors" along with the approximate dates of their brief brush with RBOC fame are as follows:

- *Asymmetric Digital Subscriber Line (ADSL)—1993.* Better known as the technology that local phone companies use to provide high-speed Internet access, this technology was first utilized as a way to deliver a video stream to subscriber homes. ADSL as a video delivery technology was not able to deliver the multichannel video experience that most cable subscribers were used to seeing.

- *Hybrid Fiber-Coaxial Cable (HFC)—1994.* This is the same technology that the cable companies were installing at the time, so it was, at best, a "me, too" strategy. Pacific Bell, one of the RBOCs, became so enamored of the technology that it announced its intention to replace its entire network, including its telephone network, with HFC. But technical trials and early rollout found so many holes in the technology's ability to support telephony that the project was shelved. Ironically, it is this same architecture that is used by the cable companies to offer their nascent voice services.

- *Switched Digital Video (SDV)—1995.* SDV was supposed to provide the best of both worlds: more reliable telephone service, through the use of advanced fiber optics, and true multichannel capabilities, through the higher capacity provided by the fiber. Unfortunately, the technology proved too cumbersome to use and was ultimately shelved once the RBOCs began merging.

Misguided Efforts at Developing Video Programming

The RBOCs also invested in video by attempting to develop new programming. Six of the seven RBOCs were members of one of two consortia, Tele-TV or Americast, which sought to bring advanced television programming to the new video networks under construction at the time. Tele-TV's investors included Bell Atlantic, NYNEX, and Pacific Telesis, more commonly known as Pacific Bell. Americast included Ameritech, BellSouth, and SBC as well as GTE, The Walt Disney Company, and Southern New England Telecommunications Corporation (SNET). USWest, the only RBOC not to join one of these consortia, went its own way, buying into the existing cable content business by purchasing Continental Cablevision.

Tele-TV was the prototype of a deal for a company with more money than media-market savvy. The deal was sold to Pacific Bell, NYNEX, and Bell Atlantic by Michael Ovitz, perhaps the most influential agent in the entertainment industry at the time.

Michael Ovitz and the Bell CEOs were all successful executives. The commonality ended there. The Bell executives all had deep operations expertise and were often more comfortable speaking about technology than working a crowd. The Bell executive that most seemed to fit outside the traditional mold was Ray Smith at Bell Atlantic. But, although he spoke about moving Bell Atlantic more toward being a technology and media company, he eventually shied away from deals that would fundamentally change the financial structure of his little piece of the Bell system.

In contrast with the Bell executives, Ovitz lived for the next deal. He catered to the largest stable of creative talent in the media business by indulging their desires for more money and the right projects. Ovitz created and ran the Creative Artists Agency (CAA), the best-recognized talent agency in the film and television industries. For his success at CAA, Ovitz was paid about $20 million per year.

Against this background, Ovitz was signed up by the three Bells in 1994 to build the new video-programming venture. His first move was to hire Howard Stringer, a thirty-year CBS veteran, to run the operations of the business. Stringer was also one of Ovitz's clients. In most industries, this would be an obvious conflict of interest, but in the entertainment industry, this was just another way to capture more of the deal.

Ovitz and Stringer recruited many other industry veterans to work for Tele-TV and spent an estimated $200 million to $300 million of the Bells' money. Tele-TV began development of content for the Bell video-on-demand platform but never actually delivered any original programming.

At the height of the Bells' investment in Tele-TV, Ovitz finally got the opportunity he wanted to run a studio. Michael Eisner, Disney's CEO, was seeking to replace Frank Wells, the president of Disney and Eisner's heir apparent, who was killed in a helicopter accident. Ovitz took the opportunity and jumped ship from Tele-TV. Adding insult to injury, not only was Tele-TV deprived of Ovitz's ability to bring in talent but Disney also was part of Americast, the other video content venture supported by Bell companies.

Ovitz's presence helped to generate talent and positive media coverage for the Bells's video ventures, but without revenue from the long-delayed video network construction projects to commit to content development, both Tele-TV and Americast failed. In the end, the Bells gave up to focus on the long-distance, Internet, and wireless businesses.

Unable to develop their own video content or network, the Bells resorted to selling other video services. Bell Atlantic became a reseller and installer of DirecTV services in 1998. But the offering proved to be unprofitable, even with the use of lower-wage labor, and was dropped.

CABLE COMPANY DEVELOPMENT

The cable companies were younger than the Bell system by several generations. The community access television (CATV) market started in the late 1940s when people in rural areas were left out of the new television craze sweeping the country. The early CATV systems were no more than powerful antennas designed to pull in television signals from distant cities and send the signals into individual homes using coaxial cable, hence the name. These early systems were often set up as small family businesses, much like the early local telephone exchanges at the turn of the twentieth century.

The cable companies are similar to the local phone companies in that they have communications connections into individual homes. The similarities end there. The cable companies' business model also differed dramatically from the RBOCs. The phone system in the United States is connected to virtually every home and business. Phone services are paid for by more than 90 percent of residential households. The cable network, by contrast, connects to about 90 percent of the homes in the United States but is subscribed to by only about 60 percent of those homes. Another difference between the RBOCs and the cable companies is that the cable companies do not have a large array of business services beyond providing video transmission to hotels and condominiums. It is substantially a consumer business.

As a result of these differences (fewer subscribers, no high-dollar business services), the cable network is built more inexpensively than the telephone plant. Typical copper cable in the telephone network is depreciated over thirty to forty years and often lasts much longer. It is not uncommon for network rehabilitation work today in older neighborhoods to unearth RBOC cable that was originally placed in the late nineteenth century and is still able to serve customers more than one hundred years later.

A typical cable network in the early 1990s was designed to last only seven to twelve years. Consequently, it was built with more planned obsolescence in mind. This limited the original cost of the network but provided for a higher constant capital-spending requirement due to the need for more frequent rehabilitation.

When the Bells were trumpeting their digital video services in the early 1990s, they would frequently offer picture quality as an advantage of their networks, citing the fact that the cable networks weren't built to last like the phone network. The continual need for network rebuilds would play in favor of the cable companies, however, when it came time to add cable modem services to deliver broadband Internet connections to customers. The services were added by the cable companies as part of the normal upgrade cycle over a seven- to ten-year period. It would take the Bells much longer to add broadband as part of their normal plant replacement cycle.

Merger Mania

Cable companies at the time were often granted exclusive franchises and regulated on a local level as compared with the RBOCs, which were heavily regulated at both the state and federal level. There was some light cable regulation on the federal level, but it was not a significant burden. Somewhat less significant was the fact that cable companies typically had multiple local operational bases, which led to less union organizing, allowing the cable companies more freedom to change work rules and the size of the workforce and to keep wages in line with the market for semiskilled labor.

Because the cable companies faced little federal regulation, they faced fewer impediments in the pursuit of new ventures and business combinations than the Bells, which were tightly constrained by the MFJ until the Telecommunications Act of 1996 was passed. As a result, the cable companies entered the merger frenzy earlier than the rest of the telecommunications industry. They were old hands at it and played the experience to their advantage when AT&T, Bell Atlantic, and USWest were seeking them as merger partners.

Bell Atlantic announced a merger with Tele-Communications, Inc. (TCI) in 1993. It took the two companies only four months to realize that they were apples and oranges and wouldn't fit together. In the end, TCI's financial model, while normal for the cable industry, was too loaded with debt for Bell Atlantic to take on.

Bell Atlantic, being the conservative child of a conservative parent (AT&T), took the balancing of debt and equity financing seriously and carried a prudent amount of debt for a company its size. Bell Atlantic's debt was a conservative 49 percent of its revenue, indicating that it could more easily afford to pay back the money it borrowed, thus according it a high debt rating. A high debt rating meant that it could borrow money at lower rates.

TCI's debt was 226 percent of its 1994 revenue. This aggressive debt level meant that borrowing was expensive and that the interest due on the loans ate up a good bit of the cash generated by its operations. Bell Atlantic's interest payments in 1994 amounted to 4.2 percent of its total revenue. TCI's interest payments totaled 15.9 percent of its sales, down from more than 20 percent (on a pro forma basis) in 1992.

USWest and Continental Cablevision tried the merger game as well, consummating their union in 1996. The two companies lived under the same corporate umbrella but maintained separate business arrangements. The two companies found no synergies to keep them together and the cable company's financial needs were a drag on the telephone business. The two went their separate ways when the cable company, which became known as MediaOne, was spun off in 1998. The marriage wouldn't have lasted anyway, as the value of cable systems increased at unsustainable rates during the late 1990s. Few shareholders could resist the temptation to sell cable properties when AT&T, Charter, and others were on a drunken spree, paying liquor-by-the-drink prices for cases of cable franchises in the late 1990s.

The cable companies still held one advantage that only the Baby Bells could replicate: a connection into the homes of tens of millions of customers nationwide. Others would covet and overpay for that advantage, but none would fully exploit it in the industry boom of the late 1990s.

THE INTERNET AS A DISRUPTIVE FORCE

During this period of stability in the industry, the Internet became more and more popular. As use of the Internet increased, its potential as a disruptive force in the communications industry became clear. The history of the Internet has been traced in entire volumes, so a few paragraphs here won't do justice to the full story. However, several aspects of the Internet's development are relevant to how the telecommunications industry reacted to its rapid popularization in the 1990s.

Most important, the Internet was perceived by the vast majority of its users as free. The initial development work that led to the Internet was paid for by the federal government. The commercial Internet was separated from the defense-related MILNET in 1984. It was later renamed NSFnet because the National Science Foundation agreed to take on the cost of maintaining the network backbone. The NSF began the commercialization of the Internet because it recognized that the original research purposes of such a broadly accessible computer network could be valuable to commercial enterprises. However, it was still a not-for-profit venture.

Because large organizations bought access to the Internet, it appeared to be without cost to most users. The costs were buried in somebody else's budget. Later, dial ISPs would become more common, selling access to individuals.

Also important was the fact that the Internet offered any-to-any connectivity with only one circuit. This kind of connectivity has been the rule in the voice network since the beginning, but it was not available in the data world until packet-switching technology became widely used in the early

1980s. Packet switching was a corporate-only phenomenon until the Internet was popularized. Any-to-any connectivity enabled a single user to access multiple content sources with minimal effort, something not previously available at a price point that would appeal to consumers.

The Internet was bringing about a fundamental change in the telecommunications network. Through the mid-1990s, the vast majority of the resources in the nation's telecommunications network were used for voice calls. By 1995, though, it became clear that the amount of data sent across the network was increasing exponentially and would eventually eclipse voice. The fantastic predictions about Internet traffic doubling every ninety days wouldn't come true (see Chapter 4 for a recounting of this fallacy), but data traffic exceeded voice on a bandwidth basis in the late 1990s and on a revenue basis only a few years later.

The problem for most carriers, particularly the RBOCs, was that data traffic generated less revenue for equivalent capacity than voice, which caused disruptions in the business models of the established carriers. Some adapted; some did not.

The potential of the Internet to increase traffic was noticed by MCI, which managed NSFnet for the National Science Foundation. MCI began investing to meet the Internet's potential long before the local companies.

The difference in readiness to accept the Internet as a revenue opportunity between the long-distance and local companies was one of the most important reasons that the dot-com investments of the late 1990s were, in large part, wasted. Although long-haul capacity in the network increased to meet the Internet hype, most end users were still connected to the World Wide Web with slow dial-up connections through the dot-com boom. Estimates at the end of 1999 indicated that less than 1.8 million of the 105 million households in the United States had broadband access to the Internet. An additional one million high-speed lines connected U.S. businesses to the Internet.[5]

Although the number of broadband subscribers was growing quickly, it wouldn't be quick enough to stanch the red ink at the dot-com companies. Many of the glitzy new services created by dot-com companies needed high-bandwidth connections to work properly. These dot-com products and services, once accepted by the public, would drive more subscribers to pay premium rates for broadband connections, thus helping the carriers pay the bills piling up from their investments in the late 1990s. Beyond the frauds and the mere silliness of many dot-com business plans, this chicken-versus-egg scenario alone accounts for most of the Internet's failure to reach its potential as quickly as was expected by many people in the late 1990s.

AT&T BUILDS AN INTERNET

In contrast to the new long-distance carriers, AT&T was managing down its customer base. As the former monopoly, it couldn't add to 100 percent market share. It had nowhere to go but down, so it used its cash to pursue the dream of becoming a computer business.

AT&T correctly determined as early as the 1960s that the ability to connect computers to a widespread communications network was the key to untold services that would revolutionize the world. Unfortunately, it was also holding on to the monopoly belief that it should be AT&T's network to which everyone connected. Eventually, the Internet would prove its base hypothesis correct. But its premise that everyone should run their computers on AT&T's network was evidence that it wasn't yet ready for a competitive market.

AT&T entered the computer manufacturing business in the 1980s. It built minicomputers based on the UNIX operating system it owned (developed, of course, at AT&T's Bell Laboratories). The machines worked well enough, but AT&T didn't succeed in building a retail channel to sell the machines. It was just not up to the bruising competition that has marked the computer hardware industry from its beginnings. In the end, it was unusual to find AT&T computers outside the old Bell system, the RBOCs being accustomed to buying from AT&T.

Because it couldn't compete in the larger market using its own home-grown computers, AT&T decided to buy into the computer business with its 1991 purchase of NCR, formerly National Cash Register. It proved inept at managing another computer business as well, especially since it installed all the executives from AT&T's failed computer business in key management positions, shoving aside the people who made NCR a success. AT&T admitted the failure as part of the second divestiture of AT&T in 1996 when both Lucent (formerly AT&T Network Systems, the telecommunications equipment–manufacturing arm of AT&T) and NCR were spun out of the mother ship.

RBOC REACTION TO THE INTERNET

When businesses, research organizations, and universities connect to the Internet, they rent circuits from an ISP. The ISPs don't own the network that provides the final link from their local Internet access point to the customer's location. They rent that capacity from the RBOCs. Thus, the RBOCs initially gained revenue from the Internet in proportion to their old business model. But when consumers started using the Internet, they did so through dial-up access, not through expensive circuits. Dial-up connections had been used for private bulletin board systems and various business applications in the past, but not in such large numbers.

Once millions of people started using the Internet through dial-up connections, the incumbent local exchange carriers' (ILECs') long-held engineering assumptions that supported their business model began to fall apart. (In this book, the term *incumbent local exchange carrier* includes the RBOCs and the independent [non-RBOC] local phone companies that at one time offered monopoly local phone service.) During the previous one hundred plus years, the ILECs' networks were engineered based on the average phone call lasting less than three minutes. All of the network capacity beside the line that goes to your house was built for the average user to make about one hundred phone calls per month lasting on average three minutes. Conversely, Internet users would go online and stay there for hours. This caused the ILECs to have to add capacity to their networks without additional revenue to pay for it.

As consumers began to notice that their primary lines were tied up with Internet use and not available for voice use, many ordered second phone lines. This became an attractive source of additional revenue for the ILECs but was a short-term fix with long-term problems. The high demand for second lines also stretched the long-held engineering assumptions that the phone company needed to place about 1.5 lines of capacity for every house or apartment in a neighborhood. Once second-line orders took off, the phone companies ran out of capacity in many neighborhoods. The cost to add a phone line to the network is about $1,000 to $1,500 and hasn't changed significantly in recent years. So the RBOCs added this capacity at, say, $1,250 and charged customers an additional $20 per month to rent the lines. A quick payback calculation shows that it takes 62.5 months for the rental of that line to pay back its initial cost. This payback is fine if the use of the line is relatively constant over the useful life of normal telephone facilities, which is about thirty years.

Unfortunately, the same customers who could afford second lines became the ones who ordered broadband Internet access when it became available in the late 1990s. So, the additional line revenue begat a cycle of stranded assets that will become more acute as broadband access becomes the standard rather than a luxury in the first decade of the twenty-first century. This will become a drag on the return-on-assets of local companies for some time (or until the assets are written down).

Reaching Beyond Dial-Up Service

The dial-up connections became a great way to get the initial generation of Internet users online. As the potential of the medium was explored by more Web developers, however, the dial connections quickly became too slow. The World Wide Web became, for many users, "the World Wide Wait." The RBOCs had an answer that they believed to be brilliant. They spent billions of dollars in the late 1980s and early 1990s adding capabilities to their network and developing support systems for what they considered to be the next generation of phone service, a technology known as integrated services digital network (ISDN). ISDN gave users the capability of maintaining up to a 144 Kb/s (144,000 bits per second) connection to the Internet versus about 28.8 Kb/s on standard modem technology at the time.

While a fivefold increase in throughput seemed impressive to most users, the price of the upgrade was too high. The terminal adapters (ISDN modems) required to support the service cost as much as $800 and the service was usually charged on a per-minute, per-channel basis, with all three ISDN "channels" required to reach the 144 Kb/s speed. The billing was complicated and often wrong. The service was also subject to installation errors, because, aside from the money put into the network, it was still an underused service. The plant upgrades and employee training were never put to use and tested to the point where the installation process was smooth. (In fact, many industry watchers referred to ISDN as standing for "I Still Don't Need It.") The few knowledgeable telephone customers who sought out the service often couldn't find a representative in the phone company's business office who knew the product well enough to fill out an order for the service.

By 1998, broadband access to the Internet was beginning its march across the country with speeds averaging 1 Mb/s, or seven times faster than the best that could be achieved with ISDN and at similar costs. The terminal equipment for the early users cost about $250 and, by the turn of the century, was often included in the setup of the service.

Why weren't the local companies ready? Because they couldn't make the mind shift, and when confronted with the facts about Internet growth and settled on a technology (ADSL), they couldn't get their (large) organizations around the problem fast enough. ADSL was a viable technology alternative for the time but has always lagged behind cable modem as the broadband Internet access technology of choice.

If any organization could muster the capital required to build a full-coverage local Internet infrastructure, it was the Bells. But they were pulled in several directions simultaneously. In addition to their normal network replacement programs, they were:

- Selling new telephone access lines at a fast pace
- Upgrading to video in select areas
- Developing ADSL services for data delivery
- Still rolling out ISDN

These capital allocation decisions became further complicated when the Bells were given the option to invest in the development of long-distance services by the Telecommunications Act of 1996.

TIME FOR A CHANGE

"For time and the world do not stand still. Change is the law of life. And those who look only to the past or the present are certain to miss the future."
—JOHN F. KENNEDY, AMERICAN PRESIDENT

The end result of this period of stability was that the brightly drawn lines between industry segments no longer made sense. Technologies were available to allow each type of company to offer services in competition with the others. Only regulatory boundaries prevented them from competing—regulatory boundaries that were about to come down.

The Internet was poised to play a role in bringing down the walls that existed between industry segments. Everybody wanted a piece of the untold riches that the Internet was going to bring. Each had solutions that turned out to be valid, but they were all going after the same consumers in the process. And the FCC didn't have the experience or the tools to guide the industry into the Internet age.

Other forces were also in the works to change the various segments in the industry. Cellular phones became the hot new electronic gadget in the mid-1990s. Wireless phones were fast becoming an integral part of the phone network rather than just a way for doctors to receive calls on the golf course. They had the potential to disrupt the traditional notion of the natural monopoly of the local carriers by giving most citizens a choice for phone service that, albeit still expensive at the time, offered features that the landline network couldn't match.

And Moore's Law was still at work during this period making computers smaller and more portable. Moore's Law, as stated by Gordon Moore of

Intel, asserts that the price performance of computer processors doubles every eighteen months. Thus, the same chip will fall in price by half in eighteen months or the same dollar amount will buy double the chip speed every eighteen months. The first true portable (laptop/notebook) computers were made available during this period. The ability to easily move computers and the data they held would bring about communications needs that the floppy disk couldn't accommodate.

The telecommunications industry in the mid-1990s was like Germany in the late 1980s before the Berlin wall came down. The companies in each walled garden were aware of the presence of the others, but they did not realize the full extent of their differences because of the artificial boundaries that separated them. Once the walls came down, Germany and the telecommunications industry had some of the same outcomes. Billions of dollars were spent trying to reshape the industry. Jobs in artificial industries were lost. The social safety net developed holes. In the telecommunications industry, many people lost jobs they had held for years and were counting on to provide them with retirement funds.

Land grabs took place in both Germany and the telecommunications industry. Authorities and others made up the rules as they went along because no one had lived through a situation like this before. There was a rush of purported do-gooders and opportunists. One facet of the times was an inability to tell them apart. Investment scams, whether legitimate but poorly managed opportunities or out-and-out frauds, happened alongside each other, often in the same company.

But before this scene could be played out in the telecommunications industry, the U.S. Congress had to break down the walls. It brought the barriers down, but it didn't create the effective adult supervision needed to prevent the telecommunications industry from resembling East Berlin in 1990 or the Wild West of the United States of the late nineteenth century.

NOTES

1. Merriam-Webster online dictionary, www.m-w.com.
2. "Trends in Telephone Service," Industry Analysis and Technology Division, Wireline Competition Bureau, FCC, May 2002, pp. 10-10 and 10-16.
3. From AT&T's and MCI's reports to the SEC on Form 10-Q for first quarter of 1997.
4. "Trends in Telephone Service," Industry Analysis and Technology Division, Wireline Competition Bureau, FCC, August 2003, p. 16-3.
5. "High-Speed Services for Internet Access: Status as of December 31, 2002," Industry Analysis and Technology Division, Wireline Competition Bureau, FCC, June 2003, p. 10.

CHAPTER 3

THE TELECOMMUNICATIONS ACT OF 1996

"Revolution is an abrupt change in the form of misgovernment."
—AMBROSE BIERCE, AMERICAN AUTHOR

"Any change is resisted because bureaucrats have a vested interest in the chaos in which they exist."
—RICHARD M. NIXON, AMERICAN PRESIDENT

Twelve years after divestiture, all the goals set out for the telecommunications industry had been met. The long-distance market was competitive, if oligopolistic. The local companies were providing lifeline service at reasonable rates and the pace of technical innovation in the telecommunications network overall quickened significantly after the early 1980s.

But other factors, unforeseen at the time of divestiture, changed the way the network was being used. The Internet and, to a lesser extent, wireless phones were being adopted rapidly by individuals as well as businesses. The Internet, in particular, was being hailed as a potential medium for all sorts of commerce. This latest development, doing business over the Internet, begat one of the largest spin cycles in the history of American punditry. The resulting market mania would rival the railroad stock manias of the nineteenth century and the South Seas bubble of the eighteenth century.

On top of changes in the way the network was being used, the carriers in the industry wanted to change the way they did business. One result of the period of stability was that the carriers, particularly the RBOCs, were growing slowly, if at

MONOPOLY	1880
	1890
	1900
	1910
	1920
	1930
	1940
	1950
	1960
	1970
	1980
	1981
	1982
	1983
DIVESTITURE	1984
	1985
	1986
	1987
STABILITY	1988
	1989
	1990
	1991
	1992
	1993
	1994
	1995
BOOM	**1996**
	1997
	1998
	1999
BOMB	2000
	2001
	2002
RECOVERY?	2003
	2004
	2005
	FUTURE

all. An obvious way for the carriers to grow was to be allowed into other markets. In 1995, when most of the debate about the Telecommunications Act of 1996 was going on in Congress, the Bell video efforts still held great promise (although this would later be proved false hope). Other carriers wanted the regulatory freedom to do to the RBOCs, and others, what the RBOCs were apparently going to do to them.

In the face of the ongoing and potential future transformation of the nation's telecommunications needs, the U.S. Congress decided change was required. What was at stake? The immensity of the wireline network infrastructure in the United States is not widely understood. The total investment in the network (local, long distance, and cable) approaches $400 billion. In addition, $40 billion to $50 billion in annual capital investment is required to maintain it. In 1996 the telephone and cable industries combined employed 1.1 million people, roughly equal the total employment of the computer services industry; yet the communications industry held roughly ten times the amount of financial assets as the computer services industry. The telecommunications industry counts virtually everyone in the United States as a customer. And, even after the walls between the service providers were breached, most of those citizens are still customers of more than one company in the industry.

No ship that large turns around as quickly as both politicians and commentators expected. Congress can and did set deadlines for action to be taken but couldn't change the ingrained attitudes and behaviors of an industry with so many large and entrenched players.

The result of Congress's deliberations became the Telecommunications Act of 1996. The act broke down most of the artificial boundaries between the walled gardens in the industry but created little in the way of new rules to supervise the former residents once they were released into the general population and began mixing with each other.

In breaking down the prior regulatory structures, the act fed the fires of economic and social change (the Internet was both) and catalyzed five sweeping trends that changed the industry forever. These trends sent shock waves through all of those who used, invested in, or were employed by the industry.

GETTING INTO THE ACT

Given the money involved with any industry this size, interest in the Telecommunications Act was high. There were few out-and-out foes of the legislation. The new-age carriers, cable companies, and independent wireless carriers were in favor of opening new markets but wanted to do so on their own terms, which generally included protection from the industry giants. The long-distance companies and the local monopolies wanted the ability to get into new markets but, of course, had an interest in protecting the smartly groomed turf within their own gardens. The RBOCs spent the most money lobbying Congress, but they were—and still are—the best-financed companies in the industry. Results also show that the RBOC lobbying dollars paid off. The RBOCs won almost everything they wanted and lost few important battles.

With competing interests from each of the established segments (as well as the nascent mobile carriers) and so much at stake, Congress had a tough job balancing the interests of the individual industry segments with those of the businesses and consumers that used the network. On top of managing market forces, Congress supported established public service obligations such as universal service and 911 emergency services.

The writers of the Telecommunications Act of 1996 must have understood that there were many imponderables in its results. Wisely, they tried not to overly constrain the market. Unwisely, they left too many gray spaces to be arbitrated by the Federal Communications Commission and the courts. The relationship between Congress and the FCC was not great at the time, but the FCC certainly did not deserve what it got in the act.

The FCC was created by Congress to oversee the implementation of the original Communications Act in 1934. Until competitors began knocking loudly on AT&T's door in the late 1960s, the FCC's job was mostly confined to regulating the broadcast airwaves used by radio and, later, television. The FCC was responsible for programs such as universal service and the review of AT&T's tariffs, but the real work of regulating the telephone industry was done at the state level.

All of that changed in the run-up to AT&T's first divestiture. Instead of cursory reviews of AT&T's tariff filings, the FCC was tasked with creating and regulating a truly competitive national market. Since AT&T was still the dominant carrier (it would retain that official designation until 1995), the regulation looked much like it had before, just with more players in the market. The FCC also had the "helpful" hand of the judicial branch of the government. The judicial branch became involved when it brokered the deal that started AT&T's first divestiture as a reaction to a federal antitrust suit. Having two branches of government involved was helpful to the regulators, as one could easily blame the other for any problems that arose.

Congress solved the issue of jurisdiction over the industry in the Telecommunications Act of 1996. The FCC was the logical choice to oversee the implementation of the act and was given the lion's share of the regulatory responsibility. The act specifically removed many items from state jurisdiction. When the FCC tried to give some of the responsibility back to the states in 2003, it was rebuffed by the courts.

The workload was beyond anything the FCC had dealt with before. The FCC was given a significant amount of specific work to do within prescribed time frames that didn't correspond with the difficulty or the gravity of the decisions to be made, particularly given the lack of specificity in the act.

> *"What hath God wrought?"*
> —SAMUEL F. B. MORSE'S FIRST TELEGRAPH, 1844

The Telecommunications Act of 1996 rewrote large sections of the Communications Act of 1934. The Telecommunications Act is subtitled:

> An Act to promote competition and reduce regulation in order to secure lower prices and higher quality services for American telecommunications consumers and encourage the rapid deployment of new telecommunications technologies.

With these grand ambitions in mind, the act changed virtually all the rules and regulating structures governing the industry erected previously by the legislative branch (the Communications Act of 1934 and the FCC) and the judicial branch (the Modified Final Judgment that governed the breakup of AT&T). The Telecommunications Act officially ended fourteen years of regulation of the old Bell System companies by the judicial branch under the MFJ, or the AT&T consent decree, as it was also called.

The opening statements of Section 253 (of the Communications Act of 1934, as revised by the Telecommunications Act of 1996) succinctly set the tone for the Telecommunications Act:

> (a) IN GENERAL—No State or local statute or regulation, or other State or local legal requirement, may prohibit or have the effect of prohibiting the ability of any entity to provide any interstate or intrastate telecommunications service.

Most of the remaining verbiage of the act qualified that statement and specified the implementation steps, but the effect was the same. From February 1996 onward, each of the walled gardens within the industry would be open to the public. The walls around the gardens would be breached, if not completely destroyed. General regulatory relief was also a stated focus of the act, but most of the deregulatory steps taken beyond replacing the MFJ and blowing down the walls between the gardens were to reduce or remove only the most anachronistic of the FCC's rules. Each of the four major industry segments felt the impact.

Commercial Mobile Radio Service (CMRS) (Cellular Telephony)

The mobile phone business was just beginning to heat up at the time the bill was drafted, so few points in the act directly affected this corner of the industry. The act allowed, but did not require, the FCC to classify mobile carriers as local exchange carriers. The act also allowed mobile services to be marketed jointly with local exchange service.

While competition developed in the mobile phone marketplace, it was more due to the personal communications services (PCS) auctions than anything included in the Telecommunications Act. The PCS spectrum included radio frequencies newly allocated to mobile services and sold at auction by the FCC in 1995 and 1996. The addition of the PCS spectrum to the existing cellular phone systems in the United States more than tripled the capacity of the mobile phone network. Before the PCS auctions, most market areas were duopolies, meaning that only two providers held spectrum in any given market. After a two- to three-year construction phase following the auctions, the emergence of these additional carriers more than doubled the number of national mobile phone carriers, causing true competition to emerge.

The bottom line was that more variations of the basic theme of mobile voice service could be offered than ever before. These options included pricing plans that brought new customers to the business in droves. The success of this competitive marketplace has meant that for many people, particularly younger customers who have never had a landline phone of their own, a mobile phone is their only phone. The result was that more than 155 million cell phones were in use in the United States by the end of 2003.[1]

Cable

The changes in the Telecommunications Act of 1996 that were aimed at the cable industry were viewed as positive by the cable companies. Rate regulation on upper tiers of services (typically the more advanced digital video that the cable companies wanted to roll out) was reduced by the act and eliminated on March 31, 1999. For consumers, though, this meant rising rates. Other minor changes were made with the net effect of deregulating or at least loosening FCC regulations of the cable industry. Since most cable rate regulation is on the local level, FCC regulation of cable services was generally redundant.

More space in the act was spent regulating the RBOCs' video services than those of the cable companies. The drafting of the bill coincided with the RBOC's biggest push into the video market. The RBOCs never made a real dent in the video market, so most of the new rules that regulate video services offered by telephone companies (Section 302 of the Telecommunications Act) are not likely to be applied anytime soon.

The biggest problem for the cable companies came because of two sections of the act that did not directly address them. In Section 205, the FCC was granted exclusive jurisdiction over direct broadcast satellite (DBS) services. Later, in Section 207, the act directed the FCC to establish regulations prohibiting restrictions on over-the-air and DBS receivers. This meant that apartment complexes and neighborhood associations would no longer be able to prevent individuals from setting up satellite receivers. This change would be a factor in the DBS providers' ability to compete on more equal footing with the cable companies in the late 1990s.

This change in the rules was important for consumers. Although the DBS and cable video offerings are somewhat different, DBS is usually the only viable competition to cable for consumers who want more than over-the-air television programming. The DBS sector of the industry grew much faster after the act was passed, reaching 18 percent of U.S. households by the end of 2003.

Long Distance

Very little in the Telecommunications Act addressed the long-distance industry directly. This market segment was already competitive, so it was fitting that few new rules would be applied in the act. The long-distance market was also about to become significantly more competitive even before the RBOCs were allowed into it, although this did not appear to be a factor in Congress's deliberations.

The principal advantage of the act for the Big 3 long-distance carriers (AT&T, MCI, and Sprint) was that they would be allowed to more easily expand their services beyond long distance. By removing the ability of state commissions to refuse entry into the local market, the Big 3 were allowed full entry into the local market with few restrictions. They were given free rein, as it turned out, to spend billions of dollars chasing the local services market, which turned out not to be the business opportunity that was initially expected.

Most users of long-distance services never really understood where or how the line was drawn between local service and long-distance service, anyway. They only understood that local phone companies could not send a call very far without turning it over to a long-distance company. The regulatory term for calls (or circuits) that stay within the local company's service area is *intra-LATA*. Local access and transport areas, or LATAs, define the geography to be served by local phone companies. Calls (or circuits) that leave a LATA are the domain of the long-distance companies.

LATAs were the creation of a bureaucracy that needed a quick fix to a problem that never existed before AT&T's first divestiture. When the RBOCs were being divested from AT&T, regulators needed to draw a formal line between local and long-distance calling areas. Each state drew boundaries to define the service areas for the incumbent local carriers. Some states drew the LATA boundaries around each city, some to encompass much larger areas, and a few to cover the entire state. There were no federal guidelines as to how to define a LATA. In the Telecommunications Act, the long-distance companies were allowed into the intra-LATA toll business, which had been a lucrative monopoly for the ILECs. (The term *incumbent local exchange carriers* includes all the local phone companies that were granted franchise rights to offer local phone service within a geographic area prior to the passage of the Telecommunications Act of 1996. The largest of the ILECs are the RBOCs. The ILECs that are not RBOCs are known as independent local phone companies because they were not affiliated with the Bell system prior to AT&T's first divestiture.) Prior to the act, only state regulators could force competition within an LATA, even for these short-haul long-distance calls. But few states allowed the long-distance carriers into this market.

Intra-LATA long-distance calls are carried only a little farther than other local calls but carried high per-minute rates compared with other local calls that were either included in a flat-rate plan or charged on a per-call basis. ILEC annual revenue from intra-LATA long-distance services peaked in 1988 at more than $15 billion. Once the act made a national rule that long-distance companies be allowed to enter the intra-LATA market, prices were driven down. ILEC revenue from intra-LATA services began a steep decline. In 1995, the last year before the intra-LATA market was fully opened, intra-LATA toll revenue for the local companies was more than $11 billion. The entry into this market of the Big 3 and the other new long-distance providers in the late 1990s brought real price competition. By 2001, the RBOCs' revenue from intra-LATA toll calling dropped to $8.5 billion.

As in the mobile services market, the long-distance market became more competitive after passage of the Telecommunications Act. But the new competition was due more to external forces, specifically the market entrants that overlaid the rail beds and highways of the United States, than to anything contained in the act.

Local

The industry segment that saw the most change as a result of the Telecommunications Act was the local services market, particularly the RBOCs. Two sections of the law, in particular, had the most impact on the ILECs:

1. Section 101 of the Telecommunications Act—Resale and unbundling obligations

2. Section 151 of the Telecommunications Act—RBOC long-distance approval

These two sections would govern the balance between the prize (gaining long-distance approval) in the open telecommunications market and the price (resale obligations) the RBOCs would have to pay.

Most independent (non-RBOC) ILECs were also required to follow the resale and unbundling rules but were not required to prove competition before being allowed to sell long-distance service. They had less to worry about in the form of competition because their service areas were generally outside metropolitan areas and thus less attractive to competitors.

Resale and Unbundling Obligations

Resale and unbundling both refer to the requirement that the ILECs sell their services to CLECs for use by the competing carrier in its own telecommunications services offered to customers.

The difference is that *resale* involves a complete local telephone service that is assembled by the ILEC and then sold, as is, by the CLEC. *Unbundling*, as the name implies, means that the CLEC can have its choice of certain individual network elements owned by the ILEC without having to buy the complete service. The unbundled network elements (UNEs) can be ordered in any grouping necessary to provide service. A CLEC that installed its own switch, for example, could use only the unbundled lines going from an ILEC switching center to a customer's home without buying the whole local service, which included the use of the ILEC switch. Defining the so-called necessary groups of available network elements would require years of effort between the FCC and the federal judicial system.

Resold ILEC service (called total service resale, or TSR) carries a higher price, as does any finished good compared with its piece parts. By contrast, using the UNE approach is like going to the warehouse and picking out the parts individually and then telling the RBOC to assemble them. Buying the individual, unbundled elements is less expensive. The CLECs learned, after some experience, that the price differential between resale and the collection of unbundled elements is significant. Thus, resale has become a less popular way of doing business.

The Telecommunications Act defines broadly what ILECs must provide to would-be competitors. The broadest statement of the ILECs' new unbundling requirements is in Section 251(c)(3):

> The duty to provide, to any requesting telecommunications carrier for the provision of a telecommunications service, nondiscriminatory access to network elements on an unbundled basis at any technically feasible point on rates, terms, and conditions that are just, reasonable, and nondiscriminatory in accordance with the terms and conditions of the agreement and the requirements of this section and section 252. An incumbent local exchange carrier shall provide such unbundled network elements in a manner that allows requesting carriers to combine such elements in order to provide such telecommunications service.

A further definition of unbundling is provided in Section 253(d):

> In determining what network elements should be made available for purposes of subsection (c)(3), the Commission shall consider, at a minimum, whether—
>
> (A) access to such network elements as are proprietary in nature is necessary; and
>
> (B) the failure to provide access to such network elements would *impair* the ability of the telecommunications carrier seeking access to provide the services that it seeks to offer. (emphasis added)

That's it. After all Congress's hard work debating competitive marketplaces and how the telecommunications incumbents should support new carriers, this is as specific as Congress could get. The FCC was in trouble. Eight years later, the word *impair* still had no working definition. The FCC attempted to define an *impairment standard* three times during these eight years but could not come up with a definition that would stand up to a court challenge.

Long-Distance Approval

The first freedom offered to the RBOCs was the ability to offer out-of-region long-distance services. In other words, the RBOCs could set up a long-distance service and sell it to customers who were not in their local service area. This option was not picked up by any of the RBOCs at the time but was used by USWest after its merger with Qwest Communications International. As part of the merger deal, Qwest sold off all its long-distance customers in USWest's fourteen-state region but was allowed to keep all its customers elsewhere.

Of course, what the RBOCs wanted was the ability to sell long-distance services to their existing local-service customers. To gain that approval, an RBOC had to convince the FCC that it complied with the new resale and unbundling requirements as specified in Section 271 of the act. The RBOCs' 271 filings would take up volumes and be rewritten several times, but at least the RBOCs had a path forward to gain approval to offer long-distance service. The process of proving that their networks were open to competitors would be involved, but the result was that millions of customers gained options for services: both existing services such as local and long distance as well as new services they had never been offered before. Chapter 5 describes these filings in more detail.

The eventual impact of the Telecommunications Act was that all carriers (mobile, RBOC, long-distance, competing carriers, and cable companies) could, for the first time, offer complete packages of end-to-end voice services. Only the Bell System had been able to do that previously, and only before the divestiture. The new choices in the market led to lower prices for virtually all consumers.

WHAT WAS LEFT BEHIND

"I'm not bad; I'm just drawn that way."
—JESSICA RABBIT,
CARTOON CHARACTER FROM THE MOVIE *WHO FRAMED ROGER RABBIT*

STATED GOALS OF THE 1996 TELECOMMUNICATIONS ACT

Based on the subtitle of the Telecommunications Act, the goals of the bill were to:

1. Promote competition
2. Reduce regulation
3. Reduce prices
4. Increase service quality
5. Encourage rapid deployment of new technology

Perhaps more important than what was in the act is what was left out.

Where's the Internet?

The idea that the Telecommunications Act was intended to "encourage rapid deployment" of anything other than lawyers is pretty far-fetched. In the minds of most people, particularly during the run-up to the dot-com boom, new telecommunications technology meant primarily one thing: the Internet. Only later did it also mean cell phones to most people.

The Internet is and has always been more a collection of connected networks than a single entity. Most people see this distributed nature as a blessing, not only for the resiliency it provides but also because it gives the network an ethereal quality that defies traditional regulation. Although individual users of the Internet can be held accountable for their actions, the network itself is available for many uses, both legal and illegal. The ethereal quality of the Internet, along with its many purposes, meant that it didn't fit into any previously defined category of telecommunications regulation. It is both local and long distance, both national and international. It carries voice traffic now (it did not in 1996), just like the telephone network. It carries video like the cable network. It even carries broadcast audio and video like traditional radio and television stations. What makes the Internet useful to many is that it is a one-stop network connection for many applications.

A fundamental flaw in the act was that it failed to deal with this inherently multijurisdictional nature of the Internet. The Internet industry, one of the nominal reasons for the act in the first place, was breaking down barriers that existed, but no new boundaries or rules were created. The bulk of the act is more focused on changes to the existing industry segments, particularly the RBOCs, than it is on shaping the new world. While it gives the FCC authority to regulate new services, the FCC couldn't keep ahead of the capital-fueled markets of the late 1990s. The Telecommunications Act dealt with the old way of using the nation's network and not with the new way, the Internet.

Many a legislator and regulator stated that the lack of regulation of the Internet was supposed to make it free to grow without regulation, guided only by competition. But that position exhibits a lack of knowledge of the industry. Virtually every other facet of the industry was highly regulated. Once the Internet was taking market share away from regulated products, conflicts were bound to arise. Nothing was put in place to address those inevitable conflicts.

In fact, the Internet was barely addressed at all in the act. The first and only substantive mention of the Internet in the act comes almost three-fourths of the way through the document, and then only in a section that deals with blocking pornography. And this part of the act, known as the Communications Decency Act, was later struck down in court as violating the First Amendment.

Almost as important as the Internet was the ability to access all the great new content out there in a timely manner. Internet users were already referring to the World Wide Web as the "World Wide Wait" by 1996. Faster access was needed. As Chapter 2 pointed out, the lack of broadband access to the Internet was one of the significant causes of the dot-com bust. Yet, there are more words in the act covering new regulations for pay-phone service than broadband or the Internet. So much for the act's stated goal of encouraging the deployment of new technology. Deregulation in the form of no regulation effectively delayed the deployment of the Internet and, thus, helped to doom most of the dot-com investments. In this case, the lack of regulation contributed to the widening of the digital divide because, until 2002, pricing for broadband connections was such that only those with higher income could afford it. (The digital divide is the difference in technology use between different socioeconomic groups. The underlying assumption is that those in poorer groups have less access to computers and the Internet and, therefore, get further behind in a competitive society. For example, someone without Internet access wouldn't be able to apply for jobs using one of the many Internet-based job search sites that have taken a large market share of the listings of good jobs.)

THE LAW OF UNINTENDED CONSEQUENCES

It is unlikely that Congress and the FCC could have prevented the tele-bomb, but they certainly could have brought some sanity to the situation had they thought through the potential results of the Telecommunications Act of 1996.

In 1936, sociologist Robert Merton published the first comprehensive, modern treatment of what is now known as the Law of Unintended Consequences. In this article, Merton took the approach of the relatively new field of social science and described the causes of unforeseen outcomes from human decision-making processes, particularly as they applied to decisions made by formally organized groups of people. Merton identified five categories of causes of unintended consequences:[2]

1. *Ignorance*—Whether willful or the result of a reasoned decision to stop seeking additional information.
2. *Error*—Ranging from a "lack of systematic thoroughness" to an obsession that prevents logical thinking.

3. *Immediacy of Interest*—The decision makers focus only on the intended benefit.
4. *Basic Values*—No further consequences are considered due to, for example, religious beliefs.
5. *Power of Prediction*—The power to compel groups to strive for the opposite result. This is the opposite of a self-fulfilling prophecy.

Congress needed to act. The bill, or one like it, had been debated for several years. In addition, 1996 was an election year: Completing a bill that could be claimed to affect the newly popular Internet could be used on the campaign trail by those seeking reelection. The bill, as it turns out, was a feel-good attempt to feign action and not a real effort to change the regulatory environment for the better.

In the Telecommunications Act of 1996, Congress provided a fertile ground for unintended consequences, particularly falling into the Error and Immediacy of Interest categories. The FCC would learn just how much of an expedient the act was while attempting to turn it into reality.

Reciprocal Compensation

While the Telecommunications Act ignored the Internet, it also failed to anticipate some of the major changes that would occur as the voice network changed. It created new rules for the ILECs and created new ways for the CLECs to interconnect to the ILECs but didn't cover the breadth of how those interconnection points would be used. The first major unintended consequence of the act was a result of the rules intended to cover financial settlements between the ILECs and the new class of competitive local carriers created by the act.

The ILECs were required to negotiate financial agreements with the CLECs for completing calls between the ILECs' customers and the new carriers' customers. Because the payments could flow either way depending on whose customer originated the call, these payments were called *reciprocal compensation*. This became problematic for the ILECs, who were used to being paid for the use of their lines on both the originating end and terminating end of a long-distance call.

The issue of reciprocal compensation could have been solved in the Telecommunications Act but it wasn't. The act specifies that such compensation arrangements have to be in place for the RBOCs to receive approval to offer long-distance service, but there is little guidance to the FCC on implementation. There is only language—from Section 252(d) of the act—that makes it seem as if Congress is punting the question to the state commissions.

The last piece of the puzzle required to create the reciprocal compensation controversy was a result of one of the FCC's attempts to help the new Internet industry get on its feet. ISPs were allowed to purchase interconnection circuits at market rates rather than having to purchase circuits from access tariffs, which carried higher prices designed to subsidize local service. (As in Chapter 2, the term *tariff* means a list of services and prices for services that the carrier offers. In the case of access tariffs, however, the services and prices are offered to other carriers, not to end customers.) This move was similar in intent to Congress banning taxation on goods purchased over the Internet in order to support the new Internet industry.

Since ISPs were not required to purchase circuits from the higher-access tariffs, they were free to purchase circuits from CLECs, or in some cases, became CLECs themselves. The RBOCs readily negotiated reciprocal compensation agreements with the CLECs because it was one of the requirements for gaining permission to sell long-distance service.

The problem developed because virtually all the traffic generated by an ISP is from customers dialing the modems of the ISP. Thus, there is a large amount of traffic going to the ISP from the ILEC (which still has most of the customers) and little originating from the ISP. This resulted in an imbalance in the reciprocal compensation payments, with most of the dollars flowing from the ILEC to the ISP/CLEC.

This created a multimillion-dollar problem for the FCC. In the first example of many resulting from the Law of Unintended Consequences, the ISPs were legally double-dipping. On the one hand, they were not considered carriers when it came to interconnection. (Long-distance carriers were required to interconnect with the ILECs using circuits purchased on access tariffs.) On the other hand, the ISPs claimed to be carriers in order to be able to gain compensation as CLECs when they completed calls for ILEC customers. The letter of the Telecommunications Act promoted the circumstances that created this situation and created nothing that would have prevented it.

The FCC allowed this illogical stance to exist for more than five years after the act was signed. Reciprocal compensation was a clear example of a situation where the application of different principles used by the bureaucracy for legitimate purposes could result in undesirable outcomes. The FCC would also struggle mightily, both internally and in the courts, to define the rules governing different facets of local competition. Eight years after the passage of the Telecommunications Act, the FCC still had not stated a difference between access and interconnect tariffs that would stand up to a legal challenge.

INITIAL IMPLEMENTATION STEPS

Whenever a government agency is overburdened, as the FCC became after the act was passed, things tend to get left by the wayside. For example, in recent years Congress has heaped new requirements on the Internal Revenue Service regarding how it conducts its business, with the result that audit rates have plummeted. This has allowed fraud to multiply and has contributed to the federal budget deficits.

The result in the case of the FCC after passage of the Telecommunications Act was that decision making was left to be pursued in the courts, a slow and expensive way to continue to define legislation. Too many issues that were supposedly decided in the act were still being bandied about in the courts more than eight years later. This occurrence clearly played to the strengths of the ILECs and, to a lesser extent, the incumbent long-distance carriers who had the money to hire lawyers to represent them in court. It left the new-age carriers at a significant disadvantage because they were not able to hire lawyers at the same rate as the incumbents. Many new start-up carriers, both at the time of the first divestiture of AT&T and during the 1990s, were able to provide valuable services but were unable to keep up with the legal requirements of operating a phone company.

MCI in the 1960s and 1970s was the exception that proves this rule. It was the only company that received timely enough rulings in its favor to act on them and be successful. MCI first challenged AT&T's regulated monopoly status at a time when that monopoly was considered not just a necessary evil but a good deal for both the consumer and the nation. A brief look at others that challenged AT&T in court reveals a list of defunct companies. Hush-A-Phone, Carterfone, Telerent, Data Transmission Co., and Phontele are but a few of the companies that are part of history, known more for lending their names to court cases or FCC proceedings in which they challenged the old Bell System than for the products and services they offered.

Following passage of the Telecommunications Act, any company that wanted to become a player in the new competitive environment needed to have enough legal staff to keep up with the volumes of pronouncements required to implement the provisions of the act. Not only was the law vague, but it also piled a significant new workload on the FCC. The Telecommunications Act alone specified twenty-two new undertakings for the FCC to complete within five years of its passage. This list doesn't include new requirements that came without time frames. Although certain regulatory requirements were lifted by the act, they in no way compensated in volume or complexity for what was put on the FCC's plate.

The FCC met the basic deadlines, but the quality of the output was not high if you gauge the decisions on how they stood up to the inevitable judicial scrutiny or their ultimate effect on the industry. As mentioned earlier, both reciprocal compensation and the Section 253 impairment standard were difficult problems to fix. Both of these issues could have been solved by Congress but instead have bounced back and forth between the FCC and courts for far too long. The outcome ultimately will be decided by the courts because the FCC was given an act so vague that opposite conclusions can be legitimately reached within the letter of the law. Any interpretation placed on the act by the FCC is only one way to look at the text as passed by Congress.

Not that these battles were all new. The rules defining local interconnection and interexchange access were gamed by all non-ILEC carriers even before the Telecommunications Act because the differences in rates between circuits purchased from access tariffs and those purchased in the open market were great and the rules governing their use were loose. MCI's gaming of the rules became an issue used by its biggest competitors (SBC, Verizon, and AT&T) in trying to slow MCI's exit from bankruptcy protection in 2004.

The Telecommunications Act purported to offer deregulation, but the result was a market with little adult supervision. The companies that wanted to play the game made and hedged their own bets to forge the existing submarkets into the brave new telecommunications world promised, but not described, by the Telecommunications Act of 1996.

FIVE LONG-TERM TRENDS

The largest effect of the Telecommunications Act of 1996 was the general opening of all markets to any carrier, new or established, that wanted to compete. Each of the companies that existed in the walled gardens would react differently based on its experience and executive leadership. However, because each subset of the industry had its own customer segments, competitor profiles, and financial requirements, many commonalities were also found in how they approached the new competitive world. During the time around the debate and passage of the act, the industry saw five far-reaching action patterns either begin or develop in the marketplace:

1. The second race to cover the nation in fiber-optic capacity

2. The RBOC mergers and subsequent search for long-distance approval

3. The search for diversification by the long-distance carriers

4. The rise and fall of the CLECs

5. Lost opportunities by the cable companies

Each of these trends started inside one of the walled gardens, bringing the perspective of that segment as it expanded to the others. But each trend spread to or affected the other market segments as well as the larger economy and society.

These five trends interacted in many ways to create the telecommunications market as we know it today. Figure 3-1 shows the periods of most activity as these trends developed. The activity heated up considerably after the passage of the Telecommunications Act of 1996. The passage of the act legitimized the business plans of the companies that followed the trends and made them part of what Michael Lewis called "the new, new thing."[3] Both the new entrants and existing carriers claimed government-sanctioned legitimacy for any new investment initiative because the Telecommunications Act was going to break down the walls preventing the company from succeeding. Images of the fall of the Berlin Wall were still fresh in the minds of Americans during this time when everything seemed possible.

Many new services and new ways of delivering and packaging existing services were created during the boom that preceded the telebomb. Many entrepreneurs and product managers tried their hands at predicting the

FIGURE 3-1.
FIVE TRENDS CATALYZED BY THE TELECOMMUNICATIONS ACT OF 1996.

The Second Race to Cover the United States in Fiber Optics

The RBOC Mergers & Search for Long-Distance Approval

The Search for Diversification by the Long-Distance Carriers

The Rise and Fall of the CLECs

Lost Opportunities by the Cable Companies

1994 1995 1996 1997 1998 1999 2000 2001 2002 2003

Passage of the Telecommunications Act of 1996

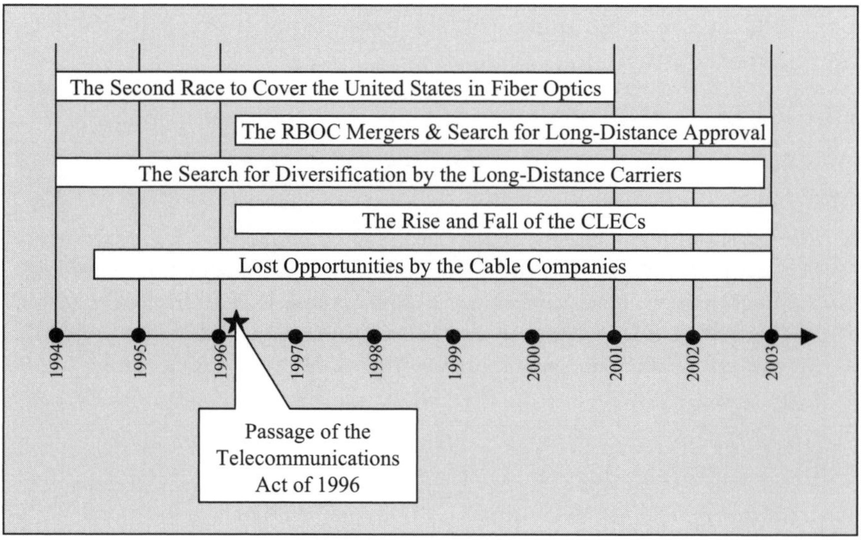

next societal and technological movement around which they could build a telecommunications product. Some developments seemed obvious, such as increasing Internet access and bundling of local and long-distance services. Others attempts ended up being ahead of their time, like telemedicine.

Not only did the number of telecommunications choices available to consumers expand; the number of companies crowding the airwaves with marketing messages mushroomed as well. The result was many confused consumers—and a few angry ones—once they figured out that the new services they just bought were not delivered by a financially stable company. In the end, it turned out that all the appropriate reagents were put into the test tube but, whether a result of poor regulation or dot-com euphoria, no one organization was able to control the ultimate chemical reaction.

Full-speed development of these trends lasted for more than four years, along with the dot-com hysteria, until the capital spigot ran dry in 2000. The trends then wound down between 2000 and 2003. The second racers were done with (or claimed victory and quickly wrapped up) their construction programs. The RBOCs' long-distance application train would chug to completion. The cable companies finally maxed out their debt limits. The shutdown of the capital markets hit the CLECs and the long-distance companies hardest. The CLECs were constrained because they were still using start-up capital in most cases. Those that couldn't become profitable or find new sources of capital went away. The long-distance companies were hit by the shutdown of the capital markets, financial scandals, bottomless pricing (courtesy of the second race), and new competitors in the form of the RBOCs.

Not until late 2003, seven years after the passage of the Telecommunications Act, did the telecommunications market come around full circle and head in the right direction.

NOTES

1. Wireless subscriber counts from the Cellular Telecommunications & Internet Association, a wireless industry association that tracks overall statistics of mobile carriers.
2. Robert K. Merton, "The Unanticipated Consequences of Purposive Social Action," *American Sociological Review*, Volume 1, Issue 6, December 1936.
3. Michael Lewis, *The New, New Thing* (New York: W.W. Norton & Company, 2001).

CHAPTER 4

THE SECOND RACE TO COVER THE UNITED STATES IN OPTICAL FIBER

"Those who do not remember the past are condemned to re-peat it."
— GEORGE SANTAYANA, AMERICAN POET AND PHILOSOPHER

"That men do not learn very much from the lessons of history is the most important of all the lessons of history."
— ALDOUS HUXLEY, BRITISH NOVELIST

The first race to cover the United States with fiber-optic cable in the 1980s was the result of an opportunity to use a new technology to enter a newly competitive market. Although the initial costs were high and the benefits were prospective, the limited number of competitors made for manageable market development. The result was a successful market that, for a time, was easily defended by the Big 3 long-distance companies. This market also delivered new services and decreasing prices to consumers much faster than the old Bell system, providing value to both investors and customers alike.

As noted in Chapter 1, Sprint, AT&T, and MCI Communications spent billions of dollars in the 1980s connecting every city in the United States to their fiber-optic networks. The Williams Companies joined them later when it built the WilTel network. WilTel was sold to WorldCom in 1994. At the end of that year, the four companies (Big 3 plus World-Com) controlled 98.2 percent of the long-haul fiber capacity in the United States.[1] (A *route mile* is one mile covered by fiber cable. A *strand mile* is one mile covered by a strand of

1880
1890
1900
1910
1920
1930
1940
1950
1960
1970
1980
1981
1982
1983
1984
1985
1986
1987
1988
1989
1990
1991
1992
1993
1994
1995
1996
1997
1998
1999
2000
2001
2002
2003
2004
2005
FUTURE

MONOPOLY
DIVESTITURE
STABILITY
BOOM
BOMB
RECOVERY?

fiber. Typically, the long-distance carriers had twenty-four to ninety-six strands in each cable. Thus, one route mile of cable would contain twenty-four to ninety-six strand miles of fiber.) The size of the long-distance network was 2.5 million strand miles of fiber. (By 1994, no other technology represented significant capacity in the network.) Even as late as 1996, those four carriers controlled 90.5 percent of all long-haul fiber strands in the United States.[2]

In the face of this continuing dominance of the largest carriers, three new carriers funded and built multibillion-dollar long-haul, fiber-optic networks. At least five additional carriers planned and built similar networks in Canada or in transatlantic and transpacific routes that landed in North America. What logic could justify such huge investments?

This second race to cover the United States in fiber is where the Internet hype that spun the dot-com bubble intersected with businesses that operated in the physical world—but with significantly more disastrous financial results. Whereas the largest of the dot-com failures (Webvan) burned through $1.2 billion in cash,[3] a typical participant in the second race burned through about $10 billion. These new carriers added immense amounts of capacity to the long-distance network even though little capacity was being added to the local networks that served as the off-ramps from the information superhighway, as the Internet became known.

The excess capacity caused a downward pricing spiral that lowered prices for all long-distance services as well as information services, such as financial and news services, which rely on telecommunications. Per-minute pricing for voice services went through the floor, causing further instability as business owners, in particular, stopped committing to long-term contracts. Why commit to a price today when the price is likely to be lower tomorrow?

Both the new and old long-distance companies came up with different ways to package the same old products, but they were not enough to save the carriers that couldn't compete on price. The market had long before run out of new ideas.

HOW DOES YOUR NETWORK GROW?

Increases in the capacity of modern telecommunications networks have been as reliable as Moore's Law has been for computers, and for just as long. The telecommunications industry has steadily developed transmission technologies through three distinct generations of technology: analog transmission over metallic circuits, digital transmission over metallic circuits, and digital transmission over fiber optics. While analog transmission systems developed steadily over time, the increases in capacity of digital systems has been exponential since the first T-1 systems were introduced in 1962. Digital transmission technologies have followed a curve much like the price performance of computer chips as predicted by Moore's Law. The fact that modern telecommunications transmission systems depend on those computer chips in addition to their own unique technologies is no accident.

Well before the second race began, the development of digital transmission over fiber-optic technology was already proceeding at a fast pace. By 1992, all major carriers in the United States were installing OC-3 carrier systems, the first generation of fiber-optic transmission technology to be broadly deployed. By 1995, the original long-distance builders were beginning to deploy OC-48 transmission systems, an improvement in transmission capacity of sixteen times in only three years and long enough before the second race heated up for investors to take note. By 2000, the most common transmission speed in the long-haul network was 10 Gb/s (gigabits per second; OC-192). This means that advances in technology increased the potential capacity of the network by a factor of sixty-four in only eight years without adding any more fiber-optic strands to the network.

In the midst of this technology transformation, three new companies (Qwest Communications International, Level 3 Communications, and Williams Communications Group) made major commitments to building out national fiber-optic networks that were essentially an overlay of existing networks. Williams had already demonstrated that it knew how to build a network and expected to repeat the process. Qwest and Level 3 also had roots in previous, successful network builds. But lightning would not strike twice for any of these companies.

Faced with an almost sure thing in the increase in capacity of the existing networks, the collective decision to spend $40 billion to compete with the entrenched long-distance oligopoly was not justifiable on any rational basis. It is true that, as with any oligopoly, there was fat in the cost structures of AT&T, MCI, and Sprint, but their cost structures were not so unbalanced as to justify the investments of Qwest, Level 3, and Williams during the 1990s.

So, why did these three companies overbuild the existing networks? In short, because they could. While touting their few unique advantages, they dumped massive amounts of transmission capacity on the market, well in excess of demand. Their actions in the market were followed by many other companies, to the point that, by 2002, an investment of $1 billion in network construction couldn't make any waves in the market. As with the dot-com companies, only a few of the early companies actually made money, but an investor who got both in and out of the game early enough saw significant value before the telebomb took most of the gains away. The Kiewit family (Level 3), Phil Anschutz (Qwest), and Gary Winnick (Global Crossing) were all early investors who pocketed billions of dollars because of the second race.

THE FUNDAMENTAL FALLACY

To attract investors, the new entrants depended on a catch phrase that passed for fact at the time but has since been debunked. Beginning in 1997, various parties interested in seeing the Internet grow began repeatedly to drop the sound bite that "Internet traffic doubles every ninety days." Although this was probably true during the early commercialization of the Internet in 1995 and 1996, it should have been obvious that growth on that scale could not be sustained. It is much easier to grow at a given percentage from a smaller base. It is easier to grow revenue from $100 to $200 than it is to grow from $100,000,000 to $200,000,000, for example. An additional $100 is easier to find than $100,000,000.

The sound bite persisted at a time when most entrepreneurs were moving too fast in the Internet land grab to spend time thinking for themselves. It was one of the dot-com catch phrases that seems passé now but had the force of gospel at the time. Previously fundamental assumptions were anything but fundamental at a time when everything was going to be changed by the Internet. The implication, believed by most, was that because the Internet was set to imminently permeate all aspects of human life, traffic would continue to double every three months for the foreseeable future. Investors were also complacent because they were making so much money in the same land grab. Even the U.S. government got into the act, quoting the statistic without any evidence to back it up.[4]

THE RACE IS ON

With billions of dollars in funding and the promise of infinitely expanding use of their infinitely expanding network capacity, the three main over-builders were off to the races. They were not alone. By 1998, both Frontier (later part of Global Crossing) and GST Telecommunications got into the act as well. Incidentally, they are called *overbuilders* because they built in addition to the existing networks, not because they built too much.

In the years leading up to and after the passage of the Telecommunications Act of 1996, the new carriers built tremendous capacity on their long-haul networks. In 1998, the last year that the FCC kept separate statistics on long-haul fiber, the networks of four new entrants (Qwest, Frontier, GST Telecom, and Williams) contained 1.7 million strand miles of fiber. Adding the rest of the Qwest build out (completed after 1998) and the later Level 3 build out, this group more than doubled the number of strand miles covering the United States in less than five years. This happened at a time when existing networks were seeing a capacity boost of sixty-four times owing only to developments in the technology used on their existing fiber-optic lines.

The result of all the building and technology evolution was that, from a gross capacity estimate of 1.5 terabits per second (Tb/s) in 1994, the nation's long-haul networks grew to a capacity of 195 Tb/s by 1998. The capacity of AT&T's, WorldCom's, and Sprint's networks at the end of 1998 was 90 Tb/s. Estimated demand in 2001 was still less than 10 Tb/s.

Adding to the folly was the lack of fiber or other broadband access in the local network. The long-haul networks were a super speedway to nowhere. The long-haul carriers could deliver multigigabits of information per second, but the local carriers that needed to deliver the data to end users had not made similar investment in extending the broadband network to homes and businesses. This became known as the "last-mile problem."

The information technology industry has a phrase to describe what happens to users of computer applications that provide too much data and little usable information: "drinking from the fire hose." The Internet became a fire hose that could direct huge amounts of data in any direction at any time. But the vast majority of users could open the tap only wide enough to receive drips of the information provided.

Although the $40 billion invested by the overbuilders was large, it paled next to the cost of rebuilding the local networks to extend broadband services to individual customers. The local telephone companies in the United States have a cumulative investment of $290 billion in their facilities. The cable companies have another $60 billion to $70 billion invested in their networks. Whereas the capabilities of new technology used by the local providers have increased greatly over the past years, the cost has dropped only marginally. The Telecommunications Act of 1996 encouraged competition in all markets but not even in the dot-com boom could enough capital be thrown at the broadband problem fast enough to match the investments of the second-race participants and the dot-com companies.

Even though the federal government could repeat the fundamental fallacy, it couldn't perform enough analysis on the situation to figure out that there was a fairly low ceiling on how high Internet traffic could grow without broadband access into consumers' homes.

PROFILES OF THE OVERBUILDERS

Against this background of great hype and little reasoned thought, the second racers started the investment cycle that led to the boom in the industry and, ultimately, the telebomb. From late 1997 to mid-2000, the dot-com companies and the telecommunications carriers fed each other's hype and developed a virtuous circle of increased promises and more investment. But, in the end, the circle was fueled by venture capital, junk bonds, and money raised from the general public through stock offerings, and not by profitable growth.

Qwest

Qwest, like Sprint before it, began as a pet project of the Southern Pacific Railroad (SPR), laying fiber along the railroads' rights-of-way. Qwest was begun in 1987 as SP Telecom, some time after GTE bought the Sprint network. In 1988, Southern Pacific was bought by Phillip Anschutz, the energy and utility investor. When he later sold SPR to Union Pacific Corporation, he kept SP Telecom, in addition to the rights to lay fiber along the national rail network. He renamed the business Qwest and built it as a carrier's carrier, selling bandwidth wholesale to other carriers who would then sell to end users. By 1993, it was also selling services directly to business customers.

Qwest became a big player in 1996 with a contract to provide Frontier with significant capacity on Qwest's new network in return for a $500 million investment.[5] At that point, Qwest began to ramp up its network build, adding almost 550,000 strand miles of fiber to its network between 1995 and 1998. The entire national network build out cost about $10 billion.

Participating in another trend of the time, Anschutz hired Joseph Nacchio away from AT&T in 1996 to create a carrier from a collection of fiber-optic assets. Nacchio was a longtime (twenty-seven years) AT&T executive who was lured away from the complacent atmosphere at the former monopoly carrier by the ability to participate in the ground floor of a start-up. Nacchio, along with Alex Mandl, was the most notable of what became a flood of executives leaving AT&T in search of greener grass.

Qwest quickly became a Wall Street favorite after its initial public offering (IPO) in 1996. The stock was bid up to fantastic levels in anticipation of the new long-distance network coming online. Qwest used this premium in the market to make two strategic investments that have proven to be its saviors.

First, in 1998, Qwest bought LCI International in a stock deal that amounted to $4.7 billion, more than forty-five times LCI's operating income in 1997.[6] LCI had more than twice Qwest's revenue in 1997 and was significantly more profitable. LCI started as a roll up of small long-distance companies during the industry consolidation that began once the oligopoly carriers made firm their control of the market. Like WorldCom, LCI merged with several long-distance resellers and with one company, LiTel, which had an underutilized fiber-optic network. LCI created what was at one time the fifth-largest U.S. long-distance company.

Qwest's second major acquisition, in 2000, was a $46.3 billion takeover of USWest. USWest, one of the original seven local operating companies divested from AT&T in 1984, was the weakest of the five remaining RBOCs (Pacific Telesis and NYNEX merged with SBC and Bell Atlantic, respectively). But *weakest* was a relative term. USWest was a profitable carrier serving 25 million customers in its fourteen-state area. In 1999, it had more than $16 billion in net assets compared with Qwest's $4 billion.[7]

The greatest benefits that Qwest received from the USWest merger were the $1.5 billion in dividends that USWest paid out every year as well as several USWest businesses that were later sold for high prices. These assets added more than $10 billion in cash to Qwest's business over the next three years—roughly the cost of its initial network build.

Level 3

James Crowe, the serial entrepreneur who started and ran MFS Communications, began building Level 3 in 1997, as a project of Peter Kiewit Sons' Inc. (PKS), a large construction company based in Omaha, Nebraska. MFS, also a Kiewit project, was successful at building and selling local fiber networks to connect businesses to the networks of the long-haul carriers. But Level 3 began as a backbone, or long-distance, network. Level 3 gave contracts for construction of their network to PKS, which took away nearly $3 billion in fees as the general contractor for the Level 3 network: the public stock- and bondholders would take on the lion's share of the risk. Level 3 funded the original network build with $3 billion from the Kiewits and a $2 billion junk bond offering. The offering was heralded at the time by the *Wall Street Journal* as the largest such offering of the decade.[8] (It would hold that record for only a few months as WorldCom placed a $6 billion offer later that year to pay off British Telecommunications as part of the purchase of MCI.) Level 3 went public in April 1998 through the public listing of shares in a PKS subsidiary that held other Kiewit businesses, including coal mines. Level 3 reported $80 million in revenue from the coal-mining business in 2003.

Level 3 spent $12 billion to build a network, more than either Qwest or Williams. The premium it paid reflected the fact that it was late to the party. Level 3 was forced to build on less desirable routes because the best ones were taken. It also had to bid up salaries to attract talent willing to leave other jobs in the telecommunications market, particularly in the telecom-rich Denver metro area, where it chose to locate its headquarters.

Because Level 3 was late to the game, it had to try a few different tricks from the other overbuilders. It made aggressive moves into local services (something it knew well from its MFS heritage), colocation and hosting. It later tried to become a software distributor.

INCUMBENTS' REACTION

The incumbent long-distance carriers' initial reaction to the overbuilders was predictable and correct. In general, they continued to build network only as needed to meet specific demand and their evolving product strategy. Only WorldCom, obsessed with doing deals rather than building a business, came completely off the tracks. While the overbuilders led the way to the boom, the incumbents stepped aside and let them invest beyond the capability of the market to absorb these multibillion-dollar investments. The overbuilders were unencumbered by the need for profits, so they could invest well in advance of demand. The incumbents had to run real businesses according to the dictates of the general investing public, not the dot-com investment community.

In looking back, the general nonreaction of the incumbents to the overbuilders should have been a warning. The curious divergence in the strategies between the Big 3 and the second racers should have been examined in more detail but instead was taken as evidence, at least by dot-com investors, that the old dinosaurs just didn't understand the new environment. The companies with a track record of success in the business were investing in other areas rather than wasting their money building bigger networks.

Sprint

Sprint essentially stopped building long-haul fiber in 1991. Between 1991 and 1998, it added only four thousand strand miles of fiber to its network.

Again, the increases in capacity brought by new technology were enough for it to expand without sinking billions into trenching new fiber. Sprint was run in a conservative fashion, befitting its origins as an ILEC. The company was run by two long-term executives, William Esrey and Ronald LeMay. Although the two looked very different, they appeared to be of the same mind. They even left Sprint over the same questionable tax-related transaction.

In terms of building stable businesses within an industry in tumult, Sprint was the winner among the long-distance companies. But, of course, it had a local company within its portfolio to even out its financial results, a lesson that Qwest also learned, but did not master until it was nearly too late.

AT&T

After sloughing off the local business, AT&T invested little in the long-distance business beyond the fiber upgrades. It built normal route expansions to its network—adding only 154,000 strand miles of long-haul fiber between 1994 and 1998, an annual growth rate of less than 4 percent. Apparently, the capacity increases afforded by new technology were quite enough to fit its growth needs.

AT&T set its sights in different directions, choosing instead to focus on other exciting new ventures. Few, if any, of those ventures paid off. Its core businesses after divestiture were long-distance and telecommunications equipment manufacturing. The equipment business, historically known as Western Electric and later to become Lucent Technologies, was renamed AT&T Network Systems. Once AT&T began offering a form of local service with AT&T Wireless, though, it became untenable to have the equipment business that sold to the RBOCs in the same corporation with a company that had the ability to compete with the RBOCs, even though, in the mid-1990s, wireless substitution for landline service was only a theory. Mobile services rates were still too high and coverage too spotty to be a replacement for landlines. But each of the RBOCs owned a mobile carrier and even the perception of a conflict was enough for AT&T Network Systems's sales teams to consider themselves at a competitive disadvantage.

On top of the competitive drivers for splitting the telecom equipment business from the phone company, AT&T's acquisition of NCR was also a failure, as described in Chapter 2, and needed to be addressed. AT&T decided to get out of the manufacturing business altogether in its second divestiture by spinning out both Lucent and NCR in 1996. One result was that the RBOCs were no longer significant customers of AT&T. A balance was maintained after the first divestiture in that the local companies bought equipment from AT&T and AT&T bought local access from the RBOCs. The revenue was not equal on both sides of the equation, but it was still significant (in the billions of dollars) to both parties. This balance was no longer in place after the second divestiture. From this point on, AT&T would continue to be the largest customer of the RBOCs but would no longer be a significant supplier.

WorldCom

In the late 1990s, WorldCom was schizophrenic. From an operational perspective, it looked like any of the other incumbent long-distance providers; from a financial perspective, it was a fraud. Before the WorldCom/MCI merger in 1998, MCI added considerable capacity to its network, but not nearly the amounts that were being built by the overbuilders. Of the amount added to the network, it can be questioned how much of that capacity was obtained from other companies through corporate acquisitions and IRUs (indefeasible right to use, a common contract structure used to lease bandwidth) rather than construction. WorldCom did buy capacity from Qwest, but those deals were on the scale of the normal course of business rather than an "if you can't beat them, join them" reaction to the overbuilders.

In an interesting irony, WorldCom was the main repeater of the fundamental fallacy that Internet traffic would double every ninety days. It built expectations in the financial markets based on that assumption. The last few mergers it completed (Brooks Fiber Properties, MFS Communications/ UUNet Technologies, and MCI) gave it a dominant position in the delivery of data and Internet services. But it didn't spend the billions that the overbuilders did to live up to the fallacy. What is clearer now is that the hype WorldCom spread was more to pump up its stock price than its network business.

WHAT GOES UP . . .

In some ways, the overbuilders were victims of their own hype, bragging about how their networks were infinitely expandable based on high strand capacity and their ability to update their networks as improvements in fiber-optic transmission capabilities became available. This hype attracted large sums of capital to their businesses, often at the expense of investments targeted at extending the broadband network to homes and businesses. It should have been a signal to customers (and a warning to investors) that supply was infinite, meaning that prices would decline. As the new capacity came online, it was dumped on a market that had no way to take up the supply. Predictably, prices dropped precipitously. If many people are trying to sell even the most popular item, the price will drop. All small merchants stuck with an inventory of Beanie Babies in 2001 learned that lesson. Once Beanie Babies were being sold by street vendors, sandwich shops, and convenience stores, the end was near.

The overbuilders built an airplane that they couldn't land. Even though the local phone and cable companies saw record growth during this period, they did not yet offer local access to high-bandwidth services at affordable prices. The local providers didn't build the bandwidth equivalent of landing strips for the high-flying overbuilders. When the ILECs and cable companies finally ramped up their rollouts of broadband technologies such as cable modems and DSL, it was too late to do the participants in the second race (or the dot-coms, for that matter) any good. Consumers and businesses wanted the bandwidth that the second racers built. Potential buyers could see the telecommunications equivalent of milk and honey on the other side of the local network, but they were not yet allowed to cross over to the Promised Land.

Without access to the product that the second racers were selling, demand never materialized. On certain popular routes, prices for long-distance services fell by more than 90 percent. All revenue projections used to justify the original business plans were shattered. The predictable conclusion of this situation was the failure or near failure of each of the overbuilders and one of the incumbents. The vicious cycle of competition, lost business, and lower revenue and profits eventually also led to the loss of many jobs in the industry. Each of the three largest overbuilders had a difficult time once the bubble burst. But, amazingly, only one of the three filed for bankruptcy protection. The smaller carriers wouldn't be so lucky.

Level 3

In 2002, Level 3 generated $1.1 billion in communications revenue from a network that cost $12 billion to build. Of the $1.1 billion, only $131 million was reported to the FCC as total toll service revenue, making it the thirty-second-largest long-distance carrier in the United States. It had $6 billion in long-term debt.

Level 3's public statements to shareholders still sounded like the shameless boosterism of the dot-com era. In its 10-K filing with the U.S. Securities and Exchange Commission for 2003, it claimed that "as a result of the rapid innovation in the underlying technology, the communications industry is visibly shifting from a utility model to a technology model." In fact, the "rapid innovations" in fiber optics had proceeded beyond the ability of the local access network before Level 3 began installing its fiber network in 1998. Partly as a result of the superfluous capacity dumped on the market by Level 3 and others, pricing in the industry is more compatible with the description of a utility model than a technology model.

Fortunately for Level 3, Jim Crowe and the Kiewits travel in the same circles in Omaha, Nebraska, as Warren Buffett. Buffett's company, Berkshire Hathaway, became Level 3's sugar daddy in 2002, providing it the cash it claimed was required to ride out the telecom slump. But with a debt level that exceeded its communications revenue by a factor of four, Level 3 had a long way to go to financial health.

Qwest

Qwest was smart enough to buy real businesses with revenue and cash flow while it still had an inflated stock price. It used these businesses to fund its vision of a new telecom carrier. It stopped paying dividends to USWest shareholders and sold other assets.

At the depths of the telecom bust, the only telecom assets that could be readily sold were directory businesses with their recurring revenue and large cash flow. Ironically, the directory business was one of the industries that were supposed to be vanquished by the dot-com companies. Qwest, Bell Canada, and Sprint all sold their directory businesses to raise cash and ride out the telebomb, with Qwest receiving $7 billion. That $7 billion, and the discontinued dividend, turned out to be the margin between Qwest and bankruptcy.

Strictly for accounting purposes, the Qwest/USWest merger was treated as though USWest acquired Qwest. The market capitalization of Classic Qwest (as it became known within the new company) at the time of the merger was $37.4 billion. The book value of Classic Qwest's assets was just more than $5 billion. The difference between market value and book value (known by accountants as goodwill) became a $32.3 billion intangible asset. This goodwill became the financial equivalent of a boat anchor, weighing Qwest down when it needed to be a nimble competitor.

Amid the accounting scandal that, in 2003, caused Qwest to restate its financial results back to the point of the merger, Qwest had to determine the value of all its assets. After looking at the real value of its various businesses, it determined that all the businesses brought into the combined company by Classic Qwest had, in essence, no value. The company wrote off all the goodwill acquired in the transaction plus $10.5 billion in hard assets, almost every dollar that was spent on Classic Qwest's entry in the second race.

Unfortunately, the one stable piece of Qwest, the local telephone business, was in disarray, since Joe Nacchio had fired all the executives who knew how to run the local business. Nacchio himself was pressured to leave as the company's stock performance worsened. Career Bell executive Richard Notebaert, CEO of Ameritech until it was purchased by SBC, came in to run the remaining company.

Through all the mergers, asset sales, and executive changes, Phil Anschutz kept a large stake in the company, even though the company bore little resemblance to what was envisioned in the original Qwest business plan. From long-distance upstart to dot-com darling to just another RBOC, Qwest's investors and customers had been taken for quite a ride, but the result enriched Anschutz just the same. At the end of 2003, he still controlled 300 million shares of Qwest, about 18 percent of Qwest's outstanding shares.

Although he was primarily a financial investor, Anschutz was close to the operations of the business. So close, in fact, that he became one of the objects of an investigation by New York State Attorney General Eliot Spitzer. Along with Bernie Ebbers, Clark McLeod, and Qwest's own Joe Nacchio, Anschutz was accused of spinning. Spinning occurs when an investment bank gives larger than usual allocations of stock in hot IPOs to the principals in a potential client. This practice was particularly lucrative during the dot-com days. While still denied by many in the brokerage industry, the practice led to the enrichment of executives and officers of certain companies and appeared to generate favor for one investment bank over another.

Anschutz settled his spinning case for $4.4 million, nearly the $5 million estimated by Spitzer as Anschutz's profit from the transactions. Rather than admit guilt and pay a fine, Anschutz donated the $4.4 million to thirty-eight different nonprofit organizations.

THE BANDWIDTH EXCHANGES

During this period, some industry analysts saw the future clearly enough to understand that bandwidth was going to become a commodity as more and more capacity hit the market. If bandwidth were to become a commodity, the reasoning continued, it could be traded in the same manner as other utility commodities, like electrical power, natural gas, and petroleum. As a result, several bandwidth exchanges were begun, most notably (later, infamously), by Enron. These exchanges ran a spot market (short-duration, short-lead-time demand), although longer-term needs could be filled as well. The customers of the exchanges were mostly carriers, with a few large corporations participating as well. Individual consumers could not participate.

The most successful exchange in the United States is Arbinet-thexchange, an exchange for long-haul voice minutes. It reported trading 5 billion minutes worldwide in 2002 and nearly 8 billion minutes in 2003.[9] The size of the business is still small compared with a market that supports 485 billion long-distance dial minutes per year originating in the United States.[10]

The logic that supported the creation of the exchanges was correct in that long-haul (not local) bandwidth would become a commodity and that it could, in fact, be traded. What the traders didn't understand were some of the fundamental differences between the markets for the other utility commodities and those for telecommunications. The starkest difference between the other utility commodity markets and the bandwidth market is that the oil, gas, and electricity markets have established local distribution networks that can handle spikes in demand. The telecommunications market didn't have such a capability for data services at the turn of the twenty-first century. As mentioned previously, the local networks didn't have enough consumer broadband capability to give end consumers the ability to demand significantly more bandwidth because their dial-up connections couldn't handle additional data loads.

Another attribute lacked by the bandwidth market was the ability to predict demand from history. Commodity traders track down all weather patterns and economic and demographic changes to minute details. Decades of historical data are available. Each trader has models that predict how demand will change based on these and other factors. None of this existed for the bandwidth market. It is hard for a market to attract traders or any sort of intermediary if there is no way to predict the market and, hence, make bets about how prices will change. The market run by Enron was billed as a carrier's carrier service, offering availability of large chunks of bandwidth between carriers. One reason it didn't work is that, even after the second race, there were still fewer than ten major long-haul fiber companies in the United States. Each one knew the other's routes (they had been burned by a lack of route diversity before) and could make a few phone calls to find out who had spare capacity available for sale. Why cut Enron in on the deal?

In the stock and bond markets, there is a job function called market maker, or specialist. The market makers' function is to maintain orderly trading. This requires that they entertain all orders for the securities they cover and maintain an organized flow of transactions at or near the market price. This function requires them to either buy securities for or sell securities from their own inventory to keep the market going.

To perform that function in the bandwidth market, dealers have to control enough bandwidth to have some available on all routes when they need to sell rather than buy to maintain orderly markets. That means having capacity available between every city pair served (that is, Boston to New York, Denver to Chicago). None of the bandwidth exchanges were well capitalized enough to maintain that kind of inventory. And none had a network behind it to soak up unmet demand. The carriers didn't like the fact that the exchanges sought to commoditize their services, and they didn't trust Enron. Period. They didn't want to participate, and they were the only entities able to provide the bandwidth required to support an orderly market.

Until there is participation by strong long-distance companies, bandwidth exchanges are unlikely to find a significant market in the United States.

TOO LITTLE, TOO LATE

Even as late as 1998, the telecommunications market still didn't realize that the long-haul network was too overbuilt to sustain all the carriers. Another company that started out as a construction consortium became the last of the companies to commit to a large build out. Velocita, originally known as Pf.net, looked at least as good on paper as most of its competitors in the second race. It had committed funding of more than $1 billion, including in-kind contributions from both Lucent and Cisco Systems. It had contracts from AT&T and others to build network capacity. Particularly for the AT&T contract, Velocita was to build an overlay on AT&T's rights-of-way and, in turn, could keep some of the fiber for its own use.

Velocita even brought in old industry hands Kirby "Buddy" Pickle and Robert Annunziata. Pickle was an accomplished job hopper, having worked at AT&T and Sprint as well as MFS, UUNet, and Teligent. Up until he left Teligent (a soon-to-be-bankrupt CLEC), he had a knack for leaving at the top of a company's prominence.

His job was to transform Velocita from a construction company into a new age carrier's carrier, like Williams Communications. But by mid-2000, even $1 billion couldn't fund the network, and no new funding was available. Velocita's CEO Pickle stated the problem succinctly two years before he joined Velocita: "Less than 4 percent of the buildings in this country have fiber running to them, and without a fiber connection you can't deliver the speed people want." In other words, he should have known better than to think Velocita had a chance to be more than a construction company.

AT&T bought the $1 billion-plus business out of bankruptcy court for $2 million cash and $35 million in AT&T stock in November 2002. In another sign of the times, this $1 billion bankruptcy case completed its trip through the financial fat farm in less than five months. Velocita learned the lesson that Bernie Ebbers finally learned. The more overspent the industry is, the more you have to spend to make a big splash. In the end, Velocita spent as much money as the largest dot-com failure (Webvan, at $1.2 billion) but the news coverage of the sale of its assets didn't even rate a listing for Velocita in the Index to Businesses section of the *Wall Street Journal*.[11]

NOTES

1. "Fiber Deployment Update—End of Year 1994," Industry Analysis Division, Common Carrier Bureau, FCC, 1995.
2. "Fiber Deployment Update—End of Year 1996," Industry Analysis Division, Common Carrier Bureau, FCC, 1997, p. 9.
3. John Cassidy, *Dot.Con: The Greatest Story Ever Sold* (New York: HarperCollins, 2002), p. 309.
4. "Behind the Fiber Glut," *Wall Street Journal*, September 26, 2002.
5. "Qwest Is Building the Basics of Better Communications," *Wall Street Journal*, December 24, 1996.
6. Operating income from LCI's 1997 10-K; deal size based on conversion ratios and share count from LCI's 8-K, dated 3/10/98 describing the merger.
7. Data from USWest's and Qwest's 10-Ks.
8. "Credit Markets: Level 3 Sells Junk Bonds of $2 Billion," *Wall Street Journal*, April 24, 1998.
9. Data from Arbinet's IPO prospectus.
10. "Trends in Telephone Service," Industry Analysis and Technology Division, Wireline Competition Bureau, FCC, August 2003, p. 10-5.
11. "Index to Businesses," *Wall Street Journal*, November 8, 2002.

CHAPTER 5

THE BIG GET BIGGER: THE ENTRY OF THE RBOCs INTO THE LONG-DISTANCE MARKET

1880
1890
1900
1910
1920
1930
1940
1950
1960
1970
1980
1981
1982
1983
1984
1985
1986
1987
1988
1989
1990
1991
1992
1993
1994
1995
1996
1997
1998
1999
2000
2001
2002
2003
2004
2005
FUTURE

MONOPOLY

DIVESTITURE

STABILITY

BOOM

BOMB

RECOVERY?

At its peak, the unified (pre-divestiture) Bell system employed more than one million people. After the breakup, parent company AT&T went into the competitive long-distance business and the local side of the Bell system was broken into seven separate companies. Each of the seven Baby Bells was still quite large, having multibillions of dollars of revenue and tens of thousands of employees. The target size for the seven RBOCs was picked for no better reason than it was the size of the largest pre-divestiture Bell Operating Company (Southwestern Bell Telephone) and the other twenty-one BOCs could be grouped into six companies roughly the same size. In other words, the number of RBOCs could have just as easily been four or eight if the structure of the original BOCs had been different.

Although the RBOCs were masters of their domain within one-seventh of the former local Bell system, they were frustrated in their attempts to grow larger organically within the industry. The Telecommunications Act of 1996 changed the rules and allowed them to grow in new and different ways. The big grew bigger through four of the largest merger transactions that swept the industry as the investment boom gained strength. The merger transactions within the old members of the Bell system were different animals than the rampant acquisitions of WorldCom or the flagrant cash burning of the second racers. The intra-Bell mergers were more of a family reunion than an investment strategy. The integration work required among companies that shared the same corporate DNA was minimal. Conversely, at World-

Com, the work required to achieve the same level of integration was much higher (and generally ignored, as we found out later).

After reuniting, the RBOCs' next challenge was to get back into the only segment of the telecommunications industry from which they had been barred—the long-distance business. The investments and time (nearly eight years) required to gain reentry into the long-distance business covered an entire investment cycle in the industry. From telecommunications boom to telebomb, the RBOCs plodded steadily along in their march toward full participation in the telecommunications marketplace.

What they found at the end of the trail, however, was completely different from the picture that they painted for themselves at the outset. Instead of becoming the fourth option for long-distance service and taking market share from the Big 3, the RBOCs found a chaotic market where bundles were required and prices were dropping.

SIZE MATTERS

The RBOCs are the largest companies in the industry by any relevant measure. Their combined revenue is larger than the gross domestic product (GDP) of Israel.[1] They have more resources and more market power than any of their competitors, including AT&T. AT&T was more aggressive after divestiture, but the sum of its bets was a smaller, weaker AT&T.

At the first divestiture of AT&T in 1984, each of the regional Bell companies took with it about 10 percent of the assets of the Bell system.[2] Ten years after divestiture (on January 1, 1994) the seven RBOCs still had roughly the same assets relative to AT&T, holding 75 percent of the total ex-Bell assets versus 70 percent ten years earlier. (The results within the RBOCs differed significantly, with BellSouth reporting $32.8 billion in assets at the high end and USWest reporting $20.7 billion at the low end.) By the end of 2003, however, SBC Communications was double the size of AT&T based on total assets while Verizon Communications was three times AT&T's size. BellSouth was about the same size as AT&T. Qwest Communications International, having written off all the assets from the Classic Qwest overbuild, was the smallest of the companies but still was larger relative to AT&T than it was at divestiture. Figure 5-1 shows all the assets of the ex-Bell companies and how the amount and ownership of those assets has changed over time.[3]

Looking at it another way, the RBOCs collectively were slightly more than twice the size of AT&T in 1984 (again based on assets). At the end of 2003, the children were almost seven times larger than AT&T. The RBOCs

FIGURE 5-1.
TOTAL ASSETS OF THE BELL COMPANIES—1993 TO 2003.

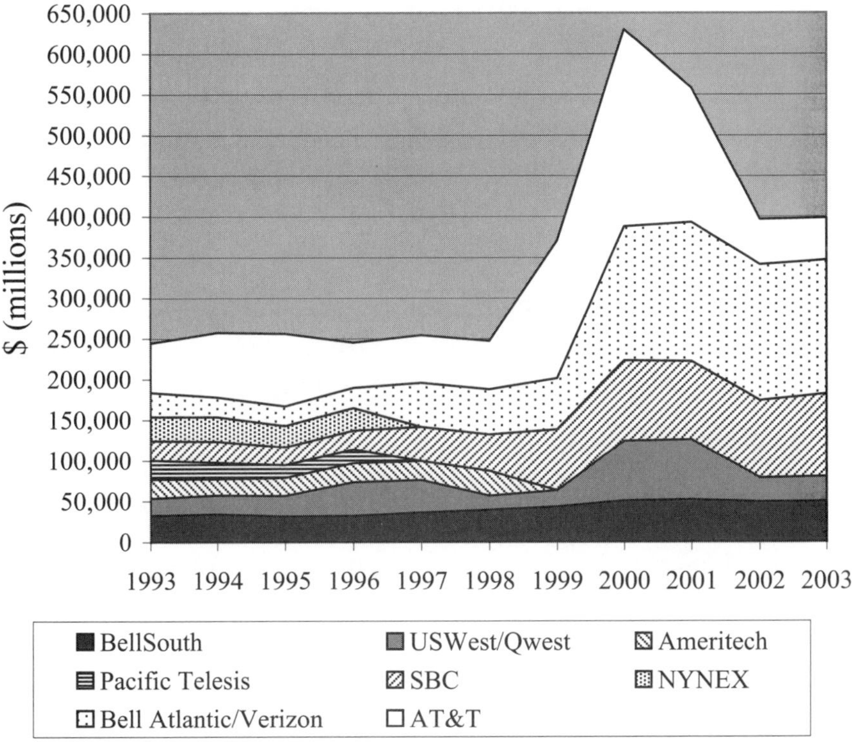

Legend		
■ BellSouth	▨ USWest/Qwest	⊠ Ameritech
☰ Pacific Telesis	▧ SBC	▦ NYNEX
⊡ Bell Atlantic/Verizon	☐ AT&T	

had very deep pockets. In an acknowledgment of this trend, by 2004, both SBC and Verizon had replaced AT&T as components of the Dow Jones Industrial Average, the most widely watched stock market barometer in the world. So when the giants decide to do something, better not get in their way.

Free to Get Even Bigger

The RBOCs have always been highly regulated companies. They are regulated at the federal, state, and (in many cases) local level. Before the Telecommunications Act of 1996, the RBOCs also lived under federal judicial regulation in the form of the Modified Final Judgment, the agreement between Judge Harold Green and AT&T that formalized its first divestiture in 1982. Under the MFJ, relationships between the companies that made up the original Bell System were tightly constrained. The Bell companies were not allowed into AT&T's business (and vice versa). The MFJ was also widely interpreted to prevent the merger of any of the former Bell System companies. The passage of the Telecommunications Act removed the Bells from any further regulation under the MFJ.

The first thing the giants did after the act awakened them from their twelve-year slumber was get bigger. The smallest and weakest of the giants were the first to go. Within two-and-a-half years of the act's passage, SBC bought Pacific Telesis and Ameritech, and Bell Atlantic bought NYNEX. The seven quickly became four. The RBOCs' individual growth relative to AT&T from this point on was propelled by the inclusion of several other carriers, most notably:

- GTE, the largest independent (non-Bell) telephone company, which merged with Bell Atlantic to form Verizon in 2000. GTE was about the same size as each of the seven original RBOCs.

- Southern New England Telecommunications (SNET), another independent phone company that served Connecticut and was acquired by SBC in 1997.

- The addition of the Qwest long-distance business, known as Classic Qwest, to USWest in 2000.

As shown in Figure 5-2, from seven companies that were the same size at divestiture (and roughly still so in the early 1990s) came two megagiants: SBC and Verizon. BellSouth, blessed with good geography, grew by benefiting from demographic trends. It also followed a less aggressive management style and maintained an internal growth strategy that may have seemed anachronistic during the dot-com boom but produced good results after the boom was over. Even though SBC and Bell Atlantic each swallowed two similar-sized companies, BellSouth maintained a market capitalization at least half of SBC's and Verizon's. Qwest, saddled with the hangover from the Classic Qwest overbuilding in the 1990s, barely made it through the telebomb.

Behind the Mergers

As a rationale for the mergers, the companies argued that they needed larger economies of scale to compete effectively. The case can be made that they already enjoyed all the scale they needed. The seven had, on average, $34 billion in gross plant, property, and equipment each before the merger frenzy began.[4] If they were able to achieve greater scale, it would be logical that their operating margins, a basic measure of profitability, would increase. But neither Verizon nor SBC was able to achieve noticeably better

FIGURE 5-2.
RBOC REVENUE—1993 TO 2003.

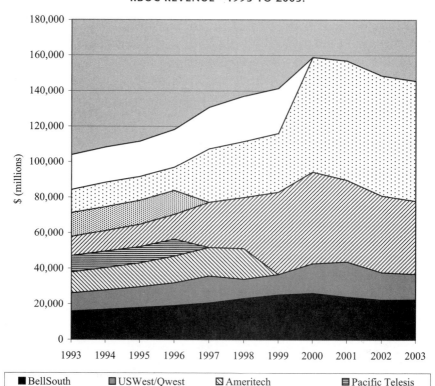

operating margins than BellSouth, which never merged. In fact, BellSouth achieved as much as 12-percentage-point better operating margins in years when its brethren were digesting mergers.

The bottom-line rationale for the mergers was that Bell Atlantic and SBC knew they would have to buy or be bought. The RBOCs are and have always been a classic scale play; that is, they have low margins but make large total profits based on serving tens of millions of customers. Even when there were seven RBOCs, each had scale in spades and knew how to use it. In an era where no one was astonished at the size of potential mergers, they instinctively knew that their size had to be big enough to matter.

There were differences, though, in how the leadership of the two most merger-prone companies, SBC and Verizon, digested the acquired companies. Each company acted from different philosophies about how to build a merged organization. At Verizon, each merger contributed new management teams to the combined company; and, after each merger, a new management structure was formed that combined the management from each company. This was best illustrated at the CEO level. Ray Smith, CEO of the original Bell Atlantic, remained CEO after the NYNEX merger but completed a succession plan where Ivan Seidenberg, the NYNEX CEO, replaced him. Seidenberg's succession happened at the time the GTE merger was announced. GTE's CEO, Chuck Lee, became co-CEO with Seidenberg after the merger while Larry Babbio, a long-term executive of the original Bell Atlantic, became COO.

SBC took a more direct approach in the Pacific Bell and Ameritech mergers. In both cases, virtually all the senior executives and many of the midlevel managers of Pac Bell and Ameritech were let go after the merger transactions were completed. SBC CEO Ed Whitacre and his management team ran the show completely.

While SBC's and Verizon's approaches to merger integration differed, the results were the same. The average operating margins (total revenue minus direct expenses) of SBC and Verizon from 2000 through 2003 were virtually identical. Both equally lagged BellSouth's performance.

LONG DISTANCE AS HOLY GRAIL

On top of the ability to merge without judicial approval (due to the MFJ), the Telecommunications Act also gave the RBOCs their next opportunity to grow. They were allowed entry into the long-distance market in exchange for opening their networks to competitors. The existing long-distance companies got nowhere near that good a deal.

Allowing every participant in the industry, new and established, to get into one another's markets was seen as a hallmark of the Telecommunications Act. As the logic went, it was better for all the walls to come down than for Congress to try to pick the winners and losers. Thus, it was believed at the time that allowing the long-distance and local companies to cross into each other's market was a fair trade. As it turned out, the investments required of the long-distance companies to cross into the local market were significantly larger than those of the RBOCs to offer long-distance service. After all, the RBOCs plus GTE had $289 billion in gross property, plant, and equipment at the end of 1995, roughly $1,100 invested for every citizen in the United States. The Big 3 long-distance companies, which controlled more than 80 percent of the long-distance market, had only $51.5 billion invested in their networks.[5]

It takes time to amass nearly $300 billion in capital and build $300 billion worth of telecommunications infrastructure. And it is particularly hard to reach that large a size without being a monopoly. Whereas the Big

3 didn't have enough money to build significant local networks, the RBOCs had the resources to make good on their ability to get into long distance.

The process required to gain approval to offer long-distance services in the Telecommunications Act was exactly what the RBOCs needed: a slow, methodical procedure to follow with relatively predictable inputs and outputs. The process is known by the section of the Communications Act that delineates it, Section 271.

A Good Fit for the RBOCs

At the time the Telecommunications Act of 1996 was passed, the long-distance market was large and still growing. The excess capacity to be dumped on the market because of the second race (see Chapter 4) was still a gleam in the eye of a small number of investors. Total long-distance market revenue in 1995, as measured by the FCC, was $85.5 billion. The RBOCs, through their ability to offer short-haul toll services within each of their local service areas (intra-LATA long-distance service) carried $8.2 billion, or less than 10 percent of the total. These short-haul toll services were lucrative for the RBOCs because they were part of their monopoly service but were beginning to slip away. From the RBOCs' perspective, that revenue needed to be replaced.

The question asked at the time was: How much of the remaining $77.3 billion market could they take? But that was the wrong question to ask. The question that should have been asked was: How much could the RBOCs get of what was left once the market became more competitive? Even without the second race, which was in full swing before any of the RBOCs gained entry into the inter-LATA market, prices were bound to drop when the RBOCs joined the Big 3 in offering long-distance services.

The overall long-distance market grew at a 5.6 percent rate in the five years before the passage of the Telecommunications Act. This rate was a mix of 8.5 percent growth for the residential market and 3 percent growth for the more mature business market.

The fact that the residential market was growing faster played well to the RBOCs' strengths. The RBOCs were stronger in this market because residential customers generally care about service at only one location, their home.

The business market is more competitive. In areas with concentrations of businesses, such as downtown areas or corporate parks, it is more economically feasible to build competing telecom networks. It is also less open to the RBOCs because even their large geographic footprint doesn't match well with large corporations. For example, Verizon, the largest of the

RBOCs, doesn't own significant local networks in large markets such as Atlanta, Denver, San Francisco, Kansas City, Phoenix, Albuquerque, and Minneapolis. So, for example, a corporation based in Atlanta with significant operations in the Midwest would be less likely to choose Verizon for long-distance service.

Nevertheless, small increases in the RBOCs' share of the long-distance market would result in significant revenue increases for the slow and steady Bells. Simply capturing 25 percent of the 1995 long-distance market (net of eventual losses in the intra-LATA long-distance market) would mean an additional $13 billion on the RBOCs top-line financial results, a 14 percent improvement based on their collective revenue for 1995.

Offering long-distance service was also a marketing imperative for the RBOCs. Because every other company was going to be allowed into the local business as a result of the Telecommunications Act, the RBOCs needed to expand their horizons or risk being the only companies without a full range of services. The RBOCs proved unsuccessful at offering video services as an add-on to local phone service. Long distance was, in fact, a more attractive market because it fit well with their existing business and customer base. It was also the next shiny penny to chase, since the Internet would not catch their full attention for several years.

Even though the financial rewards would not be as attractive as originally expected after the second race, the RBOCs could provide long-distance service (particularly residential) at a marginal cost that could not be replicated by the traditional long-distance companies.

In fact, the second race played into the Bells' hands by dumping excess capacity onto the market before the RBOCs received long-distance approval. A simple build-versus-buy analysis proved that it would be cheaper to buy the long-haul capacity they needed than to trench the fiber themselves. The RBOCs also knew the telephone service market better than any of the new start-ups at the time, giving them the requisite technical knowledge to be a savvy buyer of long-distance capacity.

The RBOCs had an existing customer service infrastructure. The call centers, customer service reps, and billing systems were already in place. They also had the advantage of existing customer relationships with 75 percent of the local service customers in the United States.[6]

THE COMPETITIVE CHECKLIST

To gain access to the long-distance market, the RBOCs had to satisfy a fourteen-point checklist of items to prove that they opened their local markets to competition. In effect, they had to support new entrants as AT&T did in the long-distance markets at the time of divestiture.

The items on the list amounted to a more significant and thorough supporting of new entrants than AT&T ever had had to provide during the development of the competitive long-distance market. The checklist, reflecting how deeply ingrained local phone service and networks are in the U.S. economy, describes each part of the local business that must be made available to competitors. Completing the checklist items cost the RBOCs hundreds of millions of dollars each.

The following checklist items are spelled out in the Telecommunications Act:[7]

1. *Interconnection.* The RBOCs have to allow each CLEC to connect to the RBOC local network for the purpose of providing service to the CLEC's customers.

2. *Access to Unbundled Network Elements.* The RBOCs have to support the CLECs by providing and maintaining certain specific elements (wire, voice channels, and so forth) that the CLECs may need to provide telephone service.

3. *Access to Poles, Ducts, Conduits, and Rights-of-Way.* Where a CLEC wants to build its own facilities to reach local customers, the RBOCs are required to allow the CLEC to use RBOC-owned or -leased real estate.

4. *Unbundled Local Loops.* In Bell parlance, an "assembled facility" is the complete voice path, or loop, necessary to connect a local switch to a customer's location. (The portion of the local facilities between the switch and the customer's premises traditionally consist of two copper wires that, when connected through the action of lifting a phone receiver from the cradle or hook, become a completed electrical circuit, or loop, from the local switch to the customer and back.) The loop is made up of individual network elements such as wires, cross-connections, and terminals. In order to facilitate competition, the RBOCs are required to make available for sale individual elements unbundled from the assembled facility. Prior to the Telecommunications Act, the incumbent phone companies generally only sold assembled facilities and only sold them as part of a working phone service.

5. *Unbundled Local Transport.* Items 2, 3, and 4 relate to the connection between a local switch (item 6) and the customer. Local trans-

port is used to deliver calls from the local switch to other carriers to provide full interworking among all other telephones attached to the network.

6. *Unbundled Local Switching.* The RBOCs have to provide access to local switching as well as individual features, such as caller ID and call forwarding.

7. *911 and E911 Services, Operator Services, and Directory Services.* CLEC customer numbers have to be available for routing by operators, if desired by the customer. Particularly important for public safety is the availability of the database that matches calling numbers to street addresses for dispatch and routing of local emergency personnel.

8. *White Pages Directory Listings.* CLEC customer numbers have to be printed in local directories, if desired by the customer.

9. *Numbering Administration.* This requirement was essentially completed when the administration of the North American Numbering Plan was transferred from Bell Communications Research (commonly known as Bellcore), which was owned by the RBOCs, to Neustar. To the extent that RBOCs participate in the administration of telephone numbers, they have to do so in a nonprejudicial manner. For example, where two area codes cover an area, like 212 and 917 in Manhattan, the RBOC cannot hoard or otherwise prevent the CLECs from having access to numbers in the more-desired area code (212 in the case of Manhattan).

10. *Databases and Associated Signaling.* Signaling provides the intelligence to route and deliver calls between the local switching system and any other connected switch. For example, when calling another local number, signaling is used to find the terminating switch that serves the dialed number, let it know that a call is coming, and determine if the line is busy or available. The RBOCs have to make these functions available to CLECs to complete calls where necessary.

11. *Number Portability.* Portability describes customers' ability to change service providers without having to change their phone number. RBOCs have to allow CLEC customers to maintain their old number regardless of who is providing telephone service.

12. *Local Dialing Parity.* The RBOCs must allow CLEC customers the ability to use the same dialing plans as any other customer in the area. This has turned out to be less of an issue than it was when the long-distance business was being opened in the late 1970s and early 1980s. At that time, the emerging long-distance carriers often required their customers to dial long strings of numbers to use their services. The fact that the services were more complicated than the simple 1+ dialing of the Bells hindered adoption of the competing services.

13. *Reciprocal Compensation.* Since before divestiture, the RBOCs lived in an environment where the long-distance business subsidized the local business. After divestiture, the RBOCs filed formal tariffs with charges for access to long-distance networks that were higher than normal rates for similar services to preserve the subsidy and make local phone service more affordable. Because the long-distance companies paid the RBOCs to both originate and terminate their calls, the RBOCs were used to charging everybody who connected to their networks. With the opening of their local networks, the CLECs were considered peers of the RBOCs. As peers, each would need to compensate the other for completing the calls that their customers originated. As explained in Chapter 3, this became a hotly debated topic.

14. *Resale.* Items 2 to 12 are the individual parts required to provide phone service. Resale refers to the aggregation of all these elements. The RBOCs are required to offer a total service resale option in addition to renting the pieces individually. This option is not used frequently, as the price is higher than for renting the pieces.

An RBOC had to prove that it made each of the fourteen items available on a nondiscriminatory basis (on essentially the same terms) to all comers in each state where it wanted to offer long distance. As the filing process proved, no one knew exactly what was required to satisfy the fourteen points. While the rules are lengthy and filled with arcane telephone terms, they still could not describe the breadth of situations that would be encountered within a series of interconnected networks that served 125 million customers in all forty-eight of the contiguous United States. The network consists of technology dating from every era since the 1880s. It serves densely populated areas such as Manhattan and some of the more rural territory across the United States.

RBOC APPLICATIONS

The Bells' Section 271 filings fit into two time frames: the early applications designed to see if the process was greased for them (those attempts failed; none got in) and the serious applications.

Ameritech submitted the first application in January 1997, less than eleven months after passage of the Telecommunications Act. The application was for Michigan (the second largest of Ameritech's five states) and was withdrawn in less than six weeks. It was resubmitted in May 1997 and soundly rejected by the FCC. SBC (Oklahoma) and BellSouth (Louisiana and South Carolina) also tried the strategy of filing in small to midsize states within their territory to test the process before going after the bigger markets.

From these first applications, the Bells figured out that the process was not going to be a piece of cake. They got the process they wanted in the Telecommunications Act, but the path was not going to be easy. Given the large number of new proceedings going on at the FCC, it was reasonable to assume that some things were going to slide through. The RBOCs' 271 filings were not among them. Congress did the FCC no favors by punting on so many decisions and leaving the hard work to the FCC (and complaining later about how slow the work was going, to boot). But the 271 filings were too big to be let through untouched. There were powerful interests on both sides of this issue, with the long-distance companies submitting arguments against the approval of the filings. All sides needed to be heard. Other than BellSouth's second application in Louisiana (also rejected), no applications were filed between November 1997 and September 1999.

Predictably, the first serious applications were for the largest markets. Bell Atlantic's application for New York was filed in September 1999, forty-three months after the Telecommunications Act was passed. SBC's application for Texas was filed in January 2000, forty-seven months after the act.

THE COMPETITORS REACT

AT&T's reaction to the first filing under Section 271 in 1997 could best be termed allergic. While admitting "we haven't seen a copy of the application," AT&T called the filing "premature" and declared that "Ameritech appears to be far more willing to devote its resources to challenging and intimidating potential local competition than to making it possible, as required by law."[8]

The long-distance providers had ample reason to rail against the RBOCs' 271 filings; the Big 3 were customers of the RBOCs in the resale business as well as competitive targets when the RBOCs gained entry into the long-distance business. The long-distance providers felt slighted by perceived RBOC foot-dragging in opening the local market, and they would eventually feel the pressure as the RBOCs entered long distance and began to take market share.

One curious exception to the long-distance providers' negative reactions came from WorldCom. WorldCom's largest corporate predecessor, MCI, was famous for the pressure it put on the Bell system, particularly leading up to AT&T's first divestiture. WorldCom provided a conciliatory, if not cordial, reaction in a news release following Bell Atlantic's approved application for New York. Phrases such as "MCI Worldcom looks forward to competing against Bell Atlantic in New York's highly competitive long-distance market" and "in approving the Bell Atlantic–New York application, the FCC has set the standard that the other Bell companies must meet" didn't fit the vituperative standard of MCI's past.

Only if you read down to the third paragraph of the news release would you get an idea of why WorldCom was toning down the rhetoric. Bell Atlantic's entry "clearly illustrates what MCI WorldCom and Sprint explain in their merger application with the FCC."[9] WorldCom knew that size mattered and the fate of its drive to become larger rested with the FCC and the Department of Justice. However, its drive to become larger would stop short of merging with Sprint. The merger was not approved and its Ponzi scheme would be discovered shortly thereafter.

WINNING APPROVAL

Bell Atlantic received the first approval among the RBOCs to offer long-distance service within its local territory. Its victory was in New York in December 1999. Bell Atlantic's application was approved forty-six months after the Telecommunications Act was passed.

The next approval would take six months. SBC's application for Texas was submitted only a few weeks after Bell Atlantic's victory. (While the FCC had ninety days to rule on the filing, SBC submitted a revised filing in April 2000, withdrawing its January filing at the same time).

SBC's first approval came in June 2000, the only approval in 2000. SBC learned from the Texas experience, though, filing in the other Southwestern Bell states quickly. Kansas and Oklahoma were filed together in October 2000 and approved together in January 2001. Missouri and Arkansas were filed together in August 2001 and approved together three months later. Thus, Southwestern Bell became the first of the original seven RBOCs to obtain approval to offer long-distance services in its territory. By then, of course, Southwestern Bell's parent, SBC, merged with two of the other original RBOCs, Pacific Telesis and Ameritech, so it still had many applications to file.

The only other approvals in 2001 were Bell Atlantic's applications in Connecticut, Massachusetts, and Pennsylvania. Once this critical mass of approvals occurred, it became a matter of when, rather than if, the others would be approved. The RBOCs can follow a successful model as well as anybody once they put their resources behind it.

As 2001 unfolded, the application floodgates were open. In the first five years after the Telecommunications Act was passed, only twelve applications were received. The scorecard on those was four approved, three withdrawn, and five rejected. The RBOCs had only gained approval to offer long-distance services in five states.

In the next thirty-one months, twenty-seven applications were filed covering all the remaining states. The scorecard for these twenty-seven filings was twenty-one approved and six withdrawn. None was rejected by the FCC. By the end of 2003, it was all over. The RBOCs were approved to offer long-distance service in each of their states.

It took almost eight years from the passage of the Telecommunications Act for the children of the Bell System to get back into the long-distance business that they were forced to give up in 1984. On January 1, 2004, the RBOCs celebrated the twentieth anniversary of divestiture having gained back the most significant market opportunity they had lost when they were separated from the mother ship.

Both the world and the long-distance market changed significantly in the intervening twenty years. Long-distance service changed from a highly profitable luxury service to a low-price, low-margin commodity. But the RBOCs were glad to be back and immediately set about the task of gaining market share.

GOBBLING UP MARKET SHARE

Once entry was gained, market share followed quickly. In the second quarter of 2001, twelve months after its entry into the long-distance market in Massachusetts, Verizon claimed that it had signed up 250,000 long-distance customers in that state. This number equaled 10 percent of the consumer long-distance market in Massachusetts. A year later, at the end of the second quarter of 2002, it reported 4.5 million customers in the former Bell Atlantic territory, double the prior year's number.

SBC claimed 2.8 million long-distance customers in the middle of 2001. At the time, it had been offering long distance in Texas for just more than a year and in Kansas and Oklahoma since October 2000. A year later, it had doubled the number to 5.6 million. By the end of 2003, the RBOCs claimed 40 million long-distance customers, more than 25 percent of the local telephone customers in the United States.

Also in 2003, around the time the RBOCs were winning long-distance entry in their few remaining states, the FCC completed its triennial review of unbundling requirements, as required by the Telecommunications Act. As part of the review, the range of facilities the RBOCs had to provide was narrowed, including a finding that the RBOCs didn't have to resell facilities that supported packet-switching technologies. This meant that for a CLEC to provide broadband Internet access to a home it must either rent an entire connection to the home or build its own network. Both the RBOCs and the CLECs disliked portions of the review. Court challenges abounded.

Clearly, the RBOCs wanted more relief from the obligations they agreed to when preparing their 271 applications, but the competitive die had already been cast. The market was bringing new products and bundles to the market—witness the all-in-one packages offered by the former Big 3, the RBOCs, and the few healthy CLECs (see Chapters 6 and 7).

The largest customers of the RBOCs were the long-distance companies. In one of the ironies of the process, AT&T, former owner of the monopoly Bell System, was one of the companies renting loops from its former children. It was renting loops it used to own. AT&T, which had taken the smart, fast-growing businesses at divestiture and left the stodgy, slow-growth local business to the RBOCs, was now on the outside looking in with the CLECs and once-upstart long-distance carriers. AT&T's long-distance business was losing revenue and market share whereas the RBOCs were poised to grow in the same business. The hare was losing steam and the tortoises were continuing to move along at their slow and steady pace.

Locked in as Providers

The RBOCs took only grudgingly to the business of becoming wholesale providers. A brief comparison of their situation to AT&T's when it supported the fledgling long-distance carriers in the 1980s paints a picture indicating continued wholesale support of the CLECs by the RBOCs for some time to come. It took Sprint and MCI until the late 1980s to reach a critical mass of fiber deployment and to be able to say they had a true national network. Until that time, AT&T provided them capacity on its networks.

The long-haul carriers had an additional incentive to build their networks. The new fiber-optic technology allowed them to gain a lower-cost position than with older copper, coaxial, or microwave technologies. It can be argued that the availability of a superior technology drove the build out of the network as much as the regulatory support given the upstarts.

Applying that lesson to the local markets, no new technology was introduced as a result of the new local competition that offered superior economics to the embedded RBOC network. Without such a new technology, the RBOCs' networks were likely to be the best choice for new entrants in the local phone market for some time to come. The only other competitors with physical connections into consumers' homes, the cable companies, were not required to offer wholesale unbundled services like the RBOCs.

Things were changing, though. The Internet, the redheaded stepchild of the Telecommunications Act, would provide a path for voice services into the homes of millions of Americans without the RBOCs or the cable companies even knowing it was there. When the RBOCs were allowed back into the long-distance market, use of the Internet to transmit voice calls was still only a niche business best left to international calling. As the Internet became more robust, finally realizing the hype poured upon it in the late 1990s, it became the preferred medium for all new and many existing forms of communication. The RBOCs ignored this at their own peril.

THE ATTRACTIVENESS (OR NOT) OF THE LONG-DISTANCE MARKET

"You Can't Go Home Again"
—THOMAS WOLFE, AMERICAN NOVELIST

In 1995 the long-distance market included $77 billion in inter-LATA revenue. The total long-distance market had almost doubled since divestiture. No end to the revenue increases in that part of the industry was in sight. Its future looked much brighter than that of the slow-growth local business.

But two things happened on the way to the party. First, many other communications providers began bundling long distance into telephone service packages. Wireless carriers, CLECs, and cable companies started offering voice service that included long distance as part of the package. This reduced long-distance service from a product in its own right to just a feature, like caller ID. This substitution caused downward pressure on both pricing and volumes for the established players in the industry. Second, and more significantly, the second-race participants dumped so much bandwidth on the market that prices declined even more rapidly, destroying the ability of any long-distance service provider to hold the line on pricing.

Was It Worth the Effort?

The result was that revenue in the long-distance market peaked with the economic cycle in 2000, dropping 9.5 percent in 2001 alone. The long-distance market in 2002 was roughly the same size as it was in 1995. Worse for the RBOCs, the residential long-distance market peaked in 1998, falling 11 percent over the next three years.

Like Williams Companies, the Bells' experience in the long-distance business wasn't as positive the second time around. The RBOCs didn't go bankrupt over the experience, but what started out as a strategic move ended up as a pure defensive play.

Revenue from the long-distance services that the RBOCs worked so hard to be able to offer didn't equal the amount of revenue they lost in the intra-LATA (local toll) market. Counting all RBOC intra-LATA revenue and SBC's and Verizon's inter-LATA revenue (Qwest and BellSouth hadn't won a 271 filing yet), the RBOCs' market share increased from 6.6 percent in 2000 to 7.1 percent in 2001. But their revenue dropped from $7.2 billion to $7.1 billion. In 2002 the slide continued, with an increase to more than 8 percent market share but no increase in revenue.

The RBOCs have yet to grow their inter-LATA business much beyond the revenue they lost in the intra-LATA market. And the revenue they have gained is significantly less profitable because of the commoditization of long distance. Of course, now that the RBOCs have 271 approvals in all their states, they can shift focus from getting into the market and gaining share to building profitable revenue. So although the RBOCs won the battle for long distance, it remains to be seen if they will win the war.

Did the RBOCs Focus on the Wrong Market?

The RBOCs' focus on long-distance approvals to the exclusion of their DSL product rollout raises a "what if" scenario. As is shown in later chapters, the RBOCs were quite slow to roll out high-speed Internet access products. Later chapters discuss how the cable companies stole a march on the RBOCs in the broadband wars, but consumers and small businesses were also hurt by the RBOCs' sluggishness. DSL was a new product that sold for premium prices; something the RBOCs had been in search of for some time. The product was in high demand almost as soon as it was announced in 1996 but didn't show up in numbers until 2000. Consumers wanted more of the Internet. Small businesses wanted to appear larger with high-speed Internet access like large corporations. And Internet content providers wanted to be able to offer richer media content that wouldn't fit through a dial-up connection. But it was several years before the RBOCs got aboard the same train.

If investment dollars had been focused on DSL rollouts more than on long distance, would the RBOCs have been better off? Certainly the consumer and small business owner would be.

NOTES

1. Israel's GDP from *World Development Indicators* database, World Bank, 2003.
2. Fred W. Henck and Bernard Strassburg, *A Slippery Slope: The Long Road to the Breakup of AT&T* (Westport, CT: Greenwood Press, 1988), p. 238.
3. Based on total assets at year end as reported by each company to the SEC on Form 10-K. The results are not adjusted for continuing operations so that the effect of various strategies can be seen in the results over time. For example, the spike in AT&T's assets in 2000 and 2001 shows the result of its failed strategy to enter the cable market.
4. Property, plant, and equipment data from Forms 10-K filed by the RBOCs with the SEC for 1995.
5. Based on gross property, plant, and equipment (PP&E) data from company reports to the SEC on Form 10-K. MCI and Sprint results include only long-distance business segments. AT&T 1995 results are from restatements in 1996 10-K to eliminate Lucent and NCR. Restated AT&T results include AT&T Wireless and Alascom. RBOC and GTE numbers include all PP&E.
6. "Trends in Telephone Service," Industry Analysis Division, Common Carrier Bureau, FCC, March 1997, p. 22.
7. Checklist items from Section 271(c)(2)(B)(i through xiv) of the Telecommunications Act of 1996.
8. Ray O'Connell, "AT&T Reacts to Ameritech's Michigan Service Application," AT&T press release, January 2, 1997.
9. Michael H. Salsbury, "MCI WorldCom Responds to FCC Decision on Bell Atlantic Long Distance Application," MCI press release, December 22, 1999.

CHAPTER 6

THE LAST STAND OF THE LONG-DISTANCE COMPANIES

1880
1890
1900
1910
1920
1930
1940
1950
1960
1970
1980
1981
1982
1983
1984
1985
1986
1987
1988
1989
1990
1991
1992
1993
1994
1995
1996
1997
1998
1999
2000
2001
2002
2003
2004
2005
FUTURE

MONOPOLY

DIVESTITURE

STABILITY

BOOM

BOMB

RECOVERY?

By the time the Telecommunications Act of 1996 was debated in Congress, the long-distance companies certainly knew that the RBOCs were coming after their market. It was speculated that once the RBOCs gained entry into the long-distance business, they would be able to take market share quickly. After all, the RBOCs owned the direct connection into consumers' homes that the long-distance companies needed to complete calls. The RBOCs also maintained a long-standing relationship with each customer.

The Big 3 long-distance companies (AT&T, MCI/World-Com, and Sprint) began looking for ways to expand beyond their traditional boundaries as a hedge against the risk of RBOC competition. The Big 3 invested heavily in some of their new businesses, but some of their other investments were only hedges, not exhibiting the commitment required to succeed in a competitive business. Paradoxically, some of the investments were too large to be sustained by the long-distance companies but not large enough to make a difference in a market where "big" is relative.

The investments by the Big 3 generally fell into three industry subsegments: wireless, local, and international. Of the three classes of investments, local service took most of the Big 3's investment dollars. Sprint PCS is the only lasting legacy of the Big 3's wireless investments.

International services experienced a land rush akin to the second race, causing many bankruptcies and disrupting the investments of every carrier in the long-distance business. International bandwidth prices, often ten times the cost of similar domestic bandwidth before the investment boom, dropped by percentages similar to those experienced in the domestic long-distance market. The resulting dollar savings to end users coincided with a bear-market-driven focus on cost cutting in corporate America. The combination unleashed a wave of cross-border outsourcing that became a political issue in the 2004 presidential election.

WIRELESS

"You see, wire telegraph is a kind of a very, very long cat.
You pull his tail in New York and his head is meowing in Los Angeles.
Do you understand this? And radio operates exactly the same way:
you send signals here, they receive them there.
The only difference is that there is no cat."
—ALBERT EINSTEIN, AMERICAN PHYSICIST (WHEN ASKED TO DESCRIBE RADIO)

AT&T

AT&T bought the McCaw Cellular business in 1994 and renamed it AT&T Wireless Services. It invested in significant additional wireless spectrum through the FCC's PCS auctions in 1995 and 1996, giving AT&T Wireless a national footprint. It was the first wireless provider to offer pricing plans for nationwide service, although it was widely and quickly imitated. AT&T spun the business out to shareholders in 2001. In 2003, AT&T Wireless was the third-largest wireless provider in the United States but it wasn't able to sustain its early advantage.[1] It sold itself to Cingular, a joint venture of BellSouth and SBC, in 2004.

Sprint

Sprint spun out its original cellular properties as 360 Communications in 1996. (The company 360 Communications is not to be confused with 360networks, a late participant in the second race. In 1998, 360 Communications was acquired by Alltel.) Sprint then purchased a significant number of PCS licenses in the FCC's spectrum auctions in 1995 and 1996. The spectrum was held either directly by Sprint or through a series of partnerships with TCI Communications, Comcast, and Cox Communications, three of the largest cable companies in the United States. Sprint and the partners controlled the spectrum in virtually every market in the United States. Using these licenses, Sprint PCS developed a national wireless network as well as a national brand and services that worked seamlessly across the country, as long as you were on the Sprint network. This approach contrasted to that of the other wireless carriers at the time, which depended on roaming agreements with other providers to offer voice services across much larger areas than Sprint could cover. (Roaming allows one company's customers to use their phones on another carrier's network. A roaming customer, though, does not have access to all of the services available on their home carrier's network when roaming.)

In 1999, Sprint finished buying out TCI, Comcast, and Cox. Rather than spin out the wireless business as did AT&T, Sprint created a tracking stock for the results of the PCS business. In 2004, after the Cingular/AT&T Wireless merger, Sprint PCS was the third-largest wireless carrier in the United States.

The Sprint PCS business is easily the most successful of the diversification efforts of the Big 3. Although not consistently profitable, the PCS business has achieved competitive market share and generates operating cash flow for Sprint. None of the other investments described in this chapter can make the same claim.

MCI and WorldCom

WorldCom never pulled the trigger on ownership in any wireless network. It made two attempts to buy Nextel Communications and might have ended up with a share of the Sprint PCS business if the WorldCom/Sprint merger had gone through. The closest MCI came to gaining a national wireless presence was the purchase of Nationwide Cellular Service by MCI in 1995. Nationwide was a reseller of wireless service. Its customers' calls were actually carried on the networks of other companies such as AT&T and Verizon Wireless. The resale business in wireless, as in long-distance services, has razor-thin margins. The business was never popular or profitable. It was disbanded during WorldCom's bankruptcy proceedings, since there were no buyers.

In 1999, WorldCom also bought SkyTel Communications, a two-way paging company based in Jackson, Mississippi, WorldCom's hometown. Along with the overall decline of the stand-alone paging market, SkyTel became a smaller company, causing WorldCom to write off most of Sky-Tel's assets. The business continues to operate in niche markets like fleet management (typically for trucking companies) and wireless e-mail.

LOCAL

Each of the Big 3 invested in building a local presence through both constructing and leasing local facilities. Their investments, although large, have taken time to generate significant competition for the RBOCs. Because the local business is much more complex than the long-distance business, the long-distance providers built local market share slowly as they figured out how to successfully operate in the different environment.

Despite the intricacies of the local business, the Big 3 had more than simple competitive incentives to jump into the local service market, particularly for business customers. First, the rate structure for business services was an enticing target. Second, the largest single expense in the long-distance providers' cost structure was for access to the ILECs' local phone networks.

Business Rates. The RBOCs' business rates were traditionally set higher than their residential rates as a way to support universal service. Universal service is a public policy goal where basic phone service should be affordable for any household that wants it. This goal was attained in the Bell System by using extra revenue from nonlifeline services, like long-distance and business lines, to subsidize basic residential service. The higher rates, and high profit margins, for business services persisted in the post-divestiture environment, making business services an attractive competitive target. A competing carrier could offer lower prices than the RBOC and still have decent operating profits.

Access Fees. Access charges are incurred by a long-distance carrier for each circuit it supports and for each long-distance call that a customer makes. Each customer location is served by a local phone company, which charges the long-distance companies to both originate and terminate long-distance calls to or from the customer. The rates charged for this access to and from the local network were set artificially high at divestiture to help the local companies support universal service, mimicking the subsidies provided from AT&T's long-distance service to the local companies prior to divestiture. From the time of divestiture through the 1980s, access fees typically represented half or more of a long-distance carrier's cost structure. That meant roughly fifty cents of every dollar paid to a long-distance company was, in turn, paid to an ILEC.

Early after divestiture, there were few ways around incurring access fees in the competitive long-distance business because the Bells owned the monopoly local service franchise. The Big 3 spent most of their cost-cutting efforts looking for ways around the cost of access paid to the ILECs. Access fees were so large that even the smallest percentage reductions resulted in huge dollar savings. Early efforts to combat high access fees ranged from simply disputing bills to detailed audits of access charges.

Later, the long-distance companies combated high access costs by building their own local facilities. These efforts didn't have the financial returns of disputing bills, though. Building local network required much regulatory work before the Telecommunications Act because the Bells' monopoly on local services was, in many local areas, government sanctioned. Add the capital outlay required to build the network, and the returns were smaller and more risky because of the extended time to payback. While the Telecommunications Act reduced some of the uncertainty of the regulatory process for any prospective local competitor, it didn't materially shorten the time to revenue from these investments.

These and other efforts to reduce dollars paid to the RBOCs became part of the long-distance companies' DNA. The possibility of reselling unbundled RBOC network elements, created by the Telecommunications Act, was attractive to the long-distance companies not only for competitive reasons but also because resold lines were not subject to access fees. The resale opportunity was only available in the consumer and small-business market, but the opportunity to avoid access fees was nevertheless a strong incentive for the long-distance carriers to enter the local market. There are few differences in how the network elements are physically assembled for resale versus access; the main differences are in how they are sold and billed. It is more of an accounting maneuver than a real distinction. But tens of billions of dollars were at stake in the competitive battle that was about to be waged for the customer.

Each of the long-distance companies developed different strategies to attack the local market, but all ended in nearly the same place. None of the Big 3's attempts to build a local presence resulted in a significant new technology for reaching customers or a significant advantage in terms of the number of local customers they signed up. Each built or bought facilities designed to serve dense business districts. Each tried several marketing strategies for selling UNE-based services to consumers with few notable successes. A description of each company's strategy and actions follows.

AT&T

Immediately after passage of the Telecommunications Act, AT&T, Sprint, and MCI filed with each state to gain CLEC status. AT&T gained approval to enter the CLEC business in all but two states by the end of 1997. It began reselling RBOC service using TSR rather than UNEs (see Chapter 5 for a description of the two different approaches). AT&T claimed that consumer demand existed for the service, but that RBOC delays and high pricing of

TSR made the offer unprofitable. AT&T stopped marketing the service and took a $633 million charge to earnings in 1998 for the costs of the project.

PROJECT ANGEL

In 1996, AT&T announced the development of Project Angel, a fixed (nonmobile) wireless technology that would allow it to connect directly to customers' homes without having to put any wires in place or resell any RBOC services. The use of radio instead of copper wires to deliver residential telephone service has been around for years. But the technology had always been expensive enough that it was cost justified only in the most remote areas, where trenching cable or planting telephone poles was not practical. Project Angel was supposed to bring similar technology to market at more attractive cost points. AT&T deployed it to 47,000 customers in ten markets, but the economics of the technology never got any better.

AT&T Wireless became the owner of the technology and sold it to Netro Corporation in early 2002 for $16 million cash and a small equity stake.[2] AT&T Wireless took a $1.3 billion charge to write down the assets and exit the business.[3]

The charge equaled more than $27,000 for each customer who used the technology.

With the arrival of new CEO Mike Armstrong in 1997, a new strategy emerged. With all the promise of the Internet and convergence talked about in the industry, AT&T's new management thought it made sense to own direct wired connections to customer locations, both residential and business. Rather than deal with its estranged children, Armstrong and AT&T decided to buy other existing local telecommunications networks.

AT&T's first move was to buy business service provider Teleport Communications Group (TCG) in July 1998. TCG was started and substantially owned by four of the largest cable companies in the United States: Cox, Comcast, TCI, and MediaOne Group. It was the largest of the competitive local service providers at the time, having been around since long before the term CLEC was in common use. TCG built networks in sixty-five major cities in the United States. At the end of 1997, it had 9,470 route miles of cable and served approximately 13,510 buildings. Like most other start-ups of this type, TCG never earned an operating profit, although it was growing quickly.[4] AT&T paid $11.3 billion for TCG and folded it into AT&T's local business.

Cable Mania

AT&T then went on what can only be described as the biggest merger frenzy in the history of the telecommunications business. It made half a dozen large deals over the next two years involving the buying and selling of cable systems serving about 20 million subscribers, nearly 30 percent of the total cable subscribers in the United States.[5] In this way, AT&T became the largest cable system operator in the United States. In the process, it bid up the price of cable systems to unimaginable heights. The excess prices paid by AT&T for these cable systems can be conceived by rational investors and businesspeople only in the context of the stock market mania going on at the time.

The first big cable deal was the acquisition of TCI and its 11 million cable subscribers, completed in March 1999. AT&T paid cash and stock worth $37.5 billion or an average of $3,415 per subscriber. John Malone, chair and largest shareholder of TCI and Liberty Media (a subsidiary of TCI), became a member of AT&T's board of directors. He was about as welcome on AT&T's board as Ross Perot was at General Motors in the 1980s after GM bought Perot's company, Electronic Data Systems. Malone left AT&T's board when it spun out his Liberty Media during AT&T's third divestiture.

AT&T succeeded in buying TCI where Bell Atlantic failed. Bell Atlantic's earlier merger offer for TCI would have been a mixed marriage of sorts between an aggressive cable company and a conservative RBOC. Armstrong wanted to change AT&T's image to be seen as more aggressive. He succeeded, but along with the aggressive image came risks that would eventually unhinge the "new" AT&T.

Two more deals were conducted over the next fifteen months. In these deals, AT&T sold specific, former-TCI properties to Comcast and Cox. These deals were valued at between $4,000 and $4,500 per subscriber. The value of cable subscribers was increasing at a rate similar to Internet stocks at the time.

The NASDAQ index peaked at 5132 on March 10, 2000. The value of cable subscribers peaked three months later. AT&T's purchase of MediaOne in June 2000 for stock and cash worth $45 billion marked the peak of the cable systems sales market with a per-subscriber price of $9,000 for each of MediaOne's 5 million subscribers. Compared with the TCI deal, AT&T paid 20 percent more for a company with fewer than half the subscribers. An extrapolation of MediaOne's potential based on general cable industry financial performance shows just how high was the price paid by AT&T. Based on historic performance, operating margins (revenue less direct product costs) could reasonably be increased to 25 percent, the high end of the normal cable industry range. If an average cable bill could be increased to $100 per month once telephony and other services were added in (from an average of $50 to $55 per month at the time), a typical customer would return $25 per month to AT&T. At that high rate, it would have taken AT&T thirty years (360 months at $25/month) just to break even on the Media-One investment. This analysis doesn't include the investment required to add the additional services required to pump up the average bill. The example also doesn't take into account the RBOC's competitive reaction to a broad-based competitor using its own facilities rather than renting the RBOCs' loops. The cable merger frenzy is discussed further in Chapter 8.

The weight of all the cable purchases and the continued investment requirements of AT&T Wireless and Concert (AT&T's international services joint venture with British Telecommunications) became a boat anchor on AT&T's financial results. The big bets, particularly on local service, were predicated on the long-distance operations' continued ability to generate large amounts of cash to invest in upgrading the local service capabilities of AT&T Broadband. Then the second race hit, scuttling those plans. Armstrong admitted that the plans to re-create the Bell system with coaxial cable instead of twisted pairs wouldn't come to fruition.

Another Divestiture

Chapter 5 describes how the RBOCs grew to be larger than their former parent, AT&T. But AT&T was getting smaller all by itself. Through 2001 and 2002, AT&T announced, planned, and completed its third divestiture in less than twenty years. AT&T Wireless, with its high capital investment requirements, was spun out to AT&T shareholders through several transactions in 2001 and 2002. The independent AT&T Wireless would last less than two years.

In its most direct admission of the failure of its local strategy, AT&T spun off the AT&T Broadband business by merging it with Comcast. As proof of the exorbitant prices paid for cable franchises only two years earlier, the largest cable company in the United States sold itself to the third-largest cable company (Comcast) at less than $4,000 per subscriber, 20 percent less than the net price paid for the franchises; effectively a $13 billion discount.

What happened to AT&T over the prior ten years? By the end of 2002, AT&T's equipment-manufacturing business (now Lucent Technologies, Avaya, and Agere Systems, among others) was gone. NCR had come and gone. The successful wireless business AT&T bought from Craig McCaw in 1994 was gone. Concert, the international joint venture, disintegrated in the face of disagreements with AT&T's partner, British Telecommunications. AT&T Broadband, the largest cable company in the nation, was also gone. Figure 6-1 shows a time line of AT&T's major acquisitions and divestitures.

In late 2003, the combined market capitalization of the spun-out companies was seventeen times the market capitalization of AT&T. That number doesn't include Comcast, since it had a sizable operation before it took on AT&T Broadband. Including Comcast, the children would be worth nearly twenty times the value of AT&T. Reflecting the changed fortunes of the companies, AT&T Wireless, itself struggling to remain competitive, was worth more than AT&T.

Once the cable fiasco was over and the third divestiture complete, AT&T settled into its one remaining business, which was long distance. But it had been declared a nondominant provider in the long-distance business in 1995 and was rapidly on its way to becoming just another long-distance company in a shrinking field of stand-alone long-distance businesses. In 1981, before AT&T's first divestiture, it employed more than one million people. At the end of 2003, it employed less than 62,000.

After the failure of his grand plan, Armstrong left AT&T in 2002 to join Comcast. The person named to succeed him at AT&T was David Dorman, an experienced executive with one big success (Business Services at Sprint) and two failures (Pointcast and Concert) on his resume. Dorman left Concert to join AT&T only two years before AT&T's third divestiture.

In becoming the CEO of AT&T, he ascended to a position that was once one of the most powerful in American business. However, after three

FIGURE 6-1.
AT&T's MAJOR ACQUISITIONS AND DIVESTITURES FROM 1984 TO 2003.

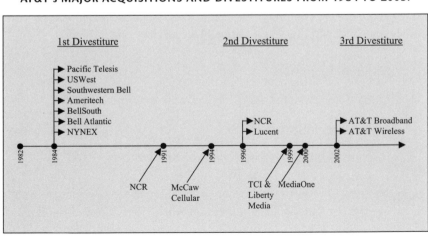

divestitures in less than twenty years, AT&T was less relevant to the U.S. economy than it had been at any time in the twentieth century.

AT&T tried to refresh its image as the quality leader in the industry and professed a focus on business customers. Even before the cable strategy failed, AT&T began reselling RBOC local loops using UNEs to provide a complete local and long-distance package to residential customers. At the end of 2003, AT&T claimed 3.5 million local customers using some mix of UNEs (for residential service) plus the TCG and other local networks owned by AT&T (for business customers).

AT&T also went back to its roots to build local market share. In 2003, it resorted to sending checks that consumers could cash when they switched their local service to AT&T. This echoed the period of stability when each of the Big 3 long-distance companies realized that the only way to differentiate its pitch was to include cash.

MCI and WorldCom

MCI's heritage was building networks and fighting against the big guys. It spent the first fifteen years of its life fighting for survival against the dominance of AT&T. It spent considerable time and money through the mid-1990s battling with the RBOCs. Its MCImetro subsidiary spent $700 million between 1996 and 1998 to build or acquire interests in eighty metropolitan area networks including twenty-seven local switches.[6] For all that investment, MCImetro generated less than $350 million of revenue in 1997, the last full year before the WorldCom merger. The subsidiary's net loss was $375 million.

WorldCom, on the other hand, built its local network the same way it built its long-distance business, by acquiring companies that had already built networks. Through the mid-1990s, WorldCom acquired several companies that were offering competitive local services, including:

- MFS Communications

- Chicago Fiber Systems, itself having been acquired by MFS

- Brooks Fiber Properties (BFP)

- City Signal Communications, itself having been acquired by BFP

In the quest for a technology that would allow the long-distance companies to bypass the RBOCs' local networks, WorldCom followed the example of Project Angel at AT&T by investing in another fixed wireless technology known as multichannel, multipoint distribution service (MMDS). MMDS had been in use for some time as a competitor to local cable systems. It had the capability to deliver about thirty channels of analog video over radio links. A few dozen of these competitive cable systems operated in the United States, but they became increasingly anachronistic once landline cable systems began upgrading to digital, effectively more than tripling their capacity.

The FCC changed the MMDS rules in 1998 to allow for two-way transmission of signals in the MMDS bands. Thus, as landline cable systems were upgraded to offer the two-way communications required to support cable modem services, it was expected that the MMDS spectrum could be upgraded in a similar way. WorldCom and Sprint both took the bait, spending about $2 billion buying up MMDS spectrum in 1998 and 1999. WorldCom's MMDS assets were acquired in the best way WorldCom knew how: through acquisition.

WorldCom rolled out service in a few second-tier markets but couldn't make the investment work. Like two other start-ups, Teligent and Winstar, which depended on similar technology, WorldCom came to the conclusion that MMDS wouldn't live up to its promise until the transmission technology could be developed further. It announced a scaled-back rollout schedule in December 2000, essentially stopping further investment.

Experience showed that the MMDS spectrum didn't have any value by itself. AT&T Wireless's write-down of the Project Angel assets seemed to indicate that fixed wireless didn't fit into a mobile strategy, either. Nextel, once a target to be bought by MCI, bought WorldCom's MMDS spectrum through the bankruptcy court in 2003 for $144 million, about one-eighth of what WorldCom spent for it.

The Last Deal

After the MCI/WorldCom merger in 1998, the strategy of the company tended toward finding acquisitions, regardless of whether the acquisition fit into the company's overall strategy to build itself into a profitable telecommunications carrier. Some of those acquisitions did add local assets to the business, however.

In September 2000, WorldCom entered into a merger transaction that signaled to the market how desperate it was to do what it knew how to do (merge) rather than to operate a successful business. WorldCom agreed to acquire money-losing, highly leveraged Intermedia Communications for a price that eventually worked out to $5 billion. Another indicator of WorldCom's problems was that the deal took ten months to complete. This time period was an eternity in the dot-com world and also a time of sharply declining stock prices. Intermedia was a rebound deal for WorldCom, the announcement coming only seven weeks after the Sprint deal officially fell through. It was a clear sign of Ebbers's desperation to do even the worst deals to prop up the Ponzi scheme that WorldCom had become.

Intermedia was an integrated carrier that offered local and long-distance voice and data services mainly to small and midsize corporate customers. But it was a financial train wreck. In 2000, Intermedia's revenue was just more than $1 billion, but the company was in debt to the tune of more than $4 billion. The company never turned a profit in eight years of operations.[7]

What became the Intermedia transaction was originally designed to be an acquisition by WorldCom of Digex, a publicly traded subsidiary of Intermedia that offered hosting and other Web-site services. Hosting was an important service in the early days of the commercial Internet because it allowed companies to offer high-performance Web sites at a reasonable cost. The hosters' data centers were located close to the major arteries of the Internet. Until the second race destroyed pricing discipline in the long-distance industry, the large and increasing bandwidth requirements of popular Internet sites mandated that the computers that housed these Web sites be located where expensive bandwidth could be bought in quantity and shared. For all but the largest organizations, these facilities were available only in hosting centers. Digex also had skills in the technologies used to create and maintain Web sites. These technologies were fast developing and in great demand as the Internet became commercialized. Digex's core competencies in these areas contributed to making the company a hot property.

WorldCom certainly had no need to buy Intermedia's network assets. But WorldCom believed it needed a hosting capability to complement its dominant position in Internet transport services. The company had other deals on the table to build the capabilities it needed in this area, but World-Com wasn't predisposed to building something it could buy. Accenture, the technology and management consultancy, was poised to help World-Com build the hosting and related services capabilities, but the deal was repeatedly stalled while WorldCom tried to find a merger deal that would get them the same assets and expertise. WorldCom's two top executives didn't understand organic growth, but they did understand that Intermedia owned a controlling interest in Digex.

DOT-COM FOOL'S GOLD

Digex was coveted by WorldCom not only for its core business, but because Digex had the financial attributes of a dot-com darling. Digex was purchased by Intermedia in July 1997, for $160 million. Intermedia got the purchase price back (and then some) in a partial IPO in July 1999 when it sold about 15 percent of Digex's stock for net proceeds of $179 million. The stock did well, as did so many Internet IPOs at the time. The stock price closed at more than $100 for the first time in January 2000. In February 2000, six months prior to WorldCom's offer to buy Intermedia, Intermedia completed a secondary offering, selling another 15 percent of the company. It netted $913.8 million, almost $86 per share. The cash from that sale kept Intermedia afloat until the WorldCom purchase.

A month after the secondary offering, Digex stock peaked at $184 per share. For all the desirability of Digex at its peak, it never made a profit. Like other unprofitable Internet IPOs, Digex sank quickly once the Internet stock bubble burst. From its peak in March 2000, Digex's shares lost over 85 percent of their value by the end of the year, closing at $22.50. The shares lost 88 percent of their end-of-2000 value by the end of 2001, closing at $2.72 per share. A few months later, the shares slipped below $1 and never saw a higher price.

The implications of the price drop for WorldCom were disastrous. Intermedia's stake in Digex was worth over $2.5 billion at the time of World-Com's first offer for Intermedia in August 2000. By the time the deal was completed in July 2001, Intermedia's ownership of Digex was worth only half a billion dollars. Intermedia, without Digex, was worthless, but World-Com still paid $5 billion for Intermedia and its 62 percent interest in Digex.

Starting in 2000, WorldCom's public pronouncements and financial statements became works of fiction, so it is hard to determine what happened with each of the built and acquired local assets. What is known is that most of the value of the local assets, as well as that of the rest of the business, was written down during WorldCom's trip to the financial fat farm from 2002 to 2004.

To gain traction with individual consumers in the local business, World-Com's MCI unit began to resell local service using UNEs from the local phone companies in 2002. It was the first company to start a large, national marketing campaign around an all-in-one package of local services, called The Neighborhood, built by MCI. MCI was not the first to offer an all-in-one package. Z-Tel Technologies (now Trinsic) and others were bundlers of resold local service before MCI. MCI's contribution was that it brought the bundles closer to the mainstream with its national brand recognition and marketing resources.

As with many of MCI's earlier consumer-oriented offers such as Friends and Family, The Neighborhood was an offering that set the tone for MCI's competitors. AT&T, Sprint, and the RBOCs soon met the offer with similar all-you-can-call programs.

Sprint

Sprint has been an integrated carrier longer than any of its competitors. In addition to the long-distance business and Sprint PCS, it has the largest independent (non-RBOC) local exchange business in the United States, serving about 4 percent of the local phone lines in the country. In fact, the local telecommunications division has been Sprint's core business since its founding. Long-distance service was part of a diversification effort for United Telecommunications in the early 1980s when it bought the Sprint long-distance network from GTE.

Sprint's long-distance business, eventually owned entirely by United, became the growth engine for the company, so much so that the entire corporation was renamed Sprint. It also made acquisitions in the local telephone business, merging with Centel Corporation in 1993. The local business has given Sprint a diversification strategy, a bond to go with the growth stocks in its portfolios: long distance and PCS. Although the local business was seen as a drag on its financial performance in the go-go 1990s, it provided Sprint a financial stability that other long-distance carriers and CLECs haven't enjoyed.

However, Sprint's ILEC business was not an effective launching pad for a broad-based national-footprint local service. Its service areas are generally outside major metropolitan areas. The largest cities it covers are Orlando, Florida, and Las Vegas, Nevada.

Upon passage of the Telecommunications Act, Sprint immediately filed for CLEC status in most states. It was approved to offer the services but generally didn't resell RBOC services. It understood (correctly) that total service resale was, at best, a low-margin business.

Instead, Sprint focused on the development of the Sprint Integrated On-demand Network, known as ION. ION was an all-things-to-all-people bundle of voice, data, and video products that was supposed to be offered over a variety of network technologies including RBOC UNEs. Using the resources of the long-distance network, the services would be delivered to points of presence in metropolitan areas. From there the services would be delivered to individual users by the Sprint local network, wireless broadband technology (MMDS), or rented facilities in areas where the first two weren't available. The target technologies for non-Sprint-owned facilities were DSL and T-1.

ION consumed a lot of money and attention at Sprint. The investment totaled about $750 million in expense and more than $1.3 billion in capital between 1997 and 2001. Not included in that sum is the $1.2 billion in cash and debt assumption spent to purchase American Telecasting and other MMDS carriers in 1999.

ION failed to reach critical mass in any market where it was deployed and became a victim of the general downturn in the industry in late 2001. After absorbing $1.4 billion in operating losses from ION, Sprint took a charge of $1.8 billion to discontinue the effort. Also in 2001, Sprint announced that it would halt the further development of its MMDS network, effectively stranding (or ION-izing) its $1.2-billion-plus investment in MMDS.[8] The MMDS investment was written off in late 2003.

After its retrenchment from ION, Sprint began retailing bundled voice services outside its traditional local area in 2003 using UNEs from the RBOCs. Sprint also hedged its bets by becoming the provider of long-distance transport services to three of the seven RBOCs.[9]

Too Much . . . and Not Enough

The bottom line for the long-distance companies is that they could not compete with the RBOCs on a large scale using the same kind of technology the RBOCs (and their subscribers) had already bought and paid for. The long-distance companies were too far behind in the capital investment required to build out a broad-based landline network. A new or different technology was required to gain scale quickly in a business that relied on scale and would much more in a competitive environment. Both Sprint (new technology: ION) and AT&T (different technology: cable) made unsuccessful attempts to build a facilities-based local business that could compete at scale with the RBOCs. MCI tried to pick its spots and become a niche local provider. But after the WorldCom acquisition, it was more focused on propping up the Ponzi scheme than investing in a telecom business.

For the long-distance companies, the internal costs (network build out, customer care, billing, and so forth) to serve consumers with completely new broadly deployed local facilities proved too high. The long-distance companies didn't have enough scale and, after all, size matters. At the peak of their investing in local initiatives, the Big 3 invested collectively at a rate of no more than $3 billion per year. Even after the telebomb, the RBOCs invested, on average, roughly double that amount per year, every year, in their businesses. At peak, in 2001, the RBOCs' collective capital spend was $36 billion.[10] Only a disruptive technology can break that cycle.

INTERNATIONAL

At the height of the investment boom, the long-distance companies were expanding in multiple directions at the same time. In addition to their reach for the local market, they were also investing to become global carriers. Each had a different strategy; each failed or exited the business in short order. The international telecommunications market has always been highly fragmented, containing more hopes and promises than actual profits. The frenzy of mergers that gripped the telecom industry in the late 1990s also hit the international markets. Most international networks in place in the early 1990s changed hands at least once.

Historically, international services were offered through either bilateral agreements between national phone companies, known as PTTs (for post, telephone, and telegraph companies), or consortia owned by several carriers. The consortium approach was most often used when building undersea cable routes. The cost of a single ocean crossing ranged from hundreds of millions to billions of dollars, so it was best to spread the risk around. Until the 1990s, virtually all the transoceanic cable in the world was laid and maintained by a consortium of this type.

A third type of organization offered international services specific to an industry. Examples included SITA (Société International de Telecommunications Aéronautiques), which served international airlines, and SWIFT (the Society for World Interbank Financial Telecommunications), which served the international financial community.

As part of the market frenzy, several of these carriers became public companies. Two of the largest were FLAG Telecom Holdings (FLAG originally stood for Fiber-optic Link Around the Globe), and SITA, which spun out its network assets and named the resulting company Equant.

The IPOs and changes in ownership created a great deal of confusion in the market and didn't contribute to improved operational results. Many of these organizations were not used to being profit centers, so it was difficult for them to start charging market rates. Exacerbating the profitability issues was the extension of the second race to these markets, particularly the transatlantic, transpacific, and intra-European routes.

The predictable result, as with the second race, was bankruptcies and corporate restructuring. Global Crossing and FLAG failed as soon as the capital markets shut down. Tycom was reacquired by Tyco, its parent company. The Big 3 also participated in the churning of assets. Each contributed to at least one consortium that intended to offer services around the world. Most of these investments by the Big 3 were poorly managed loose alliances rather than well-thought-out strategic investments. Any profitability emanating from these investments was the result of fortunate timing rather than planned action.

Sprint

Sprint contributed its international business to Global One, a consortium that included Deutsche Telekom and France Telecom, in 1996. The consortium never made money. Sprint sold out to its partners for $1.1 billion in February 2000, right before the market peaked. The sale price actually represented a small profit for Sprint, one of the few in this segment of the industry. Deutsche Telekom subsequently left Global One to France Telecom, which combined it with Equant in 2001.

MCI and WorldCom

MCI's main investment in international services came as part of British Telecom's investment in MCI in 1994. In the deal, MCI bought British Telecom North America's network operations and then contributed it and the other MCI International assets to a joint venture named Concert.

MCI's 24.9 percent stake in Concert was sold to British Telecom for $1 billion in 1998 as part of the WorldCom merger. As with Sprint and the Global One business, the price represented a premium above MCI's investment and share of the operating losses at Concert. British Telecom wouldn't be so lucky with its next mate for Concert, AT&T.

AT&T

As the United States's PTT until its first divestiture, AT&T had bilateral service agreements in place with most of the PTTs, and former PTTs, in the world. Because of those relationships, AT&T already had the ability to offer traditional services across a wider global footprint than any of its U.S. competitors. However, in a world of increasing global competition, these traditional agreements were seen as limited in two ways. First, there were typically no agreed performance metrics between carriers, just agreements on the services to be provided and financial arrangements. Second, with the age of new, Internet-based applications rapidly approaching, more knowledge of the underlying network would be necessary when developing more intricate, advanced services. Developing this understanding required close cooperation between the interconnecting carriers.

To address the weaknesses of the traditional arrangements, AT&T developed the WorldPartners alliance in 1993. WorldPartners originally included Kokusai Denshin Denwa (Japan's traditional international carrier) and Singapore Telecommunications (Singapore's PTT). By 1998, the alliance included seventeen members covering Europe and Asia.

WorldPartners was always a loose alliance that never seemed to live up to its potential. So when British Telecom (BT) was spurned by MCI in 1998, AT&T saw an opportunity. Concert had one of the largest data network footprints in the world and the largest, most advanced international inbound voice service (think 800 service in the United States, but worldwide). AT&T had attractive businesses to contribute, too. Most notable was its international direct dial voice business, which delivered significant (though declining) revenue.

AT&T decided to unwind World Partners and form a new alliance with BT. The "new" Concert, formed in January 2000, was a Hollywood marriage. It was by far the biggest bet in the international market made by a U.S. carrier during this period. AT&T contributed assets it valued at $1.6 billion to Concert and lent it $1 billion. Concert hired a CEO with dotcom credentials, David Dorman (discussed earlier in this chapter). It even advertised on billboards outside Los Angeles International Airport, just like the latest movie. It had the makings of a successful business. In 2000, Concert was the fifth-largest long-distance provider by revenue in the United States.

BT and AT&T pledged that they would place the "combined transborder assets and operations of each company, including their existing international networks, their international traffic, their transborder products for business customers—including an expanding set of Concert services—and AT&T and BT's multinational accounts in selected industry sectors" into the Concert business.[11] In fact, both AT&T and British Telecom held out certain international assets from Concert. British Telecom held out BT Ignite (a subsidiary of British Telecom that held many of its investments in Europe) and AT&T held out the global network that it bought from IBM. That reluctance to fully commit to the business along with disagreements on transfer pricing between the parents and Concert and the rapidly falling international bandwidth pricing created a financially untenable situation.

Like most Hollywood marriages, the new Concert didn't last. The agreement to unwind Concert was reached in October 2001, only twenty-one months after the venture was formed. The result, from AT&T's perspective, was a $2.9 billion write-off, essentially every dollar it put into Concert. This charge hit AT&T at the same time it was going through its third divestiture, shedding AT&T Wireless and the AT&T Broadband cable properties. With so much turbulence in its financial statements, it was easy to miss the write-off. But it was an admission that Concert was a complete failure for AT&T. The Concert business lived on as part of BT Ignite.

For their efforts at Concert, several AT&T executives were promoted to corporate headquarters. Most notably, CEO Dorman became the president of AT&T and later the chair and CEO when Mike Armstrong followed the AT&T Broadband business to Comcast.

The Bottom Drops Out

In addition to the investments of the U.S. long-distance carriers, the international telecommunications market was crowded with many other players. Other carriers included Equant (post-Sprint), Cable and Wireless, SWIFT, 360networks, and Teleglobe. Each of these organizations went through either major network builds or transitions in ownership. The companies that built or owned significant transmission assets were hit by the pricing pressure caused by the second race. Other companies that had been more buyers of bandwidth than builders of network were able to be more nimble and ride the price curve rather than being stuck with expensive fiber assets.

Prices had further to fall in the international markets because transoceanic bandwidth was much more expensive than domestic. In the early 1990s, during the oligopoly days, a T-1 from New York to San Francisco cost about $2,400 per month. The same capacity circuit from New York to London cost about $24,000 per month. A 15 percent decline in pricing took more off the price of the international circuit ($3,600) than the entire cost of the domestic equivalent. And actual percentage price declines were much greater.

The price declines brought many buyers into the market that had been unable previously to afford international bandwidth. Connectivity between the United States and most nations in the world became as inexpensive as domestic connectivity only a few years earlier. The price declines coincided with the recession of 2000 to 2002, during which companies focused on cutting costs as a way to maintain profitability. A common strategy for reducing costs became the movement of jobs or tasks previously located in the United States or other high-wage countries (such as in Western Europe) to low-wage countries like India, the Philippines, or China. Telecommunications wasn't the only enabler required to come into place, but it had previously been a prohibitive cost element of outsourcing.

Even the increased volumes brought on by new buyers couldn't make up for the price declines. The ability of the long-distance companies to fund their expansion plans was dependent not only on high volumes, but also on stable pricing in line with the old model.

The overbuilders had large fixed investments and no incentives to hold the line on pricing. The publicly traded new entrants had an additional incentive to continue to drop prices in the short term: the relatively small revenue gains they generated propped up their fantastic stock market valuations for a little while longer. Thus, as in the domestic market, the international fiber overbuilders were more to blame for price erosion than any competition brought about by the RBOCs' entry into the long-distance market.

Each of the Big 3 curtailed or abandoned their international ambitions. More dramatically, each of the independent, publicly traded international overbuilders went into bankruptcy as the telebomb deepened.

SPACE: THE FINAL FRONTIER

By 2000, virtually every corner of the telecommunications market had been addressed by some entrepreneur or existing company seeking to expand. Among the most expensive and riskiest ventures were those that attacked the global mobile phone market with low-earth orbit (LEO) satellites.

Global satellite phones that connect to the public switched telephone network (PSTN) have been around since the early 1980s. One organization, Inmarsat (originally the International Maritime Satellite Organization), is a government-sponsored consortium of national phone companies that launched satellites and provided service through bulky phones with large antennas. Its satellites were placed in geosynchronous earth orbit (GEO), 22,500 miles above the equator. GEO satellites are effective at providing stable coverage over wide areas of the earth. What they lack is quality of service. The voice signal has to be carried at least 45,000 miles, inducing delay characteristics that are quite annoying in human conversation.

In the 1990s, two new companies, Iridium and Globalstar, attempted to solve the delay problem by placing their satellites much closer to the earth, about 750 miles up (hence the term *low-earth orbit*, or LEO). This took care of the delay problem and allowed the satellites to be much lighter, but the satellites had to be in constant motion and had to be powered, so they could be guided to and kept in the right trajectory around the earth. They also had a life expectancy of about five years because of the wear and tear of constant motion around the earth. By contrast, GEO satellites had a life expectancy of ten years or more.

The Iridium satellite fleet contained sixty-six satellites plus a few hot spares floating above the service fleet, to be moved into place if one of the active satellites failed. The name Iridium corresponds to the seventy-seventh element in the periodic chart. Originally, the service fleet was expected to include seventy-seven satellites. The number was reduced to sixty-six later in the design phase, but the sixty-sixth element was dysprosium, not likely a memorable brand name, so Iridium stuck. Iridium's sixty-six satellites compared with less than ten for Inmarsat. The cost put Iridium at a disadvantage up front. Iridium's business plan called for the expenditure of $5 billion to launch the service, all of which was spent before the first billable call ran over the network.

One of the supposed advantages of the LEO satellite phones was that they were more portable. They were smaller and ran on power closer to that of cell phones than the bulky phones used on the GEO networks. The GEO phones were known as "suitcase phones" because of their resemblance in size and weight to bulky luggage.

The problem with the new LEO phones was that they were unable to work inside buildings or in urban canyons where tall buildings blocked the line of sight to a satellite. Although this may have been acceptable in the early 1990s, when most people didn't have cell phones, by the time the LEO networks were operational in 1998, the market had changed. The public acceptance of cellular technology between the original planning of the Iridium system and the actual launch of service had conditioned the public to assume that mobile phones would generally work inside buildings. But the satellite phones didn't work anywhere that the view of the sky was blocked by any reasonably dense object. Particularly for one segment of Iridium's intended market, international news reporters, the inability to file reports when covering wars without becoming a target was quite a problem. In the end, *dysprosium* may have been a more appropriate name for the company, as it is taken from the Greek *dysprositos*, meaning "hard to get at."

The LEO services also charged $3 per minute for their services, which compared unfavorably with mobile technology that had been broadly deployed in a competitive market during the long gestation of the LEO services. That left the LEO providers with a market that included only those with the need and money to stay in touch while in the most remote or hostile terrain.

Both the Iridium and Globalstar services were dead on arrival. Both went bankrupt. Iridium was resurrected by an entrepreneur who bought the assets at fire-sale prices with the intention of selling to niche markets. Iridium's assets, constructed at a cost of $5 billion, were bought out of bankruptcy for $25 million, a 99.5 percent discount.

NOTES

1. Rank was based on subscribers as listed in corporate reports at the end of the second quarter 2003.
2. Tory Weber, "Netro Buys In to Fixed Wireless with Project Angel Purchase," *Telephony*, January 21, 2002.
3. The write-down is covered in AT&T Wireless's annual report for 2002 to the SEC on Form 10-K.
4. TCG results from operations from its reports to the SEC.
5. Ninth Annual Report on Competition in Video Markets, FCC, 02-338, p. 11.
6. Local investment data from MCI and WorldCom reports to the SEC through 2000.
7. Intermedia operational and financial data from reports to the SEC.
8. Investment and write-off information from Sprint's reports to the SEC on Form 10-K.
9. Report of supplying three of the seven RBOCs from Sprint's report to the SEC on Form 10-K for 1996.
10. RBOC capital spending comes from reports to the SEC on Form 10-K for the year 2001.
11. AT&T's report to the SEC on Form 10-K for 1999.

CHAPTER 7

THE RISE AND FALL OF THE COMPETITIVE LOCAL EXCHANGE CARRIERS

"Competition is the keen cutting edge of business."
—HENRY FORD, AMERICAN AUTOMOBILE
MANUFACTURER

The passage of the Telecommunications Act of 1996 coincided with the beginning of the dot-com era. During the boom, billions of dollars were poured into start-up companies based on little more than a few ideas wrapped up in a business plan. The telecommunications industry took more than its share of the venture investments. Many of these companies have failed. New phone companies that sold local services in competition with the former monopoly carriers were called CLECs.

The number and type of start-ups in the wake of the Communications Act paralleled the newly competitive market after AT&T's first divestiture in 1984. Some of the new-age carriers built facilities to support local services, pumping several billion dollars into building fiber rings around the business districts of most large cities in the United States. Many more simply decided to resell RBOC services.

The CLECs that built new networks competed head-to-head with the ILECs' voice and data offerings for business, creating some new offerings, particularly higher-bandwidth products. This competition was good for businesses that were close enough to connect to the new networks, until the new carriers started going bankrupt. The resellers entered the market with me-too offerings that offered consumers few new features, so they had to compete on price—

1880
1890
1900
1910
1920
1930
1940
1950
1960
1970
1980
1981
1982
1983
1984
1985
1986
1987
1988
1989
1990
1991
1992
1993
1994
1995
1996
1997
1998
1999
2000
2001
2002
2003
2004
2005
FUTURE

MONOPOLY
DIVESTITURE
STABILITY
BOOM
BOMB
RECOVERY?

which was a good thing for consumers until the resellers started going bankrupt.

The CLECs ran into difficulties in one or more of three main areas:

1. Many attracted either too much or too little investment capital.

2. Many made bets on untried technology that didn't mature fast enough to provide reliable service or pay back investors.

3. Each CLEC was caught in the FCC's inability to write stable rules of the competitive road for the industry.

Some of the difficulties the CLECs encountered were fatal. Others were mere annoyances. But the collective burden, along with other complexities inherent in any start-up and the investment mentality of the time, combined to sink the majority of the new upstarts during the telebomb.

NEW KIDS ON A CROWDED BLOCK

According to the Association for Local Telecommunications Services (ALTS), a trade association for competitive carriers, there were more than three hundred CLECs operating in the United States at their peak in 2000. Most of these were new companies created to take advantage of the newly competitive local telecommunications market. The Big 3 long-distance carriers became CLECs. Even the RBOCs filed for CLEC status in some areas outside their incumbent territories.

Whereas the number of CLECs has declined significantly (ALTS estimated that eighty to one hundred were left as of April 2003), the number of CLEC lines in service has increased at a steady rate. The FCC's accounting for CLEC lines in service shows growth, from 8.2 million lines in December 1999 to 24.8 million lines in December 2002.

All this competition is not completely bad news for the ILECs, however. At the beginning of 2003, almost 75 percent of the CLECs' lines were provisioned using unbundled network elements provided by the ILECs. So, while the ILECs aren't getting full retail revenues from the CLECs' customers, it isn't a complete loss for the ILECs, either. Only 6.4 million of the nearly 25 million CLEC lines in 2003 were provided without using any facilities from one of the incumbents. About one-third of those non-ILEC-supported lines are provided by cable companies.

As described in Chapter 5, there are two ways that a CLEC can rent ILEC facilities to provide service to the CLEC's customers. First, it can simply resell the same service that the ILEC offers. In this option, called total service resale (TSR), the CLEC has no choice about which network elements are used and how they are put together. The second way a CLEC can rent ILEC facilities is by specifying individual pieces of the network in virtually any combination required to offer service. This second option is called UNE, or unbundled network elements.

While there are variations on the UNE theme, the basic idea is that the CLEC can either pay to specify individual network elements or pay a higher fee for the ILEC to assemble the required network elements for resale. Since TSR carries a higher cost and most CLECs have figured out how to specify the unbundled network elements they need, the resale market is in decline. In this chapter, the term *resell* is used generically to refer to either TSR or UNE resale.

In a parallel to the early days of the competitive long-distance business, the CLEC industry grew up in two segments: the builders and the resellers. Many CLECs used both strategies and, as you will read in the profiles in this chapter, they often entered several markets at the same time. Entering multiple markets generally contributed to the CLEC's downfall by increasing the degree of difficulty of their business operations.

BUILDERS

Before the term CLEC came into popular use, the industry had competitive access providers, or CAPs. They built networks along roads and utility rights-of-way to connect buildings in the business districts of major metropolitan areas to the backbone networks of the Big 3 long-distance companies. The CAPs provided direct service to some businesses, but their main customers were the long-distance companies that used the CAPs to gain direct access to customers without having to pay the high access fees charged by the incumbents. The term CAP has generally fallen from use in favor of the term CLEC, but the terms are roughly equivalent.

The step up from CAP services to equal competitor to the RBOCs proved difficult, though. As with the long-distance companies' local ambitions, the CLECs ran into trouble dealing with a multiplicity of state and local as well as federal regulations.

The construction process became a problem as well. So many companies tore up the streets of various cities to place their fiber that the highway departments couldn't keep the streets paved. Many municipalities didn't have the bureaucracy in place to enforce rules regarding placement and rehabilitation of these construction sites. The District of Columbia had such a hard time keeping up with the traffic tie-ups and poorly repaved streets that it declared a moratorium on new telecom construction in 2000, delaying the business plans of several start-up carriers.

There were many stories at the time about one CLEC digging up a street and repaving it only to have another CLEC plow up the new pavement a few months later. Not only did that situation invite traffic and political problems in the municipalities; it was a sign that the new fiber networks were going to compete with each other as much as with the ILEC. The additional networks solved the local bandwidth problem in some small areas. But many of those areas were solved more than once. And many other areas were never touched. It became a crapshoot as to whether a business owner's locations happened to be close enough to one of the new CLEC networks.

This section profiles two of the builders, nTelos and McLeodUSA, to show the variety of troubles the builders encountered. Both nTelos and McLeodUSA offered CAP-like services in advance of the Telecommunications Act of 1996. Because of their previous experience, they were seen as better bets to become stable businesses in the long term, but both made serious mistakes that can only make sense in terms of the investing euphoria of the late 1990s.

nTelos: A Lesson on Overpaying

*"Failure is simply the opportunity to begin again,
this time more intelligently."*
—HENRY FORD, AMERICAN AUTOMOBILE MANUFACTURER

nTelos began its life in the nineteenth century as the Clifton Forge–Waynesboro Telephone Company (CFW), a little independent (non-RBOC) local phone company serving three small cities in the upper Shenandoah Valley and Alleghany Highlands of Virginia. (CFW served the city of Covington in addition to Clifton Forge and Waynesboro.)

Like most of the ILECs in the early 1980s, CFW was granted licenses to provide cellular service in its landline service area. Fortunately for CFW, that territory covered two interstate highways (Interstates 81 and 64). The roaming fees generated by passing cars produced solid cash flow with few customer service obligations.

Interstate highways also make good places to plant fiber optics. This natural advantage gave CFW easy access to neighboring communities. By 1997, CFW claimed 450 route miles of fiber-optic cable along the highways of central and southwestern Virginia. This network reach and capacity made it easy for CFW to offer CAP services. CFW also joined forces with Shenandoah Telecommunications, Sprint, and R&B Communications in a consortium called ValleyNet that connected all their properties along the corridor of Interstate 81 between the Pennsylvania Turnpike and Interstate 40 in Tennessee, a distance of about 450 miles. ValleyNet was a microcosm of the second race. It focused on only one area but installed more fiber capacity in that area than would be needed for many years to come.

In February 2001, CFW merged with R&B Communications, updating its name to nTelos and buying naming rights to a concert venue in Portsmouth, Virginia. It was like PSInet and Enron, only smaller.

Even though the face of the company was changing, the management of the company still had its roots in the small local telephone business. The collective experiences of James Quarforth (from nTelos) and J. Allen Layman (from R&B) amounted to significant knowledge about managing small telephone companies but did not include experience managing more far-flung enterprises. The next tier of executives, including a chief financial officer named Moneymaker, also lacked significant experience beyond their narrow specialties.

ANOTHER SECOND RACE

For the companies that decided to build their own network facilities in the local market, an additional impediment to profitability was the fact that most local business centers were overbuilt multiple times. As in the long-haul market, too many carriers built too much capacity to be sustainable in the market. By the end of the 1990s, most cities of any size in the United States contained fiber-optic rings built by at least two companies and in many cases more.

An example of the overbuilding that occurred was in Roanoke, Virginia. In addition to its role as a communications center for the southern Appalachians (Verizon, AT&T, and WorldCom maintained hub facilities there), the city was overbuilt by Cox (the incumbent cable provider), nTelos, and KMC Telecom Holdings (a facilities-based CLEC). All this fiber is in place for a metropolitan area with about 225,000 residents and a downtown area with only a few hundred buildings.

nTelos began offering CLEC services throughout central and western Virginia and parts of West Virginia. Its offerings included voice and data services for business as well as high-speed and dial-up Internet access to the general public. It also invested heavily in wireless services. In the FCC's PCS auction in 1995 and 1996, CFW (by itself and in partnership with others) picked up licenses that covered its then-current service territory and a few contiguous areas. It paid reasonable sums (apparently less than $30 million) for the licenses and began to set up service.

nTelos's strategy included growing the PCS business beyond the original licensed area. It took a large step in that direction by taking advantage of a situation resulting from the Bell Atlantic/GTE merger. The merger included the creation of Verizon Wireless. The new Verizon Wireless included the cellular interests directly controlled by Bell Atlantic (operated as Bell Atlantic Mobile), the PCS interests of a partnership significantly owned by Bell Atlantic (operated as PCS PrimeCo), Vodafone's U.S. operations, and GTE's wireless business. Because each of these businesses was large by itself, there were many areas where more than one of the four offered service. As part of the merger agreement, Bell Atlantic and GTE agreed to divest many of the overlapping properties. The PrimeCo properties in central and eastern Virginia were put on the block.

Fortunately for Bell Atlantic, the sale of these properties coincided with the height of the dot-com euphoria and, more important, the top of the market for stocks and telecom properties. So, nTelos paid PrimeCo close to $450 million for a PCS business that included 86,000 subscribers. Admittedly, the PrimeCo areas had the potential for more subscribers and do, in fact, have more today. However, the price paid included $407 million in cash that nTelos didn't have.

One of the lessons to be learned from the telebomb is that there is an inverse relationship between the amount of cash that changes hands in a merger transaction and the success of the resulting company. When large stacks of cash have to be raised quickly to enter into this kind of transaction, generally the only place to go is the junk bond market, also called the high-yield debt market in more polite circles. Either way, it is a bad neighborhood.

In nTelos's case, it didn't directly issue junk bonds, but it agreed to sell senior cumulative convertible preferred stock to investment bank Morgan Stanley and Welsh, Carson, Anderson, and Stowe, a well-known private equity firm. Carried as long-term debt on the company's books, the preferred stock might as well have been junk bonds. Before the PrimeCo purchase, nTelos maintained an average debt level equal to 47 percent of revenue, typical of a well-managed company in the industry. The debt taken on in the PrimeCo purchase pushed nTelos's long-term debt level to 500 percent of its year 2000 revenue. Even a CFO named Moneymaker couldn't dig nTelos out of that hole.

Blame the hubris of the time on the downturn in the economy, but the PrimeCo purchase turned out not to be the fast-growing cash generator that nTelos must have anticipated. In fact, the transaction doomed nTelos. The interest and dividends on the indebtedness incurred during the expansion reached as high as 40 percent of revenue, a level that even the healthiest company couldn't hope to continue for any length of time. The interest, dividends, and capital burned in expanding the wireless business wiped out one hundred years of stockholders' equity in less than two years.

Following the trend among overspent companies in the telecom market, nTelos completed its drive-through bankruptcy in five months. The former common stockholders were wiped out, and the bankers and investors that lent nTelos the money that sent it over the edge now own the company. The slimmer nTelos business was on the edge, even after losing more than $600 million in debt during its bankruptcy. As it left bankruptcy, it carried $320 million in debt for a company with less than $300 million in annual revenue. That number compared unfavorably with MCI, which left bankruptcy with $5 billion in debt and more than $20 billion in revenue.

Ironically, where many CLECs have failed due to their inability to operate in new markets, nTelos's CLEC operations are small but have positive operating income: nTelos has chosen its markets well and provides profitable and popular data services. Its operational expenses are relatively low. It just purchased the new PCS business at too high a cost.

McLeodUSA: Creating a Debt Monster

"Neither a borrower nor a lender be; For loan oft loses both itself and friend; And borrowing dulls the edge of husbandry."
—WILLIAM SHAKESPEARE, *HAMLET,* ACT I, SCENE III

Clark McLeod was a serial entrepreneur who sold his first telecommunications venture, long-distance carrier TelecomUSA, to MCI for $1.25 billion in 1990. MCI would recycle the TelecomUSA name (see Chapter 1), and McLeod would recycle the idea of creating a competitive telecom carrier, this time in the local business.

After McLeod sold TelecomUSA to MCI, he started McLeod Telecommunications, which later became McLeodUSA. McLeod Telecommunications started as a CAP before the Telecommunications Act was passed. It later entered virtually every facet of the telecommunications business: competitive local service, incumbent local service, directory publishing, long-distance service, telecom equipment installation and maintenance, cable television, Internet service, and wireless.

McLeodUSA's geographic coverage started in Clark McLeod's home state of Iowa and soon expanded to Illinois. The company stayed near home, later offering services only in the upper Midwest and as far west as Colorado. It evidently aimed to be a big fish in a small pond, boasting in its 10-K filing with the U.S. Securities and Exchange Commission for 1996 that "the company believes that it is the only competitive access provider in the Des Moines [Iowa] market." In the 2000 census, Des Moines, Iowa, had fewer than 150,000 residents older than 18 (.07 percent of the population of the United States).

As of 1996, McLeodUSA had never made a profit. But it was reasonably lean, with only $2.6 *million* in long-term debt for a company with $81 million in revenue. Over the next four years, its long-term indebtedness grew to $2.7 *billion*.

The terms of the first tranche of debt offered by McLeodUSA in 1997 should have been a warning to all future investors. Given the company's relatively low debt levels, it should have had no problem borrowing money if it had borrowed a reasonable amount of money. But it sold $500 million face value of notes with a 10.5 percent interest rate for $289.5 million, an incredible 42 percent discount. The holders of these notes paid 58 cents to get an investment with a face value of $1 that paid 10.5 percent interest. That equates to an 18 percent return; incredible, even for the junk-bond market.

McLeodUSA's expansion then went into overdrive. Between the beginning of 1997 and the end of 2000, the company completed at least twenty-five acquisitions with a value of $3.5 billion. The acquisitions cost it almost $700 million in cash and debt assumption, with the rest paid in stock. McLeodUSA also spent $2 billion on the build out of its network. Although small compared with the second racers, McLeod built far more network than it could ever hope to sell.

The amounts paid for merger candidates predictably peaked with the dot-com era. In March 2000, as the NASDAQ hit its highest point, McLeodUSA acquired Splitrock Services in a mostly stock deal valued at $2.3 billion. For that sum, McLeodUSA received a company with less than $300 million in total assets, less than $100 million in 1999 revenue, and a history of never making a profit.

During this time, Clark McLeod's role within the organization was a combination of hunter and booster. He led the search for larger and larger acquisitions and also acted as chief cheerleader for the company's stock. His role was very much like that of Bernie Ebbers at WorldCom. And like WorldCom, once the mergers ended, there was little to cheer about.

Once mergers were beyond McLeodUSA's reach, McLeod hunted for funding instead of acquisition targets. The largest late investor in McLeodUSA was the buyout company, Forstmann Little & Co. McLeod welcomed one of Forstmann Little's investments in McLeod as follows in August 2001: "Today's announcement reflects the strength of our long-term partnership with Forstmann Little. With their increased investment and active involvement . . . , McLeodUSA is poised for its next round of growth." Less than six months later, McLeodUSA was in bankruptcy.

As the telebomb deepened, it became difficult to attract outside investment, so McLeodUSA turned to selling assets to raise cash. In contrast with nTelos, McLeodUSA's best investment was in the PCS market. Licenses that cost it $32.8 million in 1997 were sold in 2001 for net proceeds of $125.6 million, a 282 percent return on the investment. McLeodUSA never offered service in the spectrum, thereby avoiding yet another expensive build out that likely would not have paid off.

Unable to grow revenue enough to feed the debt monster or find enough new funding, McLeodUSA needed its own trip to the financial fat farm. It shed about $2 billion in debt in less than ninety days during its drive-through bankruptcy in early 2002. Like nTelos, the investors who came to the party late and bought the high-interest-rate debt ended up owning the company after its bankruptcy. In the case of McLeodUSA, Forstmann Little ended up with a 58 percent ownership stake. The shareholders, including Clark McLeod, were left with no ownership in the company. McLeod himself chose to "retire" from the company in favor of new management. Formerly ubiquitous in stock analyst circles, the company's namesake completely shrank from view.

As of mid-2004, McLeodUSA still had yet to turn an operating profit and had no identifiable segment that looked close to being profitable. Its debt load, while considerably lighter, still exceeded its annual revenue for 2003. And its revenue declined in each of the nine quarters after its bankruptcy filing in February 2002.

RESELLERS

Clearly building networks was a risky proposition in both the local and long-distance markets. But reselling the ILECs' local services wasn't any picnic, either. The ever-changing regulations were a constant problem. Also, the margins on resold services were thin, so large volumes were required to recoup fixed costs.

Because the resellers were held hostage to the availability of RBOC loops and had largely undifferentiated products, it was harder for them than for the builders to provide a differentiated offering in the marketplace. This problem was exacerbated when a company took on large amounts of debt.

The bondholders didn't want to hear complaints about the slow RBOCs; they wanted their interest payments. COVAD was an example of just such a company.

COVAD: Building a Highway to Nowhere

COVAD was an early, and possibly the largest, variant on the CLEC theme called a data local exchange carrier (DLEC). It sold DSL services that ran from its network to customer locations on UNEs. COVAD raised and spent nearly $3 billion to build a DSL presence in about 1,700 central offices in ninety-four cities in the United States.[1] COVAD built this presence without any sort of guaranteed long-term supply of UNEs from the last-mile access providers (almost always the RBOCs). This is the equivalent of building toll roads between, in, and around most major cities in the United States and then waiting for the individual municipalities to allocate funds, design, and build all of the on- and off-ramps based on the assumption that some federal government agency will tell them they must do so.

COVAD was started by Silicon Valley investors who knew the Internet well, but knew nothing about the local exchange networks that were the most important, costly, and difficult-to-provision item in their value chain. In other words, the UNE local loop was the first and only item on the critical path to implementing a DSL service. In order to gain this knowledge, COVAD hired Bob Knowling, an RBOC executive, as CEO. Knowling came to COVAD with significant network operations experience from both Ameritech and USWest.

Knowling knew how to provision local loops. At USWest, he ran the local network operations group that included the ten thousand or so outside plant technicians who did the physical placement of the copper loops and the installation of services on those loops. But he was a classic insider and didn't know how to operate from the outside. He had no experience in the new competitive environment that evolved as other carriers started to order UNEs, which used the same copper loops but required different business processes to implement. Most specifically, he knew how to tell technicians to provision loops, but he didn't know how to tell an entire RBOC organization to do the same thing.

The difference is subtle, but important. Any one of several hundred management personnel at an RBOC can order a technician to provision a local loop to a residence. The same technician wouldn't take an order from a CLEC employee. Moreover, the same technician was unlikely to have the knowledge necessary to provision a UNE in 1998. Not only were the competitive boundaries between the RBOCs and the CLECs unclear; the business processes required to provision a local loop of any kind were, and still are today, more a part of the lore of the Bell system than a defined, repeatable process. Of course, no one did know how to convince an RBOC to quickly provision services for a CLEC since this kind of competition had never existed before. And Knowling was a monopolist, a product of the Bell system, with little knowledge of the competitive market. It would take several years for the provisioning of wholesale services, as they were called, to become efficient. Until the time when wholesale provisioning processes matured, any carrier depending on resold RBOC services was at a competitive disadvantage.

At the end of the day, COVAD couldn't find enough revenue or provision the customers it did find fast enough to start recognizing revenue. COVAD never found a value-add formula that translated to customer success and the rapidly increasing revenue that its financial structure required.

Given that COVAD raised about a third of its capital in the bad neighborhood of the junk bond market at interest rates as high as 13.5 percent, it was no surprise that the company filed for bankruptcy. The reorganized COVAD, $1.4 billion lighter, emerged from its 120-day drive-through bankruptcy in December 2001. After bankruptcy, it depended as much on resale of a traditional RBOC service known as special access as it did on DSL. As of mid-2004, it had still never reported an operating profit.

CLECs that did find a way to add value to the commodity products were able to generate a loyal following. Any company entering the newly competitive telecommunications market in the mid- to late 1990s needed to have significant investment if it expected to be able to play with the big boys. While some new carriers actually believed that they could slay the giants of the industry with just a few million dollars of venture capital and a me-too product offering, these companies were generally gone quickly, some even before the general dot-com meltdown. Overinvestment was more the rule among the new entrants. Most financially successful companies, though, followed more prudent investment paths.

Trinsic: So Far, So Good

Trinsic, formerly known as Z-Tel Technologies, Inc., is one of the potential success stories among the competitive carriers. Although profitability has been elusive for Trinsic, it has avoided most of the pitfalls that have snared other carriers.

Trinsic, based in Tampa, Florida, was founded to take advantage of the competitive opportunities opened up by the Telecommunications Act. It built product offerings based on renting UNEs from the RBOCs and building a differentiated product offering on top of the resold services. It added calling cards, intelligent network features, call-routing features, voice mail, and voice recognition services on top of plain dial tone.

The Trinsic management team did not include veteran RBOC personnel. Instead, it relied on competent businesspeople and technologists who understood the network from a user's perspective rather than a carrier's perspective.

Trinsic also implemented wholesale offerings. It used its own ordering and provisioning capabilities to shorten the time to market for other carriers' UNE-based CLEC services. Both MCI and Sprint utilized this capability. The wholesale offerings were initially extensions of the technology behind the basic product set. They are an example of developing new sources of revenue with little marginal cost and an ability to mine corporate assets for revenue. Demonstrating this capability, Trinsic's wholesale services have been profitable almost from the beginning.

In addition, Trinsic has not pursued growth for growth's sake. It has completed only one major acquisition, the purchase of Touch 1 Communications in 2000. Touch 1 brought customers and a needed telemarketing capability to Trinsic. The deal was also completed with relatively little cash. Trinsic avoided the bad neighborhoods (junk bonds) into which other CLECs fell. Including its convertible preferred stock, Trinsic's debt equals about half of its annual revenue, not too far from the debt levels of the larger carriers.[2]

Although not yet fully profitable, Trinsic has made progress in a difficult environment. It is generating cash from operations and, unlike McLeod, has recovered from a decline in revenue during the telebomb. All in all, Trinsic has provided an example of how to avoid some of the traps that many CLECs have fallen into.

OPERATIONAL DIFFICULTIES

The rise and fall of the CLECs very closely tracks that of the dot-com era. Many CLEC business plans depended on being able to sell to dot-coms or on other dot-com-era business truisms such as the fundamental fallacy of Internet use doubling every ninety days (covered in Chapter 4). In addition to the overoptimism of the business cases, virtually all the CLECs found the local phone business to be more complicated than they expected. These complications generally fell into three categories:

1. Investment balance

2. Regulatory confusion

3. Technical difficulties

Investment Balance

Getting the balance of investment right was a problem. The builders, in particular, had a voracious need for capital because their business cases generally depended on being early to market—building their networks before too many other competitors entered the market. This problem fed on itself when the number of builders became such that they were competing with each other not only for capital but also for employees and rights-of-way. Chapter 4 shows how Level 3, the last company to post for the second race, paid significantly more to build a national network than Qwest or Williams. The land-rush mentality of the dot-com era often caused tunnel vision in entrepreneurs. The same was true for those building in the local and regional markets.

The problem often came down to an issue of timing rather than whether the company was over- or undercapitalized. The tunnel vision of the entrepreneurs was coupled with the desire of the venture capitalists (VCs) that funded the companies to lock in their investments at low valuations. By committing large sums of capital early on, the VCs were able to gain larger percentage ownership. If the VCs waited to put some of the money in later, the company might have a higher value, thus garnering less percentage ownership for a given dollar investment.

Toward the end of the avalanche of bankruptcies in 2000 to 2001, one result of the overinvestment was that several insolvent companies had a pile of cash on hand. One example of this was CoreExpress. CoreExpress was a project funded by Benchmark Capital, known for its "go big or go home" investment mentality.

CoreExpress began offering secure, performance-guaranteed network connections over a customer's existing Internet circuits in May 2000, after the crest of the dot-com wave. Most of the initial investment cash was still left over when the company realized that it was not going to be able to cover payments on the fiber-optic network it leased to support the service. The problem wasn't lack of cash; it was the lack of revenue to cover mounting operations costs when revenue wasn't growing.

A more prudent investment strategy would have been to commit investment dollars in stages, each successive tranche of funding being dependent

on the successful completion of financial or operating milestones. VCs usually worked that way, but they were swept up in the times as well and didn't
always follow their own rules.

The CLECs were generally unable to time their investments to the
growth of their market. However, even a more deliberate investment approach in the future will not take significant market share away from the
RBOCs anytime soon. To put it in the same terms as the spend of the Big
3 long-distance companies, the CLEC industry averaged about $10 billion
per year in capital spending between 1996 and 2002. That included the
boom years, so it is unlikely that that pace could be kept up over time. The
CLECs' $10 billion compares with an average capital spend by the RBOCs
during the same period of $25 billion to $30 billion.[3] Again, only a disruptive technology can break the cycle of dominance.

Regulatory Confusion

"Time is the scarcest resource and unless it is
managed nothing else can be managed."
—PETER F. DRUCKER, MANAGEMENT THEORIST

Although given broad opportunities by the Telecommunications Act, the
CLECs were not given a roadmap for how to get there. The fact that the
market rather than bureaucrats would decide the winners and losers was
considered to be one of the features of the act. But in the name of competition, the act left many areas too vague to be of immediate use by the CLECs.
The act listed many different ways that the CLECs should be allowed to use
the incumbent's networks to promote competition. But it didn't specify the
interconnection rules and processes in enough detail to be implementable.

As late as 2004, more than eight years after the act was passed, the FCC
was still changing the definition of what the ILECs were required to lease
to competitors. One way to kill start-ups in any industry is to change the
competitive rules frequently over long periods of time. The FCC succeeded
in doing that.

In February 2003, the FCC issued new rules as part of its "Review of
Section 251 Unbundling Obligations of Incumbent Local Exchange Carriers." This order was a scheduled Triennial Review, called for in the Telecommunications Act. It was, in effect, a self-review of the state of industry
regulations resulting from the act. This review was of particular importance
because the commission's rules governing competition in the local market
had been sent back to the FCC for reconsideration twice by federal courts.
The alterations of the rules contained in the Triennial Review included

changes of opinion by the FCC on basic issues that most thought had been decided earlier. And, worse yet, the commission punted on several other requirements, essentially tossing responsibility to the states, throwing up its hands, and wishing better luck to the state utility commissions.

One of the network elements that the FCC did a reversal on was line sharing. Previously, a DSL provider could rent just the high-frequency portion of a loop that already provided phone service in order to provision DSL service. Since both the RBOC voice service and the DSL service would run over the same telephone line, the services were said to share the line. Line sharing was desirable from the standpoint of the DLECs; because the line supporting the voice service was already in place, there was no waiting for the RBOC to install a new copper pair. Quicker service installation made for satisfied customers and shorter time to revenue for the DLEC. As part of the order, the FCC decided to make line sharing unavailable to CLECs in the future, even though three of the five commissioners stated later that they favored retaining it.

Although passed by the commission, the Triennial Review results didn't stand to logic. They were immediately challenged in federal court. The RBOCs' side won a stay of the new rules, leading to an impasse that threatened the entire UNE pricing regime set up by the FCC. Admittedly, the FCC was dealt a bad hand in the vagueness of the Telecommunications Act. But three successive commissioners (Reed Hundt, William Kennard, and Michael Powell) were unable to catch up in the eight years following passage of the act.

If the UNE pricing regime put in place by the FCC fell, the businesses of the CLEC community would suffer, and likely die. CLEC stocks suffered in advance of the June 2004 deadline for resolution set by the federal courts. Many of the CLEC stocks fell by half or more.

From reciprocal compensation to the list of unbundled network elements to access reform, the inability of the FCC to find acceptable implementation steps slowed the pace of competition. Regardless of the type of CLEC, builder or reseller, they were dependent on the ILECs for, at a minimum, interconnection, and, in most cases, much more.

The CLECs were more dependent on the implementation of the Telecommunications Act than any other segment of the industry. They didn't have any established businesses with steady cash flow to tide them over until the FCC and the courts sorted out how to implement the act.

Congress decided that the ILECs must share in the burden of opening up their former monopoly markets. The FCC has, so far, been unable to find a legally defensible way to implement the admittedly vague will of Congress.

Although legal title to the local Bell assets surely rests with the RBOCs, those assets were built over time with money paid by subscribers who had no choice but to buy from the monopoly and whose rates were determined by regulatory authorities that kept others out of the business. The regulatory logic then follows that when competition becomes feasible the regulators can use their power to require reasonable support of competitors by the monopoly incumbents. But the question remains: How long should the incumbents support the CLECs?

By way of an analogy, AT&T supported the new long-distance carriers for some time after divestiture, but only until MCI's and Sprint's interexchange networks were built, a process that took about ten years. When that process was completed, the long-distance business was a neat little national oligopoly, easy to regulate at the federal level. As long as the competitive balance of the Big 3 was in check, the rest of the industry couldn't stray far from the normative behavior of the big dogs at the head of the pack.

The local market is nowhere near as orderly, which makes it less susceptible to national rules. The competitive dynamics have many more varieties because there isn't one national market for local service. The Telecommunications Act has defined roles for state commissions, but there are more than fifty local markets. Each community has its own competitive dynamics. While any given CLEC may be able to establish a presence in one or more communities, there are likely to be communities within the same state that have, effectively, no competition. CLEC competition on its own isn't likely to ever, by itself, prove to be enough to remove, at the federal level, the obligations of the ILECs to support their competitors.

The practical answer for the CLECs was that the CLECs would have to put relatively more energy into building a capability to ensure compliance by the RBOCs than would the Big 3, which already had large staffs devoted to such compliance. The long-distance companies that survived the first race to cover the United States developed both regulatory and operational capabilities designed specifically to keep AT&T's and the RBOCs' power in check. COVAD, for example, might have been better off hiring a CEO or COO with long-distance operations expertise to bake RBOC-management skills into every corner of a company that was so deeply dependent on the RBOCs for its success.

Each CLEC played the regulatory game differently. Trinsic hired regulatory staff. Others spent liberally on outside attorneys to advocate for them. Still others bet their businesses on specific regulatory outcomes that they thought were most likely. COVAD, for example, depended on the FCC beginning to enforce UNE rules and generally failed in that regard.

Regardless of the regulatory approach a CLEC followed, the bottom line is that the long-term future of the CLECs is still at the mercy of the RBOCs because of the regulatory failings of Congress and the FCC. Until the UNE rules are rewritten in a way that will pass a court challenge, the RBOCs' legal teams will always have the upper hand. Among the publicly traded carriers that depend on the market structure created (or, more appropriately, allowed) by the Telecommunications Act, the roller-coaster ride of Pac-West Telecomm (see Chapter 10) is likely to be the norm as regulation in the industry continues to change. It is a lesson in the price of uncertainty.

Technical Difficulties

Like the dot-coms, many CLECs committed to technologies that weren't ready for prime time in the search of some sort of competitive edge. Some technologies just took time to develop; others may never be commercially viable.

Local Multipoint Distribution Service
The most common failed technology was millimeter wavelength fixed wireless. Known as local multipoint distribution service (LMDS), it is a short-range technology that requires near line of sight between base stations and customers. For this reason alone, the deployment of LMDS should have been limited. The Big 3 long-distance carriers had enough trouble with the more-stable MMDS, which works at lower frequencies and is thus more stable and flexible. Others were not forewarned.

Two start-up carriers were the poster children for difficulties with wireless technologies: Winstar Communications and Teligent. They both wanted to be facilities-based carriers with networks based on millimeter wavelength technology. While they waited for the wireless equipment to reach a state of operational readiness, they began reselling RBOC local facilities. The radio equipment never reached production readiness, and the resale model had razor-thin margins that didn't fit their operational model. Both companies went into Chapter 11 bankruptcy protection, Teligent in 2001 and Winstar in 2002.

Powerline Networking
Another technology that resurfaced during the investment boom was powerline networking. Powerline networking involves sending telecommunications signals over electrical supply lines. Sending those signals in the form of electrical impulses over a medium designed to send electricity seems logical. That simple logic has been used to take many investor dollars in the years since divestiture. In reality, the characteristics of telecommunications

signals differ greatly from those of electrical power supply. Because they are so different, the networks of wires used to send the two types of signals have grown up very differently over the one hundred–plus years since their original deployment. The wires used to carry current to toasters and refrigerators are designed to do one thing and do it at minimal cost with maximum safety.

One characteristic of home wiring is that the typical new house today has about twenty electrical wires leaving the breaker box that is placed at the electrical service entrance to the house. In houses built in the first half of the twentieth century, that number could be as little as four. The twenty circuits in the modern house typically feed power to over one hundred electrical outlets or other built-in electrical fixtures. The appliances that use residential electrical power range from something as simple and predictable as a lightbulb to power hogs such as stoves, ovens, garage door openers, and power tools. This variety of uses combined with the continual changing of the mix of appliances using power at any given time makes for an electrical system with constantly changing power use. The wires used for telecommunications depend on stability in order to be useful; stability that cannot be found in electrical power lines.

One of the lessons that the RBOCs learned in their original deployments of DSL technology in the early 1990s was that the telephone wiring within homes was generally not "clean" enough to carry sensitive high-speed data signals. Telephone wiring within the home also contains many circuits that branch off from each other in order to reach all areas of the house. The change of state that occurs when phone handsets are taken off hook (picked up) and placed back on hook (hung up), as well as the changes in electrical signals when phones are dialed, all interfered with the DSL signal. In order to make the service work, the wiring from the network interface (where the phone line enters the home) to the DSL modem had to be free of telephones, called a home run. If even the telephone network requires conditioning to deliver high-speed data signals, imagine the changes required for powerline networking. Consequently, it is not likely to be economical to use electrical service wiring for data networking. The advent of cheap, in-building wireless networking, known as wi-fi, or wireless fidelity, further reduced the need to rewire homes to offer powerline networking.

The bottom line for powerline networking is that, although it is technically feasible, other technologies have been developed to deliver telecommunications signals more efficiently and cost-effectively than power lines. Fiber optics in the long-distance and metropolitan networks and wireless in the home network will continue to be more cost-effective.

Voice Over IP

Voice over Internet protocol (VoIP) is a technology used to transmit voice conversations over the packet-switched Internet rather than using traditional, circuit-switched networks. This technology finally reached a level of maturity that made it commercially viable in large-scale deployments by 2002. Any company that depended on the technology before then either was confined to niches of the market or failed.

From the technological difficulties of VoIP in the late 1990s, though, came technical and market developments that made VoIP the only contender to break the RBOCs' monopoly on landline local exchange service. Better technology for smoothing out inconsistencies in IP networks was developed in reaction to initial demand. That technology, combined with ever-cheaper bandwidth and the need by carriers and customers to find ways to make services more efficient, made VoIP a viable alternative to RBOC copper for all but the most complex or sensitive voice services.

At a time when any idea that could be expressed on a cocktail napkin could attract venture capital, VoIP, LMDS, and powerline networking all seemed like good bets to some investors and engineers. Among the three, only VoIP is likely to achieve broad market success. The others, like wi-fi, may fill technology gaps in certain areas but will never become broadly deployed within the carrier networks.

THE STEALTH CLEC

One way to avoid many of the operational difficulties encountered by the CLECs is to avoid the UNE/resale business entirely.

As the United States discovers broadband Internet connections, more and more applications are being developed to make use of the bandwidth that is finally reaching households and small offices across the country.

VoIP has been subject to great R&D spending since the Internet became commercially viable in the mid-1990s. Early VoIP services offered low-quality connections and required advance arrangements between the parties to a call. Hence, they were used only when the savings were considerable, as in international calling.

VoIP services have developed into commercially viable systems that, while still not as reliable as traditional phone service, are nearly as easy to install and use. The cable companies have begun to install VoIP services and sell them alongside cable modems as part of a complete, converged package of services.

The combination of now-ubiquitous broadband access and the lack of regulation make the Internet fair game for all kinds of services. Enter Vonage, the stealth CLEC. The Vonage service supports voice telephony over an existing broadband Internet connection, generally either cable modems or DSL. There are no unbundled network elements to rent, no access charges, and no colocation requirements. Fewer interconnection agreements are required. Vonage entered the voice market offering a complete service with unlimited local and long-distance service for $40 per month when the incumbents and most competitive providers were offering the same service for $50 per month. The service attracted more than 150,000 customers by mid-2004. In an attempt to break with the RBOC and CLEC competition, Vonage reduced its price for all-you-can-call plans to $25 per month by late 2004. Vonage's fees were on top of any ISP charges, but the total still compared favorably with traditional voice offerings for customers who already had broadband Internet.

Time will tell if Vonage can compete with the ILEC's and CLEC's voice services, but its cost advantage is bound to induce many customers to try the service.

NOTES

1. COVAD operational data from its reports to the SEC on Form 10-K for 2001.
2. Long-term debt, convertible preferred stock, and revenue from Trinsic's reports to the SEC.
3. "The State of Local Competition 2003," Association for Local Telecommunications Services (ALTS), April 2003, p. 10. CLEC data include local spending by AT&T, MCI, and Sprint. RBOC data from 10-K filings.

CHAPTER 8

LOST OPPORTUNITIES BY THE CABLE COMPANIES

The cable companies were in a much better position to compete with the RBOCs than the CLECs and even the long-distance companies. The cable companies already owned a connection into most homes in the United States, they had the local bandwidth that the rest of the industry (including the RBOCs) needed, and they had new voice and video products to sell. But they were too distracted by mergers and acquisitions to finish implementing the new services.

The cable companies were able to find $90 billion between 1996 and 2002 to invest in upgrading their networks. The strongest of the cable carriers were able to borrow on good terms; the others resorted to the junk bond markets. In the end, however, every major cable company took on significant debt to finance its contribution to the telecom investment boom. The building binge that followed amounted to a complete overhaul of the cable infrastructure in the United States. The rebuild gave the cable companies a huge technical advantage over the RBOCs in delivering new, innovative services to consumers. The cable companies weren't able to maintain the initiative, though; they were too busy getting bigger.

The RBOCs merged with regularity during the late 1990s, but the Bell-on-Bell mergers required relatively little in the way of integration work since the RBOCs had similar management structures, information systems, and technology. More significantly, very little cash traded hands in the Bell transactions. The cable companies, however, spent immense amounts of cash bidding up the price of a cable subscriber to unsupportable heights. There were more than twenty transactions within the cable industry in which a minimum of $1 billion worth of subscribers changed hands.

Before the telecommunications boom, cable franchises

MONOPOLY

1880
1890
1900
1910
1920
1930
1940
1950
1960
1970
1980
1981
1982
1983

DIVESTITURE

1984
1985
1986
1987

STABILITY

1988
1989
1990
1991
1992
1993

BOOM

1994
1995
1996
1997
1998
1999

BOMB

2000
2001
2002

RECOVERY?

2003
2004
2005

FUTURE

traded hands at approximately $2,000 per subscriber. Even with all the great new services that the cable companies offered as a result of the Internet and the cable network upgrades of the 1990s, it was still hard to justify a price higher than about $3,000 per subscriber. Against that backdrop, the major acquirers of cable systems bid the prices up, mirroring the unsupportable prices paid for dot-com stocks. AT&T's purchase of MediaOne in 2000 set the top of the market at $9,000 per subscriber.

Once the hype met reality, AT&T and many other cable companies felt the financial strain of the cable system purchases. AT&T spun off its cable operations. Adelphia Communications went into bankruptcy, and the other cable companies had difficulty servicing their debt. The operating model of the cable industry had always depended on high debt levels, but the use of expanded debt to finance mergers instead of the aggressive pursuit of new revenue caused the cable companies to miss an opportunity to steal a march on the rest of the industry. And the hangover from the acquisition binge will be felt at some cable companies for years to come.

The bottom line for customers of the cable companies is that the high and continuing interest payments required of the companies will force upward pressure on their rates for some time to come. Cable rates regularly increased through both the boom and the telebomb. With no new competitors on the horizon, that trend is likely to continue.

EFFECTS OF THE TELECOMMUNICATIONS ACT ON CABLE

Overall, the Telecommunications Act of 1996 was a positive event for the cable industry. The act didn't add significant constraints or new threats to the cable business other than its support of DBS video services. Perhaps the worst item in the act for the cable companies was a provision making it easier for individuals to put satellite dishes on their property. DBS services are the biggest competition for the cable providers in the provision of video services to the home.

One of the positive aspects of the act was that the procompetitive changes made it easier for the cable companies (and, indeed, all carriers) to offer a broad range of additional communications services. In one of the few purely deregulatory sections of the act, prices for the cable companies' advanced video services were deregulated. At a time when the Internet was just beginning to show the promise of new but untried services, the cable companies had an expansive view of the possibilities. They summed these possibilities up in one word: convergence.

EARLY CONVERGENCE

To the cable industry, convergence meant offering many different kinds of new services (voice, video, data, and images) over one integrated network. Perhaps the biggest and most publicized early effort at convergence was Time Warner Cable's Full Service Network (FSN) project in Orlando, Florida. FSN was designed to provide advanced interactive services including video on demand, interactive shopping, and video games, in addition to normal broadcast video.[1] The project covered four thousand customers in Seminole and Orange Counties and provided television set-top devices that included advanced software and a color printer (for printing coupons and other online content).

The FSN service was rolled out in late 1994 and was generally a hit with customers. However, it was a financial disaster for Time Warner. The expensive set-tops (Time Warner wouldn't admit to a cost figure) couldn't pay for themselves with the small amount of additional revenue they generated. The advanced network was shut down in 1997, with the usual declarations by Time Warner that the project was a success and many valuable lessons were learned.[2] The FSN, like other cable companies' efforts at mastering convergence, ended up becoming an expensive demonstration project, whether or not that was the original intent.

Like AT&T's bets on computers connected to a closed information distribution network (see Chapter 2), the FSN was directionally correct and technically feasible, but still economically flawed in that the costs were too much for any one company to bear. Developing the services and offering them to a relatively limited set of subscribers over a closed network led to a cost position that was untenable. The ability to offer services developed by others over an open network made more sense. The broad commercialization of the Internet would finally make the hoped-for opportunities realistic, albeit in a different economic model.

Other services, such as telephony and advanced digital video, also appealed to the cable companies as possible candidates for bundling together. (Virtually all the customers of the cable companies were individual consumers rather than businesses.) The ability to bundle many services for sale to consumers also appealed from the competitive standpoint of being able to beat the ILECs. Remember that as late as 1998, the RBOCs were still considered to be a credible threat to the cable companies' video market.

The rub for the cable companies was that for all the new services to work, the cable network had to be upgraded to two-way digital transmission, not an inexpensive proposition. In order to complete the upgrades, the cable companies, always strapped for funds, needed additional financial strength. Given their chronic lack of cash, they would need near flawless execution to pull off the upgrades and get the revenue from these new services flowing quickly. One way to gain the required financial strength necessary to attract outside investment was to become larger, which they did. The fact that all the cable companies had similar financial structures that size alone couldn't change was beside the point. This was the 1990s after all and the cable companies joined the RBOCs and WorldCom in the belief that size matters.

But first, let's look at why the cable network technology had a leg up on the telephone network as the Internet age approached.

CABLE'S ADVANTAGES

Despite the mixed results of the FSN, the cable companies had a more convincing argument than did the ILECs that their networks could handle converged services. As mentioned in Chapter 2, the cable networks' constant need for rehabilitation was historically a drag on their financial performance and customer satisfaction scores. That problem played in their favor, though, when it came time to add high-speed Internet access services. The services were added as part of the normal upgrade cycle over a seven- to ten-year period (roughly 1994 to 2002). It would take the Bells much longer (thirty to forty or more years!) to add broadband as part of the normal replacement cycle for their network.

The cable companies' new services were developed on the same basic transmission technology that they had used for years to deliver video signals. This relatively stable network platform delivered much higher bandwidth to individual users than that of the ILECs. The ILEC network depended on much older designs. The engineering principles used in the telephone network first came to practical use before the 1930s and were intended to support a single voice path to each home in a service area.

Cable plant, on the other hand, has always been designed to deliver multiple, higher-bandwidth channels—or carriers, as they are known in the cable business—to each home. The original engineering work for the cable network was completed more recently (the 1950s and 1960s) than that of the phone network. Also, the newer hybrid fiber-coaxial cable systems used from 1994 on were of much higher capacity than traditional cable plant and modern telephone networks.

While both networks (phone and cable) were originally designed to transmit analog signals, it is easier to assess their relative capacity in the modern telecommunications network by comparing their digital equivalent capacity. The analog voice network is designed to carry voice circuits of roughly 4 KHz. As first digitized, voice circuits require bandwidth of 64 Kb/s (64,000 bits per second). So as designed and later upgraded to digital, the phone network can deliver 64 Kb/s without further network engineering—or "line conditioning" as the engineers call it.

Cable networks, on the other hand, are generally designed to carry 120 video channels, each taking up about 6 MHz of analog spectrum. Each 6-MHz carrier on a cable network can be digitized to carry about 27 Mb/s (27,000,000 bits per second) of bandwidth. Thus, the cable network can deliver almost 3.25 gigabits per second (120 x 27,000,000 = 3.24 Gb/s) to an individual home versus 64 Kb/s for the phone network. (This example is based on a 750-MHz system, the most typical capacity today. The example assumes digitization of the entire system, which is not typically seen.)

The cable network delivers its bandwidth to homes in a service area via one single network path. Each of the 500 to 750 homes in a typical modern service area taps into the same stream of bandwidth and, thus, can view the same programs. By contrast, the phone network generally maintains a separate network path for each line it serves. There is a separate pair of wires installed in the network for each telephone line. The bandwidth delivered on one telephone line is dedicated only to that line.

To make a more accurate comparison of the relative capacity between the two networks, the cable bandwidth should be divided by the number of homes it is designed to serve. The final comparison is 3,240,000,000/750 = 4.32 Mb/s per home for cable versus 64 Kb/s for the phone network. Even with an upgrade to DSL, the phone line is rarely capable of greater than 384 Kb/s and tops out at 1.5 Mb/s. And DSL can only reach about half of the ILECs' subscribers without additional line conditioning.

The cable design not only delivers more bandwidth per user; it allows different users to take more than their pro rata share of the bandwidth at times, making the cable technology more accommodating for common Internet tasks such as downloading graphics or large files.

This analysis is simplified in many ways; nevertheless it shows how the cable network can offer more services on its existing network than can the phone network. The digital upgrade of the cable network meant more (and cost less) than the comparable upgrade to the telephone network. However, the cable companies still needed to find the cash to roll out the promised new services.

THE URGE TO MERGE

"If the dream is big enough, the facts don't matter."
—DEXTER YAGER, AMWAY SALESMAN AND MOTIVATIONAL SPEAKER

Given the potential advantages of the cable network, the cable industry was a natural place to invest. But where to start? In general, the strongest competitors in any industry are able to attract the most capital at the most attractive rates. Since combining businesses was seen as a way to gain financial strength, merger and acquisition departments across the industry were put to work.

Most of the large cable systems in the United States have changed hands at least once since 1990. Some have changed hands four or more times. All the mergers resulted in a rapid consolidation of the cable industry. In 1994, the ten largest cable companies (known as multisystem operators, or MSOs) controlled systems serving 32,055,000 cable subscribers. By 2003, the ten largest MSOs served 59,574,000 subscribers, an 86 percent increase. Comcast led the pack with a 702 percent increase in subscribers, having sucked up the cable systems of three of the other 1994 top ten (Continental Cablevision, TCI Communications, and Jones Intercable). Adelphia Communications (365 percent) and Cox Communications (255 percent) also had significant increases. Charter Communications, which didn't even exist in 1994, acquired enough systems to become the third-largest MSO.[3]

Another way to explain the concentration in the industry is that in 1994, the top ten MSOs served 53 percent of the basic cable subscribers in the country. By 2003, the top ten served 83 percent of basic cable subscribers. By comparison, at the end of 2001, the RBOCs served 87 percent of the telephone lines in the United States.[4]

The cable industry started its bout of mergers before the RBOCs, in part, because of regulatory freedoms (they didn't have to worry about the restrictions of the MFJ) but also because a more fragmented industry structure made for more numerous merger candidates. The pace quickened as the RBOC mergers went into full swing. The cable industry understood the trend toward larger competitors and wouldn't be left out. The increasingly easy money made available as the U.S. economy eased into the euphoria of the dot-com era also greased the way for many buyouts of cable franchises.

The cable industry consolidation included many junk bond offerings to raise cash needed to complete transactions. Some deals were all stock or a mix of stock and cash, but many of the deals included a large cash component to induce the sellers to enter into the transactions. The indebtedness incurred to complete the mergers added to an industry structure that already included significantly more debt than the ILECs carried. By contrast, each of the RBOC mergers was an all-stock transaction. Since no cash traded hands, the RBOCs didn't have to hang out in the bad neighborhoods where junk bonds are sold. The RBOCs didn't have to raise large sums of cash to buy anyone out.

There was a mania of sorts in the pattern of these mergers. The dot-com era was in full swing, and the possibilities seemed limitless. So, too, were the prices that would be paid for brick-and-mortar businesses, such as cable franchises, that could claim a connection to the Internet. Figure 8-1 shows the per-subscriber prices paid for cable companies during the dot-com era. Both the price per subscriber and the frequency of the deals accelerated at the same pace as volume and prices on the NASDAQ. The top prices paid neatly follow the level of the NASDAQ index through the investment boom and telebomb.

Each of the largest cable companies joined in the feeding frenzy except Time Warner, whose ownership structure was so complex that it was not conducive to complicated merger transactions. A comparative analysis of

FIGURE 8-1.

PER-SUBSCRIBER PRICES PAID IN MAJOR CABLE MERGERS AND ACQUISITIONS, 1994 TO 2002.

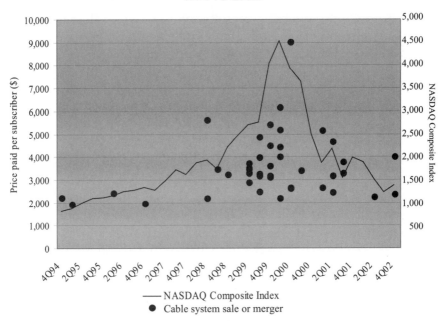

SOURCE: Cable deal information from the annual reports to the SEC on Form 10-K of Cox, AT&T Broadband, Comcast, and Charter. Each dot represents one transaction in which cable systems changed hands.

Time Warner's cable business and financial statements was attempted for this book, but complex ownership structure and continual reengineering of the corporate structures above the cable entity over time made that all but impossible.

PROFILES OF TWO MAJOR MSOs

To help you understand how the cable companies operationalized "size matters," this section profiles two major MSOs that grew larger over the past decade: Comcast and Charter. Assessing the differences in their strategies and results gives a hint about what is likely to happen to the cable industry giants in the future.

Comcast: Running with the Big Dogs

By 1996, Comcast was well on its way to becoming a diversified telecom carrier, owning interests in local networks (Teleport Communications Group, or TCG), cellular (Comcast Cellular), and PCS (through its Sprint PCS partnerships), as well as its cable franchises. During the mid-1990s, Comcast conducted several deals that added more than a million subscribers to its business. The deals (with MacLean Hunter Limited and E. W. Scripps) were completed at prices of about $2,000 per subscriber, the norm at the time.

In 1997, Comcast began raising cash and selling noncore businesses to prepare for a push to become a much larger cable company. The first large increment of cash came in June 1997, in the form of a $1 billion investment from Microsoft, whose CEO, Bill Gates, understood the power of broadband networks. Microsoft was investing in making its popular software titles more Internet friendly. But it also saw the synergy of broadband with its software business. The Internet was perceived by Microsoft as an additional marketing and sales channel as well as a way to guard against piracy by tracking licenses through always-on Internet connections.

After the Microsoft investment, Comcast began selling off its interests in other communications businesses to raise cash and clear the decks for the bigger deals to come. TCG was sold to AT&T in 1998. Comcast Cellular was sold to SBC in 1999. The partial ownership of Sprint PCS was also sold.

Comcast's move to become the largest cable company in the United States began in earnest in 1999 with its purchase of Jones Intercable and the announcement of Comcast's acquisition of Lenfest Communications.

Those two mergers, along with several smaller ones in 1999 and 2000, increased Comcast's subscriber base by two-thirds in less than two years.

The per-subscriber prices paid in Comcast's 1999 and 2000 cable acquisitions showed a steady acceleration, partly in reaction to the increasing pressure that AT&T was putting on the buy side of the market and partly in reaction to Comcast's desire to cluster its cable franchises together to gain operational efficiencies. *Clustering* is a cable industry buzzword for operating systems in contiguous geography. This rationale was used by Comcast to explain the extreme price of more than $6,000 per subscriber paid in the Lenfest acquisition. Lenfest's cable systems were located in the greater Philadelphia area, which Comcast considered its home turf. The earlier Jones deal, not necessarily a clustering play, was done at $3,288 per subscriber.

Comcast's biggest deal, however, was the merger with AT&T Broadband in 2002. Once AT&T admitted that its broadband acquisition binge wasn't sustainable, it sought a buyer for the business. Comcast was the obvious choice, having been a significant bidder for MediaOne back in 2000. It was also the largest cable company after AT&T itself and Time Warner (which wasn't in a position to make such an acquisition). Comcast, which more than doubled in size in the transaction, picked up the AT&T Broadband business for less than $4,000 per subscriber in stock and debt acquisition. While that price seems a bit steep now, it was more than $1,000 per subscriber less than the net amount AT&T paid for the business.

At the close of the transaction, Comcast became by far the largest cable company in the United States, with 21.3 million subscribers, nearly 30 percent of the cable subscribers in the country. It also had nearly $35 billion in debt, more than $1,600 for each of Comcast's subscribers. By contrast, the RBOCs averaged less than half that amount of debt per subscriber.

Including the AT&T deal, Comcast's subscriber numbers increased at an average annual rate of 31.3 percent between 1993 and 2002. It is interesting to note that, taking out the effect of the mergers, Comcast's core subscriber numbers grew at only 2.2 percent per year, on average. In the face of competition from direct broadcast satellite, merging was the only way to get larger.

During this period, however, Comcast was able to significantly increase not only its overall subscriber numbers but also its average cable bill. Its revenue per subscriber increased, on average, 8 percent per year from 1993 to 2002, growing from $34 a month to $60 a month. Both rate increases and the addition of new services helped Comcast's top-line (revenue) growth.

The buildout required to offer the new services took its toll on Comcast's operating margins, however. (The analysis of operating margins in this chapter uses earnings before interest, taxes and amortization, or EBITA. The measure includes depreciation in order to reflect the critical nature of capital expenditures in maintaining the network. It does not include taxes because corporate tax rates are often reflective of factors well outside the operations of a cable network. Likewise, amortization is not included. Many of the merger and acquisition transactions included significant amounts of "goodwill" in recognition of the price paid above the asset value of the business. The amortization of this goodwill, particularly as the companies adopted SFAS 142, had the ability to skew financial results dramatically [Time Warner is the poster child for goodwill gone bad] and reduces the comparative value of financial statements for the purpose at hand.) From EBITA margins of 24 to 28 percent in the late 1990s, Comcast's margins dropped to the teens before the AT&T Broadband acquisition. The addition of AT&T Broadband, which was a significant money loser for AT&T, depressed results in the short term for Comcast. The extent to which Comcast can rebuild its EBITA margins to pay down the debt piled up over the course of more than a dozen significant acquisitions will determine its ability to survive, or thrive, or not. With debt service (interest expense plus current debt repayment obligations) that amounts to nearly $20 per month per subscriber in 2004, Comcast was vulnerable to any unfavorable economic factors including competition or increased interest rates.

After selling off most of its noncable assets to finance the expansion of the 1990s, Comcast needed to look for other new sources of cash. In February 2004, it made a bid for The Walt Disney Company, an embattled and undervalued entertainment company with a saner debt/revenue ratio and diverse assets, many of which could be monetized. The Disney bid was a large and risky proposition that was clearly more necessary for Comcast than Disney. Investors knew that Disney's stock was undervalued and quickly factored a higher price for Disney by bidding Disney's stock up 15 percent and Comcast's down 8 percent. The proposed merger later unraveled when Comcast was unwilling to increase its bid.

Charter: A Classic Roll-Up

Charter Communications was started by Microsoft cofounder Paul Allen in 1998. Its stated mission was to be a classic roll-up, buying underperforming assets and turning them into world-class operations. Charter's entry into the buy side of the market for cable franchises at the same time as AT&T and Comcast contributed to the steep increases in cable franchise prices between 1996 and 2000.

Charter entered into more than twenty significant system purchases and swaps over the next four years. It went from essentially zero subscribers in 1997 to 6.5 million at the end of 2002.

The prices that Charter paid for the systems, although not outlandish compared with prices being paid by AT&T and others, were still high given the traditional value of such franchises. Charter paid more than $4,000 per subscriber in some cases, particularly odd for a company whose stated strategy was to buy undervalued assets.

Through the purchase and operation of these franchises, Charter amassed $17 billion in debt. Because it had large cash needs and no track record operating cable franchises, it ended up going to the high-yield debt markets. Charter sold its junk bonds at an average interest rate of more than 10 percent. Even if Charter turned the cable properties it bought into world-class operations, that much high-yield debt would still be a major drag on the company.

Joining the likes of Enron and WorldCom, Charter went through its own legal issues regarding inaccurate financial statements. Charter engaged in aggressive accounting tactics in which it counted more revenue than it should have and deferred expenses to later periods in order to improve its current financial results. Charter subsequently fired CFO Kent Kalkwarf and COO David Barford in the midst of the accounting scandal and re-stated its financial results for 2000 and 2001.

Charter was successful at increasing revenue in its new franchise areas. Its revenue per subscriber increased 15 percent on average from 1999 to 2002, outpacing gains at Cox and Comcast. Unfortunately for Charter, however, revenue was gained but operating income did not follow. Its EBITA margins averaged less than 10 percent, among the lowest in the industry. Specifically for Charter, slim margins meant that little money was left over after operating the business to make principal and interest payments on the debt gained in the acquisition process.

Although Charter's total debt in 2003 was less than Comcast's, it represented more than $2,600 for each subscriber. At 10 percent interest, the annual interest bill (not counting debt repayment) amounted to $260 per subscriber. That meant $22 from each subscriber's monthly bill was required just to pay interest on the mountain of debt.

Without a significant reduction in total indebtedness, it is unlikely that Charter will be able to survive in its current form, much less prosper from the opportunity to gain revenue by offering new services. Until the right solution is found, it is likely that majority investor Paul Allen will prop the company up.

ALLEN VS. GATES

Paul Allen's telecommunications investments stand in high contrast with those of his high-school buddy Bill Gates, in both style and results. Allen's investment style is to buy controlling interests in his companies. This style requires that Allen or his company, Vulcan Capital, must take an active role in the management of the companies. It also means that there are fewer eggs in his basket. When problems arose, Allen was on the hook to be part of the solution.

Gates, on the other hand, follows classic investment theory, diversifying his investments (putting his eggs in many baskets). He invested in Comcast and AT&T Broadband (when they were separate companies) as well as Teledesic (an ill-fated LEO satellite data provider). Neither Gates nor Microsoft took active management roles in any of these companies; any messes created are for others to clean up.

The result of Allen's investment style is that as Charter's fortunes have sunk, so has his investment. Gates's results, although mixed, follow the industry as a whole. Microsoft's original investment in Comcast has done well. Its investment in AT&T Broadband performed poorly but held its own after the Comcast merger. Teledesic quite literally never got off the ground. The bottom line for Gates and Microsoft is that they roughly broke even on their telecommunications investments (not bad considering what else happened in the industry). And they did so with less risk than Allen.

DELIVERING NEW SERVICES

From 1996 through 2003, the cable industry spent nearly $90 billion in capital expenditures, upgrading its facilities to deliver the latest services, according to National Cable & Telecommunications Association (NCTA) industry statistics. The construction binge amounted to almost a complete overhaul of the cable network in the United States. The companies' finances took a beating during this time from construction outlays as well as merger-and-acquisition costs. By the companies' historical financial standards, it was just business as usual. The cable industry is used to taking much bigger bets than both the ILECs and the traditional long-distance companies.

The network upgrades came in the wake of earlier, more far-reaching experiments in convergence that failed to live up to their potential. Like the Internet after the dot-com bubble, the emerging reality of convergence was more practical. The services that the cable companies added fell into three categories:

1. Digital video services

2. Voice telephony

3. High-speed data

Digital Video Services

With the rebuilding of the cable networks, the cable companies gained the ability to provide digital video. Digital video offers higher picture quality as well as capacity for more channels. By adding two-way capabilities, the upgraded network can also support pay-per-view and interactive video services.

The upgrades were important more as a competitive reaction to DBS services than as a revenue enhancer. Even with the addition of the improved video services, take rates (the number of customers who subscribe to the service divided by the total number who have the service available to them) were stuck at about 20 percent of subscribers in upgraded areas at the end of 2003. The cable companies saw only marginal increases in revenue from digital service tiers. The digital services require an upgraded set-top box to decode the digital services. Customers who receive a set-top box rarely commit to purchase significant additional services. For the cable company, though, the digital set-top box represents an investment of several hundred dollars per customer in the digital revenue stream, further eroding margins.

Voice Telephony

The cable companies were slow to offer voice services. Only Cox and the former AT&T Broadband equipped a significant number of their systems for telephony services by the end of 2002. The take rates were initially high for the cable systems that offered the service but leveled off once price competition set in among the local service providers. Even with a rollout schedule slower than cable modems, cable telephony was in place for 2.2 million customers across Cox, Comcast, and Charter by the end of 2002.[5] That represented more than 1 percent penetration of the landline telephone market in the United States and about one-third of the non-ILEC lines installed in the United States. Competition kept that number from climbing substantially in 2003.

Beyond the investment constraints inhibiting rollout, another major reason that telephony services are not more widely available on cable systems is rooted in the technology used to support the service. Initial implementations of telephony over cable plant were circuit switched, meaning that for every phone call placed, bandwidth was allocated between the subscriber's phone and the cable companies' local phone switch. This bandwidth was available only to that call, and not released for other uses until the call was disconnected. This type of network looked and worked much like certain types of equipment in the traditional phone network. No surprise, then, that it also had a similar cost structure.

It is easy to enter a market with undifferentiated technology (technology that is the same as competitors offer), but it is harder to provide a compelling offer or establish a competitive edge without better technology or a lower-cost position.

The potential for a lower-cost position was offered by using packet voice (generally VoIP) technology. This technology takes voice conversations, digitizes them, and breaks the digital signals into groups, or packets. The packets can then be sent over the existing IP network used to support cable modem services. Additional savings are also offered because the process of breaking the digital signal into packets allows silence to be compressed or eliminated, saving bandwidth. Whereas circuit-switching technology has been in the cable network for a number of years, the packet voice technology was placed in the network more recently and was only considered robust and reliable enough to be used for voice calls as of 2002.

The incumbent telephone carriers, who have been building regulated phone networks for more than one hundred years, have built networks that are extremely reliable. The cable networks must approach (but not necessarily meet) this level of reliability before consumers will accept them. Among the technological hurdles for the cable networks to surmount to increase reliability was the mundane issue of how to power their telephone systems. When the power goes out at a consumer's home, phone lines provided by an ILEC generally still work. This reliability has come to be expected, particularly when phones are relied on for services such as 9-1-1 calls. Cable networks, on the other hand, were never designed to work when the power is out because cable's video signal is of little value if you can't turn on your TV.

Packet voice technology could be a disruptive technology that beats the RBOCs' voice offerings. It enables a lower-cost position and approaches the services of the ILECs' networks. If it can approach the reliability provided by the incumbent carriers, VoIP is likely to be a valuable addition to the cable companies' bundle of converged services.

It is, however, likely to be only an addition to a converged bucket of services rather than a service sold by itself for two reasons. First, local dial tone is considered a commodity by most users. It is expected to work and it is expected to be cheap. Years of regulatory guidance toward subsidized residential service have conditioned users to expect inexpensive, reliable phone service. Thus, margins on the service are low and only attractive in combination with other services. Second, the incumbent phone companies already offer a low-cost, valuable (if commoditized) service. The cable companies do not have an opportunity to offer significant discounts below the incumbents' subsidized commodity rates.

Unfortunately for the cable companies, in the ten years it has taken them to add telephony to their converged bag of tricks, the incumbents have become much smarter. The incumbents have long-distance approval, and they have the resources to spend on marketing, including win-back campaigns. If the cable companies had focused on cable telephony while the RBOCs were preoccupied with proving that their markets were open to competition, cable telephony could have a much larger market share now. If they had deployed new services more aggressively, they might also have had fewer opportunities to get in trouble in the junk bond markets looking for fast cash fixes to score their next acquisition target.

High-Speed Data

High-speed data service offered via cable modem is much more common than cable telephony services. The idea of using the cable network to distribute data was discussed in the industry as early as 1993. The cable network already acts as a common network to distribute signals to all connected, just like the Ethernet technology used in local area networks. Allocating bandwidth to data services was not difficult. Early cable modem services were even able to use the old coaxial cable plant before it was upgraded to modern hybrid fiber-coaxial plant. The cable upgrades of the late 1990s and early 2000s markedly improved raw data capacity, but the service still needed to be packaged and priced for the consumer market.

The cable industry rallied around a standard (called DOCSIS for "data over cable system interface specification," first published in 1995) to offer cable modem service. Technical standards like DOCSIS create a common song sheet for all suppliers to the industry. When the manufacturers of network gear can make and sell the equipment to a larger number of carriers, they can lower their price points because some of the cost of preproduction R&D is borne by the carriers and because the fixed costs of production setup can be spread across many units. The cable industry was thus able to offer its version of high-speed Internet access sooner and at lower cost than the RBOCs. The RBOCs wrestled with DSL standards for much longer, not settling on de facto standards until nearly five years after the first DOCSIS specification was published.

The combination of low price and high speed became very successful in the market, almost immediately pulling customers away from dial-up connections to the Internet. Cable modem services also compared favorably with the ILECs' DSL service, offering higher bandwidth and wider availability.

Broadband Internet access services (both cable and DSL) became water for the desert traveler at the turn of the twenty-first century. Anyone who was a more-than-casual user of the Internet in the 1990s grew frustrated by dial-up connections. The supposed advantages of the Internet were hard to justify during those long moments while users waited for Web pages to download. During those long waits, the increased cost of broadband became easier and easier to justify. Broadband access solved many of the problems of dial-up connections: pages loaded faster, file downloads were accomplished in seconds rather than minutes or hours, and worries about the size of e-mail file attachments all but disappeared.

Broadband was the final missing piece of the puzzle in the democratization of telecommunications services. The combination of fast, last-mile access to the Internet combined with cheap long-haul rates put all telecommunications services into the realm of possibility for both consumers and small businesses. Broadband enabled the Internet for the masses by offering consumers an option for access to the Internet that rivaled the access already enjoyed by businesses and universities.

Included in the benefits of broadband was the ability to support widespread telecommuting for the first time. Until broadband became available, telecommuters were also hampered by slow, expensive dial-up connections. Once access to e-mail and corporate files was enabled (and secured) over high-speed, open connections, the location of many U.S. jobs became irrelevant. Once location became irrelevant, the work could be done at home, or even in another country. As high-speed Internet connections became more prevalent and less expensive around the world, offshore outsourcing became a trend in corporate America.

Cable modems will be pointed out by supporters of the cable companies as a shining example of their product innovativeness, but the cable modem was in fact a marginal development that ran on top of existing cable technology. The digital upgrade made it better, but it would still have been a competitor for DSL without the upgrade. Because of dot-com machinations and the ever-changing ownership situations, cable modem services were not rolled out as aggressively as they could have been.

It is true that cable modem services handily outpace the incumbent telcos' DSL technology in providing broadband Internet access to consumers, but that is more attributable to the telcos' inactivity than to anything brilliant about the introduction of cable modems.

The ILECs were slow to invest in rolling out the electronics that supported DSL service. But even once the electronics were deployed, fewer than half of their subscribers could receive the service without upgrading the network, making broad rollout of DSL service much more time-consuming and expensive than for cable modems. With cable, once the network was upgraded and the electronics to support high-speed Internet service was deployed, essentially 100 percent of the customers were eligible for cable modem service.

Although cable modem service has been offered since 1996, it has begun to contribute meaningfully to financial results only since 2001, reaching 15 percent of revenue at Cox in 2003. Cable modem services have been a financial success for the cable companies. Other new services offered on the upgraded networks have yet to find as broad a market. A look at the market for telecommunications services gives a clue about how the additional services might contribute to future revenue.

WHAT DO CUSTOMERS BUY?

Eight years into the new environment created by the Telecommunications Act, the variety of new services, marketing channels, and provider choices has increased. With all the investment and attempted expansion, what did customers actually buy? A look at the changes in customer spending behavior can be broken into two parts: changes in spending on existing services and spending on new services.

Basic Services

Overall spending for traditional services has remained flat, growing at 7 percent overall (less than 1 percent per year), through the period following the Telecommunications Act. That overall stability masks significant changes within the categories. Local telephony has maintained its slow-growth pace while cable rates have climbed much faster, increasing at an average rate of 8 percent per year. Keep in mind that the average monthly household expenditures increase through both increased take rates and increased prices. Long-distance rates have, predictably, dropped. Table 8-1 shows how spending for these basic services has changed since the passage of the Telecommunications Act.

New Services

Several new services took off in the late 1990s. To say that these services were introduced or broadly deployed based on the provisions of the Tele-

TABLE 8-1.
AVERAGE MONTHLY SPENDING ON BASIC TELECOMMUNICATIONS SERVICES, 1996 TO 2002.

BASIC SERVICES	1996	1997	1998	1999	2000	2001	2002	INCREASE FROM 1996 TO 2002
Local Telephony	$30	$32	$33	$34	$35	$36	$36	20%
Long-Distance Service	21	25	23	21	18	15	12	−43%
Cable	16	17	18	19	20	21	23	49%
Total Basic Services	$67	$74	$74	$74	$73	$72	$71	7%

SOURCE: Telephone rates from the FCC. Cable rates from the NCTA. All statistics are adjusted to show average expenditure per household. While virtually all households have phone service, only about two-thirds have cable.

communications Act, however, would be a stretch. Particularly in the cases of the wireless and Internet access business, both existed before the act, but neither was strongly influenced by the act. Digital video, though, was specifically deregulated by the act. That deregulation has not guaranteed success, but has given consumers the opportunity to try the new services and the cable companies the opportunity to raise rates. Table 8-2 shows how the market for these new services has developed.

Each of the new services has seen dramatic growth, with wireless service being the leader. Ironically, wireless is a corner of the telecommunications market that the cable companies sold out of to raise cash for their landline investments. Internet access has shown dramatic growth, also. Digital video services, deregulated by the Telecommunications Act, have not proven to be a significant revenue generator.

Overall Spending

Figure 8-2 shows the total average each household spends for all telecommunications services. Based mostly on increased take rates for services like

TABLE 8-2.
AVERAGE MONTHLY SPENDING ON NEW AND ADVANCED TELECOMMUNICATIONS SERVICES, 1996 TO 2002.

NEW SERVICES	1996	1997	1998	1999	2000	2001	2002	INCREASE FROM 1996 TO 2002
Internet Access	$1	$3	$6	$9	$11	$13	$15	1,400%
Digital Video	0	0	0	1	3	5	7	N/A
Wireless	9	11	14	17	23	29	35	289%
Total New Services	$10	$14	$20	$27	$37	$47	$57	470%

SOURCE: Wireless figures from the FCC, Internet access, and digital video extrapolated based on company reports.

FIGURE 8-2.
AVERAGE MONTHLY SPENDING FOR TELECOMMUNICATIONS SERVICES,
1996 TO 2002.

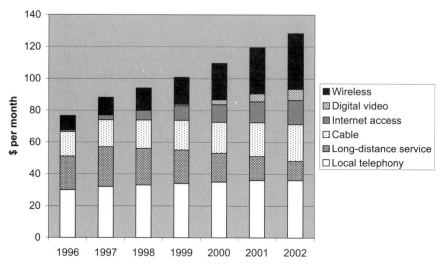

Internet access and wireless phones, the average U.S. household now spends 68 percent more per month on communications services than it did in 1996. Assuming that consumers perceive additional value in the marginal dollars spent (otherwise, why would they spend the money?), the industry has increased its usefulness and reached its goals of bringing new products to market. On a segment-by-segment basis, however, the investments required to achieve those gains were not always in proportion to the revenue increases. How well a company matched its investments to the services it wanted to offer in large part determined its success in the market.

WHAT IS A CABLE SUBSCRIBER WORTH?

"2 is not equal to 3, not even for large values of 2."
—GRABEL'S LAW

None of the cable companies were able to realize the potential value that led them to pay $4,500 to $9,000 for a cable subscriber. Mergers in the cable industry were not a way to create value. The cable companies spent more time and money on merger-and-acquisition activity than on product development. It is extremely hard to provide a cogent story as to why cable systems reached such stratospheric prices, particularly when the mergers cost the cable companies an opportunity to steal a march on the RBOCs.

The escalating valuations were based in part on dot-com-era hype about convergence. If you believed in convergence, it was logical to believe that the cable companies were in a position to capture some of the existing telephony revenue as well as revenue for new services such as data and advanced video. But if you add up all the potential revenue the cable companies could reasonably have hoped to gain from the telecom spend of the average American, it is still impossible to support a $9,000-per-subscriber valuation.

Services generally offered or within easy reach of the cable companies are:

• Basic cable

• Digital cable

• High-speed Internet access

• Local telephone service

• Long-distance telephone service

Basic cable and local telephone service are well-known commodity services. Their prices are subject to extensive study and regulation. They are unlikely to increase at rapid rates. Long-distance telephone service is less regulated but no less a commodity, thanks to the second racers. Its price, particularly in a bundle of services, is decreasing, not increasing.

High-speed Internet access is also subject to some competition, with DSL and other offerings in the same markets. In addition, if the cable companies want to replace dial-up Internet access, they must find price points closer to those of America Online (AOL) and the Microsoft Network (MSN) as they draw more customers away.

Digital cable is a largely unregulated service, but it offers little differentiation from direct broadcast satellite services, so pricing in this market is also competitive. Neither the take rates nor the revenue from these services has met the expectations of the cable companies.

Table 8-3 provides a look at the revenue potential if a high-end customer were to take all of the potential services offered by the cable company. It is based on the average amount that customers pay for these services, not the most that a customer pays. Obviously, heavy pay-per-view users and international callers, for example, will be well above these numbers.

Operating margins (EBITA) in the industry are unlikely to return to their historic norms, but they can return to about 20 percent across the industry. At that level, a high-end customer could be generating $27.40 in

TABLE 8-3.
PER-SUBSCRIBER REVENUE POTENTIAL FOR CONVERGED CABLE CUSTOMERS.

TELECOMMUNICATIONS SERVICE	AVERAGE MONTHLY BILL
• Basic cable	$ 35[1]
• Digital cable	14[2]
• High-speed Internet access	40[3]
• Local telephone service	36[4]
• Long-distance telephone service	12[5]
Total	$137

[1] Source: NCTA industry statistics, includes basic and extended basic cable tiers.
[2] Average spend among subscribers. Source: cable company financial disclosure reports.
[3] Median industry pricing.
[4] Source: FCC industry statistics.
[5] Based on 240 minutes per month @$.05/minute.

operating income per month, or $328.80 per year. Using 10 percent cost of capital as a discount rate, that subscriber is worth $3,288 ($328.80/.10 = $3,288).

Although the cable companies are getting closer to the Holy Grail of the $100-per-month cable bill, inflation and competitive pressure on pricing have reduced the attractiveness of that proposition. In the real world of 2003, average cable bills were still about $65, less than half of the high-end customer's bill. Given current operating margins for the cable operators, the average customer is worth less than $1,500.

The perfect storm that hit the telecommunications industry also hit the cable sector. Once it became clear that cable property values were not rising to the levels promised by $6,000 and $9,000 per-subscriber prices, the merger-and-acquisition deal velocity cooled down just like the dot-com mania. Not only were the prices asked for by the few sellers in the market unrealistic; competition from the major acquirers dropped out of sight. AT&T was busy retrenching. Charter was overextended. Comcast was busy digesting its acquisitions.

The weight of periodic interest payments on the mountain of acquired debt became enough of a drag on the cable companies that they were unable to acquire more or to capitalize on the increased strength that size gave them. For the issuers of junk bonds, this effect has been accelerated by the high interest rates paid on their bonds. The cable network rebuilding frenzy also cooled down, having peaked in 2001, according to the NCTA. So the acquisition of more debt was unlikely. The question remains: Which companies can live with what they have?

"I had great difficulty figuring out how the South, having won every battle, could possibly have lost the war."
—COLGATE DARDEN, FORMER GOVERNOR OF VIRGINIA, ON HOW THE CIVIL WAR WAS DISCUSSED IN THE SOUTH IN THE EARLY DAYS OF THE TWENTIETH CENTURY

The cable companies won the battle to upgrade their networks to handle modern services and to have enough carrying capacity to satisfy modern telecommunications (that is, Internet) demand. But the distractions inherent in their frequent mergers and high debt levels left them exhausted after the battle and unable to continue on the initiative. If the next battle were only among the cable companies, as in the days of the walled gardens, then a competitive stasis would have been reached by the end of 2003 for all but the most overextended carriers. But the cable companies' performance as a competitor and as an investment is no longer solely compared with the other cable companies but also to their direct competitors, the RBOCs, the CLECs, and other companies in the industry. Winning the broadband battle was important. Winning the overall competitive war is still a long way off.

The ability of the large cable companies to establish themselves on firm financial ground by shedding debt gathered in the wake of the Telecommunications Act will be the prime determiner of their ability to become effective competitors in the telecom business. And cable subscribers will be footing that bill. Looking at which companies have less of a mountain to climb in 2004, Time Warner and Cox could see the top of the mountain; Comcast and Charter couldn't see the crest yet.

NOTES

1. "Show Home to Feature Full Service Network," *Orlando Sentinel,* February 17, 1995.
2. "Time Warner Cable to End FSN Test," *Orlando Sentinel,* May 1, 1997.
3. "Cable Television Developments," National Cable & Telecommunications Association (NCTA), December 2002, www.ncta.com.
4. "Trends in Telephone Service," Industry Analysis and Technology Division, Wireline Competition Bureau, FCC, August 2003, p. 7-4.
5. Telephony subscriber data from company reports to the SEC on Form 10-K for the year 2002.

CHAPTER 9

THE CRASH

"Bad times have a scientific value. These are occasions a good learner would not miss."
—RALPH WALDO EMERSON, AMERICAN ESSAYIST AND POET

Contrary to popular belief, the crash in the telecommunications industry started well before the stock market peak in 2000. Even before the Telecommunications Act of 1996 was passed, the industry landscape began changing at an ever-faster rate. Many segments of the industry became anachronisms with the advent of the Internet and cheap mobile phone service. The Telecommunications Act of 1996 hastened the exit of a large number of companies in the industry and the second race finished off a few more.

During the period of stability—from 1988 up to the time of the Telecommunications Act—there were only two telecommunications carrier bankruptcies. Both bankruptcies were in the long-distance business, which was opened to all comers in 1984. Once the rest of the market became competitive, the Darwinian creative destruction began. As the teleboom became the telebomb, what started as a trickle of bankruptcies in the late 1990s became a flood by 2001, when thirty-four carriers filed for bankruptcy protection.

While the noncarrier dot-coms blew through the economy barely leaving a trace, many of the bankrupt carriers were billion-dollar ventures. The telecom carriers spent far more money than the nontelecommunications dot-coms chasing the dreams of a new Internet-enabled world. In terms of money taken directly from investors and spent developing businesses that eventually failed, the telecommunications industry wasted far more investor dollars than the noncarrier dot-coms. As a whole, the telebomb likely wasted more real

	1880
	1890
	1900
	1910
	1920
	1930
MONOPOLY	1940
	1950
	1960
	1970
	1980
	1981
	1982
	1983
DIVESTITURE	1984
	1985
	1986
	1987
	1988
	1989
	1990
STABILITY	1991
	1992
	1993
	1994
	1995
BOOM	**1996**
	1997
	1998
	1999
BOMB	**2000**
	2001
	2002
RECOVERY?	**2003**
	2004
	2005
	FUTURE

investor dollars than any, and possibly all, of the previous stock manias in the U.S. equity markets.

Chapters 4 through 8 describe how the industry dominos stacked up within each segment of the telecommunications market. This chapter shows the order in which the dominoes fell across the segments and explains the trends among the dead carriers that caused the dominoes to fall when they did. This chapter also provides a different view of the competitive landscape by analyzing what happened to the $220 billion of incremental investment that flowed from the telecommunications industry during the boom (and the telebomb).

MARKET EVOLUTION

Between the passage of the Telecommunications Act of 1996 and the end of 2003, a total of 104 telecommunications carriers filed for bankruptcy (see Table 9-1). Beyond the 104 bankruptcies, there were scores of other carriers that left the market through either purchase or merger with (usually) healthier companies. A complete list of carrier bankruptcies from 1988 to 2003 is included in Appendix B.

TABLE 9-1.
TELECOM CARRIER BANKRUPTCIES, 1988 TO 2003.

TYPE OF CARRIER	YEAR								TOTAL
	1988–1996	1997	1998	1999	2000	2001	2002	2003	
Long-distance	2	4	1	2	1	4	4	1	19
Paging		1			1	2	1		5
Fixed wireless			2	1		1	1	1	6
Satellite—LEO			1	2	1		1		5
Wireless			2					3	5
CLEC				1	3	12	11	1	28
International				1	1	9	3	1	15
Integrated				1			5	1	7
Internet service providers						5	4	1	10
Cable						1	2	1	4
Satellite—GEO							1	1	2
Total	2	5	6	8	7	34	33	11	106

SOURCE: Bankruptcy data collected from SEC filings, FCC filings, bankruptcydata.com, and company Web sites. Bankruptcydata.com is published by New Generation research, an independent publisher of information about bankruptcy and turnaround investing. The population includes telecommunications carriers with a significant presence in the United States. The list excludes companies whose main revenue came from equipment manufacturing or retailing, construction, telecommunications services (such as antenna towers), software, or content.

Within the list of bankrupt carriers, it is clear that individual segments of the market experienced difficulties at different times, based on what was going on in the industry. Some segments experienced their own survival of the fittest, whereas others became entirely extinct. Looking at each of the segments and explaining why the companies within the segment faced bankruptcy at that particular point helps to build an understanding of how the industry as a whole developed during the late 1990s and early twenty-first century.

Long Distance (Phase 1)—1997 to 2000

Before the Telecommunications Act, the long-distance business was already competitive. The number of carriers was, in fact, expanding. But the industry was changing and not all carriers were able to adapt to the new environment. The long-distance providers were taken out in two groups. The first group fell within the first few years after the Telecommunications Act. It was mostly resellers that didn't have the wherewithal to expand or change course in the face of increased competition. The second and larger group went out after the second race destroyed all pricing power within the industry. It is reasonable to think of the bankruptcies as an ongoing reaction to the sea change in the industry interrupted for a time by the ease of obtaining investment dollars to keep marginal operations afloat during the dot-com era.

Paging and Fixed Wireless—1997 to 2002

While the long-distance business experienced bankruptcies continually throughout the boom and bust, it is still an identifiable industry segment (although not for long). The first industry segments to be obliterated, or nearly so, were the anachronisms: fixed wireless video and paging. The bankrupt fixed wireless companies provided analog video (MMDS) services that were competitive with cable systems before the advent of digital cable. The fixed wireless cable companies' capacity to transmit more channels was constrained by the radio frequency spectrum (licensed from the FCC) of the MMDS bands. The companies' spectrum and a few other assets were bought out of bankruptcy by WorldCom, Sprint, and others, but for different uses than to transmit analog video.

The paging business became a victim of cheap, ubiquitous mobile phone service. Why pay $10 to $15 per month for a one-way numeric pager, when a wireless phone could be had for $20 per month, sometimes less?

LEO Satellite—1998 to 2002

The next industry segment to fall off the cliff was the LEO satellite companies. These were the first multibillion-dollar bankruptcies of the telecommunications crash. In each case, the networks worked as advertised, but the companies couldn't add customers fast enough in the face of a terrestrial mobile phone business that improved dramatically between the original planning of the LEO systems in the mid-1990s and their commercial availability in 1999 and 2000.

CLEC—1999 to 2003

The market crash also hastened the expiration of companies in several additional niches that were created after the Telecommunications Act. The capital crunch that resulted from significantly lower stock market valuations also exposed the weaknesses of companies that had not adequately planned for the new competitive industry.

First to go after the stock market turned were the CLECs. According to the Association for Local Telecommunications Services (ALTS), the CLEC industry went from more than three hundred carriers in 2000 to about one hundred at the end of 2002.[1] The implosion of so many carriers included twenty-eight bankruptcies and many merger and buyout transactions arranged to stave off bankruptcy. The loss of two-thirds of the CLECs, however, did not stop the industry. In terms of both access lines and revenue, the CLEC segment of the industry grew during this period. The ones that went away ran into trouble because they still depended on fresh capital (having little-to-no cash flow) at a time when the venture capital ATMs were closing.

The fact that the CLEC segment of the industry was growing even among the failures of so many companies was an indicator that the industry was, indeed, facing survival of the fittest and not a general slaughter. That growth was jeopardized in 2004, however, when the federal courts again blocked a set of UNE resale rules set forth by the FCC. The result of the court's decision and the Bush administration's decision not to appeal the ruling was an almost certain increase in the rates that CLECs would have to pay to rent UNEs.

Internet Service Providers—2001 to 2003

Quickly following the CLECs in their decline were the ISPs. The CLECs and the ISPs were vulnerable because they did not establish profitable business models before the telebomb hit. Most had not diversified beyond dependence on RBOC services quickly enough to be able to weather a general economic downturn. The ISPs were able to hold out longer because they had cash flow from their Internet access customers and reciprocal compensation from the RBOCs, but they were generally never profitable. The ISPs also depended on fresh capital, albeit less so than the CLECs.

Two of the oldest names in the Internet service industry, Genuity and PSINet, succumbed to bankruptcy. Genuity traced its corporate heritage back to one of the first Internet providers, Bolt, Beranek, and Newman, later known as BBN. PSINet offered Internet access services beginning in 1989, well before the commercialization of the Internet.

Integrated Carriers—2002 to 2003

Integrated carriers, the next market segment to get hit, generally operated established businesses in one or more industry segments but overexpanded into another one. The company nTelos, profiled in Chapter 7, had profitable investments in ILEC and CLEC services, but was tripped up in the expansion of its PCS business. The only ILECs to go bankrupt fit into this category. They were able to stay out of trouble for a while after the market crash given the steady cash flow of the local phone business, but the extended downturn eventually caught up with them, sending four into bankruptcy in 2002.

Long Distance (Phase Two) and International—2001 to 2003

The second wave of failed long-distance carriers generally included the second race participants. Williams Communications, Velocita, Global Crossing, and 360networks all failed after their primary investment, fiber-optic networks, became essentially worthless when pricing in the industry fell apart.

The pricing problems hit the international long-distance market harder than the domestic business, with nine international carriers going bankrupt in 2001 alone. Every independent, publicly traded carrier that depended on international telecommunications for the bulk of its revenue filed for bankruptcy during this period. (Equant, although publicly traded, was majority owned by France Telecom.)

Several businesses in traditional segments of the industry failed as well (GEO satellite, terrestrial wireless, and cable), but these were anomalies within the segments and not, generally, signs of a larger trend.

There are commonalities in the bankruptcies that cross industry segments. Indeed, the segment lines were blurred to such an extent by 2003 that categorizing each of the bankrupt carriers was a challenge in itself.

WHAT CAUSED THE BANKRUPTCIES?

In general, overinvestment was rampant among the new and newly expanded carriers. How the companies reacted when the overexuberance of their business plans became apparent determined whether or not the companies lasted—as well as how long. Some revised their business plans and tried to adapt, some went directly out of business, and some committed fraud to cover the problems.

In addition to the failures caused by general overinvestment and fraud, there were a number of business failures in the telecommunications industry that followed the style of the dot-com failures that became acute during the same period. The distinguishing characteristic of the dot-com failures was that no amount of investment was appropriate for the businesses they purported to enter.

A closer look at each type of business failure reveals the basic character of some of the businesses that entered the industry in the late 1990s. It is also interesting to contrast those that failed with those that have narrowly avoided bankruptcy (at least so far), such as Level 3 and Charter Communications.

Overinvestment

As should be apparent at this point, many companies simply spent too much money in advance of any real demand for their services. They were generally caught believing that the Internet was open to a land grab. They thought they were paving the information superhighway, but they were, in many cases, sending bulldozers into the wilderness. Lost in that wilderness with the capital spigot cut off, they eventually died of cash starvation. Like the Big 3's investments in local services, these investments were larger than most investments in Internet businesses but were still not large enough to create lasting value. Big is relative and size matters.

For example, e.spire and XO Communications were two companies that wanted to offer competitive services and thought they could slay the giants. They spent $1 billion and $4.5 billion, respectively, to build networks targeted at different buyers. Those buyers never showed up. Like Velocita, e.spire and XO aspired to follow in the footsteps of the second racers, despite the fact that the second racers became the poster children for over-investment.

e.spire: Great at Building, Not at Selling

The company e.spire began life as the generically titled American Communications Services Incorporated (ACSI), a CAP offering local access services to long-distance companies. It also offered high-bandwidth services to some large businesses and eventually branched out into offering its own voice services. The company laid fiber around the business districts of second- and third-tier cities in the southeastern United States under the theory that it would avoid competition by staying out of the top metropolitan areas. Unfortunately, several other companies, such as nTelos, had the same idea.

e.spire was founded by industry veteran Anthony Pompliano, Sr. Pompliano had been in the industry since 1960, spending most of that time with Western Union International, the perpetual laggard and erstwhile competitor to AT&T before MCI took that mantle in the 1970s. AT&T and Western Union competed in the telecommunications industry through most of the twentieth century in the same way Microsoft and Apple Computer competed in the computer operating system markets in the 1990s. Which is to say that there was no real competition.

AT&T consented to Western Union's presence in the market, even performing actions that resulted in propping up Western Union when it seemed likely to fail. Microsoft did the same, investing $150 million in Apple in 1997, during a downturn in demand for Apple's products. Both Apple and Western Union lived in perpetual second place in their respective markets, attracting small but loyal followings, but never able to push to the front of the line.

Pompliano and the other executives who ran e.spire had many years of experience building and operating networks, but little to no sales experience. The result was a large and expensive network with no traffic on it. e.spire went about its business doing what its executive knew how to do. It planted 185,040 strand miles of optical fiber between 1993 and 2001. This ambitious construction program cost e.spire about $900 million.[2] The company started building networks before most of the industry in 1993. Because it gained experience constructing local fiber networks early, it was in demand to share its lessons learned with other companies trying to do the same in the late 1990s. This type of consulting became a line of business for e.spire, contributing 28 percent of its 1999 revenue. Of course, once the market crashed and carriers stopped building networks, this line of business quickly faded.

The network itself never generated enough revenue for e.spire to be profitable. In fact, e.spire barely covered its operating costs. When it entered bankruptcy in March 2001, its debt roughly matched the cost of building the network, meaning that it had recouped the cost of maintaining the business but had not paid back any of the construction cost. In total, the network that cost $900 million to build generated less than $700 million in revenue over its eight-year operating history before bankruptcy. In 2000, e.spire generated $261 million in revenue from the network. In the same year, service on its nearly $950 million debt was more than $124 million, almost half of that revenue.

Although e.spire lasted almost a year beyond the peak of the market, it eventually filed for Chapter 11 bankruptcy protection in March 2001. Its assets languished in bankruptcy court for seventeen months, an eternity by modern standards. The network was eventually sold for $68 million to Xspedius Communications, an integrated carrier that was looking to expand. It remains to be seen if Xspedius paid a low enough price (about 7.5 cents on the dollar) to make a business out of the assets it found at the bankruptcy yard sale.

XO Communications: Big Dreams for Smaller Customers

XO Communications Inc., like e.spire, started building networks before the Telecommunications Act of 1996. Originally called Nextlink, XO was formed in 1994 by wireless entrepreneur Craig McCaw (who also founded the business that became AT&T Wireless). XO's chosen market was small and medium-size businesses (in contrast with e.spire's focus on small and medium-size *cities*). XO defined its market for voice services as companies with fewer than fifty access lines. As with most companies that started before the passage of the Telecommunications Act, it also offered CAP services.

XO's focus on smaller customers meant that its subscribers would have a smaller average bill than a large business would. Smaller customers with smaller bills not withstanding, XO's network ambitions were almost as large as the second-race participants. Between 1994 and its bankruptcy filing in June 2002, XO built or acquired local fiber networks in twenty-five of the largest thirty cities in the United States. The company also gained access to long-distance fiber connecting the cities.[3]

As part of the network build, XO made by far the largest bets on LMDS, a fixed wireless technology, spending more than $800 million to acquire licenses in each of the top thirty markets in the United States. The technology was intended to work in a similar fashion to MMDS (discussed in Chapter 6), but LMDS signals are in such a high frequency that they are attenuated (the signal strength is diminished) by simple environmental phenomena such as raindrops and tree leaves. While it is not strictly a line-of-sight technology, the signals cannot penetrate buildings. XO has yet to make significant use of the technology.

All of this network acquisition and construction by XO cost more than $4.5 billion. To finance the network and its operation, XO took on long-term debt of about $5.5 billion. By contrast, XO generated less than $3.2 billion in total revenue from its inception in 1994 through filing for bankruptcy.

The first clue of impending trouble for a potential investor should have been the fact that XO's revenue wasn't even covering the interest payments on its debt until the end of 1999, more than two years after its IPO. Interest payments were still 37 percent of revenue at the time of XO's default in November 2001.

It was clear that XO needed help, but in late 2001, it was hard to find anyone willing to invest in CLECs, particularly ones with that much debt. XO bucked the trend by attracting two major investors.

Up through the time of the default, one of XO's biggest investors was the buyout firm Forstmann, Little. (As described in Chapter 7, Forstmann, Little was also a large investor in McLeodUSA, becoming its majority shareholder after bankruptcy.) Through various classes of stock, Forstmann invested more than $1.5 billion in XO. As XO's finances deteriorated, Forstmann and Mexican carrier Telefonos de Mexico (commonly known as Telmex) devised a rescue plan in which Forstmann and Telmex would provide $800 million in new financing and would end up owning nearly 80 percent of XO. The remainder of the ownership would be split among the various classes of debt holders that had lent the company $5.6 billion. The debt would then be canceled as would all the old common and preferred stock.

The recapitalization plan proposed by Forstmann and Telmex clearly favored the sources of the new cash investment (Forstmann and Telmex) over the existing investors when it came to the distribution of ownership in the new company. While the Forstmann proposal was being debated by XO management, famed corporate raider Carl Icahn began buying XO's senior bonds, paying as little as 50 cents on the dollar for the bonds ($500 for a bond with a face value amount of $1,000). Once he amassed 85 percent of the senior debt, he challenged the Forstmann plan. The Forstmann plan needed the blessing of the senior debt holders, and Icahn refused.

Protracted negotiations with counter proposals from Icahn and Forstmann did not result in a deal to restructure the company. XO filed for bankruptcy protection on June 17, 2002. Icahn, holding senior debt, which has first rights over other investors in a bankruptcy, emerged the victor with more than 80 percent of the common stock in the "new" XO whereas the other stock and bond holders, including Forstmann, got little or nothing.

Forstmann, Little wrote off its entire $1.5 billion investment in XO. In the final analysis, Forstmann tried to do a new-age deal when, during the dot-com bust and the telebomb, the market was tired and wary of tricky financial deals. The financial services industry, having been burned badly during the past few years, was moving back toward traditional ways of doing business. Icahn knew that and, through his ownership of the senior debt, became the most privileged investor at the table. This meant that he didn't need to negotiate much with Forstmann, whose ownership of stock placed it farther back in the line.

Before bankruptcy, XO carried $5.6 billion in long-term debt. Upon emerging from bankruptcy, XO carried less than $600 million. Although XO was $5 billion lighter, as of early 2004, the company had yet to turn a profit. In fact, it slipped back into a dot-com habit when it announced the purchase of the telecommunications assets of Allegiance Telecom in 2004. Allegiance was another bankrupt CLEC with declining revenue and a history of operating losses.

Fraud

In addition to overinvestment (whether in building networks or in acquisitions), some companies couldn't admit the failures of their business plans and resorted to producing false financial statements.

WorldCom is the most commonly cited example of this type of bankruptcy. It built the biggest financial fraud in the telecommunications industry and took many honest industry executives down with it. Looking back, it is clear that nobody was asking questions when WorldCom's stock was on the rise. The board of directors and so-called independent accountants, who were not independent at all, failed to diagnose and correct mistakes that were made by a CEO who, it was eventually proved, knew no more about running a modern telecommunications carrier than he did about yacht building or timber farming (Bernie Ebbers's other business interests).

The root cause of WorldCom's downfall was that the company took on immense amounts of debt (about $40 billion) to make acquisitions, many of which make sense only when put into the perspective of Ebbers's ego. Capital costs (the interest on WorldCom's debt) became so high that profitability was affected. Ebbers wouldn't admit that WorldCom might miss the profitability estimates he had given to the financial community, so he instructed his CFO to meet the targets no matter what.

Adelphia Communications Corp., the sixth-largest cable MSO, also had problems rooted in the egos of its senior executives. The founder of the company, John Rigas, and his three sons, along with a few other executives, were accused of spending company money for personal gain. The group of executives also received loans from the corporation, as did Bernie Ebbers at WorldCom. But overshadowing even Ebbers, the Adelphia loans were alleged to be somewhere between $2.5 billion and $3.4 billion compared with the $400 million that was received by Ebbers from WorldCom.[4]

Before the market crash (and Sarbanes-Oxley, the act of Congress passed in 2002 requiring stricter corporate governance practices), it was common for corporations to offer loans to senior executives, especially when an executive was going through a transition that required personal financial sacrifice. But the magnitude of the loan guarantees at Adelphia was astounding and certainly went beyond any definition of good corporate governance, even if the guarantees didn't break any laws.

Global Crossing and Qwest Communications International (even though Qwest has not filed for bankruptcy) may not deserve to be in this category, but they certainly engaged in aggressive accounting by treating bandwidth swaps as current revenue but deferred expense. The accounting treatment, signed off by the Arthur Andersen accounting and audit firm in both cases, treated what were essentially barter arrangements trading bandwidth of equal value as two transactions, one a purchase of capacity by the company and the other a sale of capacity. The sale transaction became immediate revenue, but the cost of the purchase transaction was accounted for over a period of years. The net effect of this accounting treatment was similar to that used by WorldCom to hide costs by spreading them out over time.

Global Crossing had every incentive to increase its revenue to keep the company alive. Shortly after its bankruptcy filing in January 2002, it listed $12.5 billion in assets, but had taken in less than $3 billion in revenue over the prior year. Global Crossing was overleveraged like nTelos and e.spire, only on a much larger scale.

Dot-Com-Style Failures

The dot-com-style failures were generally CLECs who believed that, between the Internet and the ability to resell cheap RBOC services, they would find a business model that would allow them to fell the Goliaths of the local marketplace. Many started with a general approach to the market and thought they would figure out the rest along the way. The mentality at the time, particularly within the venture capital community, was that the land rush was on and that if a company didn't jump on the bandwagon, it would be forever playing catch-up.

Certainly by 1998, the entrepreneurs and investors should have seen that the cumulative investment of other companies was already too much. But such dot-com-era truisms as the fundamental fallacy (that Internet traffic was doubling every ninety days, discussed in Chapter 4) enabled normally circumspect businesspeople to see what they wanted to see. The net effect of this change in perspective during the dot-com era was that placing bets on untried companies entering the telecommunications market amounted to legalized gambling, with the odds of success for an undercapitalized company being better at the casino.

The CLECs suffered from the general inability of the market to fulfill the Internet hype and the slow response of the RBOCs to the new local resale business. This slowness of customers and the RBOCs to accept the new carriers meant that the capital required to reach financial breakeven increased dramatically. Additional capital was required so that the companies' bills could be paid during the wait while many issues were ironed out with the Bells. The result was that many of the carriers that amassed large amounts of capital found themselves at the nickel slots when they thought they could afford baccarat.

The dot-com-style bankruptcies in the telecommunications industry generally followed the same paths as the dot-coms of other industries: a business plan that fit on a cocktail napkin, either too much or too little up-front funding, and a crowded market of companies that depended in one way or another on the RBOCs for service.

The RBOCs weren't exactly waiting for the CLECs with open arms. While the RBOCs had the carrot of long-distance approval in front of them, they also had thousands of people, complex operations processes, and many, interconnected legacy support systems that needed to change to meet the requirements of the new world created by the Telecommunications Act. While there may have been individuals who did their best to sabotage the CLECs, the RBOCs actually got behind the new way of doing business as quickly as could be expected by those with experience trying to get RBOCs to adopt major change.

The dot-com carriers should have learned the lessons of the new long-distance companies from the 1980s. The new long-distance carriers had large staffs of access coordinators whose job was to make sure the ILECs did their job. The access coordinators were the tugboats of the industry, working any angle they could to get the Queen Mary turned around and pointed in the right direction. Adding people to dot-com businesses was antithetical to the idea that the Internet was going to change everything. Any proposal to add people to a dot-com business was met with skepticism by investors and management and was seen as an admission of failure in the capital markets. Yet, many of the original dot-coms that have become large businesses, such as Amazon.com, have recognized and accepted that certain parts of their business must be stocked with people.

Most of the companies that followed the dot-com mentality were those with dot-com-like business plans. Some others' business plans were set to address second-order effects of the problems encountered by businesses trying to use the Internet. Net2000 is an example of the former, and Core-Express is an example of the latter.

Net2000: A Strategy Like So Many Others

Net2000 started life as a reseller of Bell Atlantic services in 1993. It, along with other resellers, needed to search for a new business model when Bell Atlantic stopped paying bounties to most aggregators that brought in new business. Becoming a CLEC seemed an obvious thing to do. Net2000 didn't invest billions of dollars as did so many of its brethren; it simply became a wholesale buyer of integrated voice and data services rather than simply a middleman, as was the case in the older resale model.

The change in strategy and investments initially seemed to pay off. Net2000 at least doubled its revenue every year from 1997 through 2000. But the revenue increase was more a result of the dot-com bubble than any lasting advantage. The company's business strategy could have been copied from any other dot-com company at the time. Net2000's strategy, as stated in its report to the SEC on form 10-K for 2000, was generic:

- "Offer bundled services on a single invoice."

- "Increase customer satisfaction and loyalty through our proprietary Web-enabled self-care system."

- "Utilize state-of-the-art, readily expandable information systems."

- "Continue to focus on excellence in customer care to maintain high customer retention rates."

In other words, not only was Net2000 not differentiated from any of the hundreds of other CLECs, its business strategy was indistinguishable from any of the thousands of other dot-com companies. It also spent money like a dot-com. In each of the three calendar years before it filed for bankruptcy, it spent more than its entire revenue in selling, general, and administrative expenses. SG&A expenses are also known as corporate overhead expenses and are shown on financial statements after revenue and the cost of operating the core business. The total of Net2000's operating costs and SG&A was more than two times its revenue in each year from 1998 to 2000.

Its stock, which was offered to the public for the first time in March 2000, just as the NASDAQ was peaking, traded as high as $37.25 per share. Net2000 filed for bankruptcy November 16, 2001, about eighteen months after the NASDAQ peaked. It completed the sale of substantially all its assets to Cavalier Telephone sixty-six days later. Few of Net2000's investors realized that the "2000" in its name was an expiration date.

CoreExpress: Bad Bet on Bandwidth

Whereas Net2000 may have been able to carry on with more funding (and greatly reduced expenses), CoreExpress actually ended its brief run with cash left in the bank, as described in Chapter 7.

CoreExpress's main product was designed to directly attack one of the characteristics of the Internet that slowed its adoption by mainstream businesses. The Internet is great at connecting users around the world. The communications protocols developed in its early days were primarily focused on making sure that data packets got through the underlying communications media (wire, fiber, radio, and so forth). The protocols were not designed, however, to control whether groups of packets got through together, quickly, or at the same rate.

While the Internet had a built-in resilience, it was expressly not designed to provide better service to some users than others. Whether this was a function of the focus on reliability or on the egalitarian spirit of the Internet's early days can be (and probably has been) debated. The result of this characteristic was that businesses, used to dedicated circuits with predictable speed and reliability characteristics, were not adopting the Internet for corporate communications as fast as had been predicted.

To bridge this gap, CoreExpress developed its Extranet service, which would use a high-bandwidth, highly engineered network to provide guaranteed levels of service. In and of itself, this idea might have flown, but CoreExpress also made another bet—that it would be able sell spare bandwidth on its network to raise revenue while the Extranet product was building momentum. The bet on the bandwidth market eventually sank the ship.

CoreExpress received venture capital support from Benchmark Capital. Benchmark had a reputation for making large investments. For example, it backed Webvan, which was the biggest pure play Internet failure of the dot-com era.

Benchmark led the funding of the CoreExpress venture with Morgan

Stanley Dean Witter. CoreExpress leased fiber from Williams Communications. CoreExpress lit the fiber with Nortel equipment that was received in exchange for equity rather than cash. The routers and other gear needed to provide Internet services were obtained from Cisco under the same type of deal. Finally, Benchmark provided the cash that allowed CoreExpress to build and scale its operations. CoreExpress received a total of $573 million in start-up funding, including the in-kind contributions.

CoreExpress had bright technical leaders, including CEO Mike Gaddis. It also had good sales and marketing leadership with experience in tele-bomb survivors MCI and Savvis as well as the dot-com darling, Digex.

CoreExpress's problem was not a lack of skills, but a lack of timing. CoreExpress joined a crowded bandwidth market just as the price of long-haul transport was dropping. The bandwidth market was only supposed to be a hedge for CoreExpress, tiding it over until the Extranet business kicked in. Instead, the additional bandwidth became a boat anchor. The bandwidth business never realized significant revenue, and the Extranet business, still in its infancy, couldn't carry the freight for the whole network.

When CoreExpress realized that the Extranet business wasn't growing fast enough to make up for the lack of bandwidth revenue, the company knew that it wasn't going to be able to survive on its own. CoreExpress sold its business to Williams Communications, the largest supplier of fiber-optic capacity to CoreExpress and its largest creditor, in November 2001. The failure of CoreExpress and other companies like it weighed heavily on Williams. Williams filed its own bankruptcy petition less than six months later.

SURVIVORS (FOR NOW)

Certain aspects of Level 3's business (described in Chapter 4) also fit the dot-com category. As a second-race participant, Level 3 overinvested in building its network. But it also saw itself offering more than bandwidth, drinking the same Kool-Aid as, for example, the RBOCs that offered content over their video dial-tone networks and AT&T, which believed that linking computers to its own closed data network was the key to future prosperity. To achieve that dot-com vision, Level 3 invested in CorpSoft and other businesses that offered software over the Internet. The hope was that Level 3 could leverage its network to deliver software content. This acquisition did not lead Level 3 closer to profitability, and its bandwidth business didn't gain significant traction by itself.

Charter Communications (described in Chapter 8) was in the same boat as Level 3 in that Charter could not recover its initial investment in the normal course of operating its business. What kept Level 3 and Charter afloat? Both shared ties to high-profile investors. Paul Allen, the second-richest Microsoft investor, was a founder of Charter and its largest shareholder. By mid-2004, he had already sold his other major telecommunications investment, RCN, at a loss, so it was unlikely that he would walk away from Charter. However, it would be difficult to work the business into a profitable venture.

Level 3 was also able to garner an investment from a high-profile investor: Berkshire Hathaway. Berkshire Hathaway is chaired by Warren Buffett, the famous investor. Although it was important to Level 3's image to get an investment from Buffett, the size of the investment, $100 million, was not exactly a strong endorsement. At the end of 2002, Berkshire Hathaway had more than $12.5 billion in cash, so $100 million was pocket change to Warren Buffett. An example of a serious investment for Berkshire was the $1.5 billion it spent in 2003 to purchase Clayton Homes. In perspective, Berkshire's investment in Level 3 was the equivalent of damning Level 3 with faint praise.

Also, Berkshire's investment was not in Level 3's common stock but in a convertible bond offering that carried junk bond interest rates. This indicated less of a vote of confidence than buying the common stock. The only rational explanation for the investment was the Omaha connection between the companies. Walter Scott, Jr., the chair of Level 3's board, was also a member of the board of directors of Berkshire Hathaway. Scott and Buffett both lived in Omaha. Scott needed help to shore up a Level 3 that was reeling from the effects of the second race on its revenue. Bringing in a marquee investor like Buffett made Level 3 look like it might be a telebomb survivor (for a while).

Buffet took advantage of the recovery in the market in 2003 to convert the bonds into Level 3 shares, which he promptly sold. The bulk of the bond issue that Berkshire bought into was converted in June 2003. As a result, 161 million shares, including more than half of Berkshire's, hit the market beginning in late June 2003. Predictably, when that many shares hit the market, the price of the stock declined. In July and August of 2003, trading volumes for Level 3 shares surged and the price dropped precipitously.

Clearly Berkshire was selling the shares it received when it converted the bonds, bringing the price of Level 3's stock down in the process. It was a classic situation of supply and demand. When there is more supply than demand for any good, the price goes down. If Berkshire received an average of $5.50 per share for its 29-million-plus shares, its total return on the $100 million investment (proceeds from the stock sale plus a year's interest on the bonds) was about $170 million, a 70 percent return in just over a year.

In a July 8, 2002, press release regarding Berkshire's investment in Level 3, Buffet was quoted as saying, "Liquid resources and strong financial backing are scarce and valuable assets in today's telecommunications world. Level 3 has both. Coupled with the management of Walter Scott and Jim Crowe, in whom I have great confidence, Level 3 is well equipped to seize important opportunities that are likely to develop in the communications industry." Buffett, a famously disciplined investor, obviously changed his mind over the next eleven months.

Level 3 was the biggest spender among the second racers, spending an estimated $12 billion on its network. Level 3's investment was only one of the many that flowed as a result of the Internet, the newly expanded mobile services market, and the Telecommunications Act. How much money was actually spent? The investments that led to the crash contributed many dollars to the U.S. economy that the investors never saw in return. But who received the money that was spent?

FOLLOWING THE MONEY

From 1996 to 2003, the telecommunications industry spent more than $620 billion on capital projects, an average of more than $75 billion a year. Figure 9-1 shows the spending by year and by industry segment. Annual capital spending more than doubled, from $50 billion in 1996 to a peak of $121 billion in 2000. It returned to near $50 billion in 2003.

Whereas the stock market saw a large boom, followed by the telebomb, and then a return to more normal trading patterns, capital spending (which indicates investment in the industry) shows a different pattern. The boom is apparent, but there was no bust, only a return to normal investment amounts. Within those amounts, though, the spending patterns changed with decreased investment in traditional telephone networks and increased investment in the newer (mobile) and the more aggressive segments (cable) of the market. CLEC spending, however, showed a nice round bubble in its rise and fall, returning in 2003 to about the same level as it began in 1996.

Separating the Bubble from the Beer

The telecommunications business has always consumed large amounts of capital. It is the nature of the business that copper wire and electronics degrade over time, new buildings must be served, and newer generations of

FIGURE 9-1.
TELEBOMB CAPITAL SPENDING.

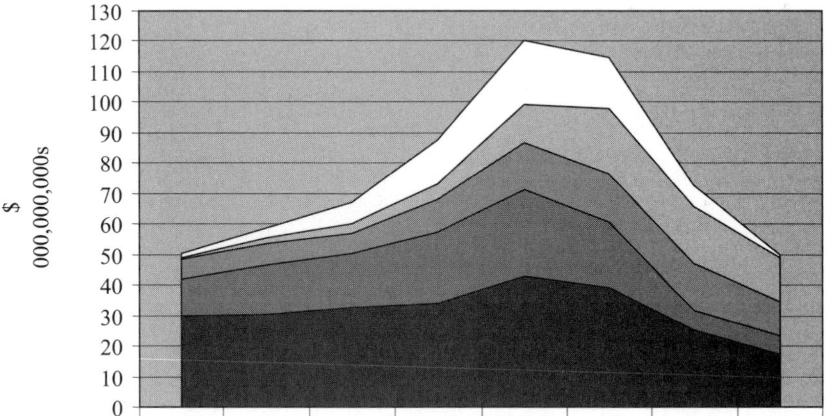

$000,000,000s	1996	1997	1998	1999	2000	2001	2002	2003
☐ CLEC	1.6	3.4	6.7	14.5	21.1	17.0	7.0	1.0
▨ Mobile	0.5	2.0	3.3	4.9	12.8	21.2	19.0	14.4
▨ Cable	6.4	7.0	6.3	11.0	15.0	16.0	15.0	11.0
▨ Long-Distance	12.2	16.2	17.7	23.2	28.9	21.4	6.5	6.1
■ RBOC	29.6	30.3	32.8	33.9	42.6	39.1	25.3	17.3

SOURCES: Long-distance and RBOC figures come from company reports to the SEC. Cable investment data from NCTA. CLEC investment data from ALTS, except 2003, which is the author's estimate based on reporting CLECs. RBOC figures include GTE. Wireless investment is for those companies reporting separately to the SEC. The mobile investments of the RBOCs and AT&T Wireless are included with parent company before they were reported separately.

technology prove to be more cost effective than old ones. An industrywide capital spending level of $50 billion per year is a reasonable approximation of steady-state spending to maintain the health of the network. That level of spending coincides with actual spending in both 1996 and 2003. If industry spending had stayed steady through the seven-year period from 1996 to 2003, the industry would have spent $400 billion in the normal course of business. No small sum, but an amount required to keep the nation's communications infrastructure modern and functioning.

If $400 billion would have been normal, then the difference between that typical spend and the $620 billion total that was actually spent could be considered the amount of investment brought forth by the new environment created by the Internet, new wireless spectrum, and the new regulatory environment brought on by the Telecommunications Act. Thus, the $220 billion incremental capital spend represents a reasonable proxy for the total investment by the new and existing competitors to get into the various markets that were opened to them in and around 1996. Figure 9-2 shows the bubble spend using the same data as in Figure 9-1.

FIGURE 9-2.
TELEBOMB CAPITAL SPENDING.

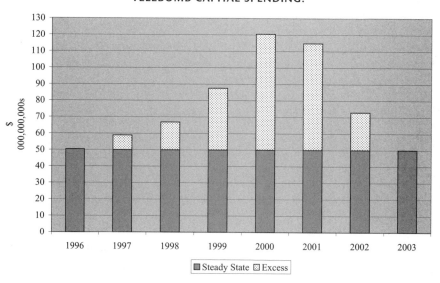

The carriers spent their investment capital building networks and services. Many of the carriers spent all their capital and still didn't develop viable businesses. Other companies struggled through the bust and came out on the other side intact and prepared to compete in the changed market. Chapter 10 discusses some of the factors that will determine future success or failure of those that made it through the telebomb. This section is focused on a different aspect of the large capital spend of the industry during the telebomb: Where did all the money go?

The following is an analysis that estimates where the money went. Forensic accounting has not advanced to the point where each dollar can be efficiently traced. In many cases, it is also not possible to differentiate between normal capital spending and money that was part of the speculative bubble. Given these caveats, this analysis shows that the bulk of the money ended up in the hands of four groups:

1. The equipment providers who sold new equipment to the carriers

2. The employees hired to build and operate the new businesses

3. The construction companies that built the networks

4. The investment banks who raised the capital

The nature of capital spending in the telecommunications industry is that money is spent to place equipment (electronics and support structures;

buildings and, in the case of wireless, towers) and transmission media (landline only, generally copper or fiber). The equipment is then integrated into a network that is placed in service. Software is written and customer service capabilities are developed to make sure that customers can be activated and service can be maintained and billed. How did each of the groups offering these services make out?

Equipment Providers

Networks don't work without hardware, electronics, fiber, switches, routers, and structures in which to house them. Although the domestic carriers are fairly easy to track, the equipment providers are a larger population including many small manufacturers and many companies both large and small that are located overseas or owned by foreign companies. This section looks at the two largest suppliers of telecom equipment through the bubble, Nortel Networks, and Lucent Technologies. They are representative of the suppliers of equipment to the U.S. carriers. They are, or were, integrated manufacturing companies, making many of their own components.

For the purpose of following the money, Nortel's and Lucent's results were used as proxies for the sale of equipment to U.S. carriers. Both companies sold the bulk of their products in the United States, although they also sold internationally. No other companies sold as much equipment to carriers in the United States during the boom. Cisco surpassed Lucent and Nortel in size, but it sold more to corporate customers and other end users of Internet-related hardware than to carriers.

Nortel's and Lucent's combined revenue from 1996 to 2002 was $262 billion compared with total capital spend within the U.S. telecommunications industry of $572 billion over the same period. Keep in mind that most of the dollars counted by the equipment manufacturers, particularly during the boom, came from the capital budgets of carriers. Thus, a dollar spent by a carrier on, for example, optical transmission systems, became revenue for the equipment providers.

The combined revenue of Lucent and Nortel more than doubled from 1996 to the peak in 2000. Figure 9-3 shows the sharp peak in revenue at the top of the bubble. The down slope during the telebomb is also quite dramatic in that it is much steeper than the decline in carrier revenue over the same period. Carrier revenue is mostly based on monthly recurring revenue from providing telecommunications services. The equipment providers' revenue derived mostly from one-time revenue recognition from new sales. While both segments saw a sharp drop-off in new sales after the

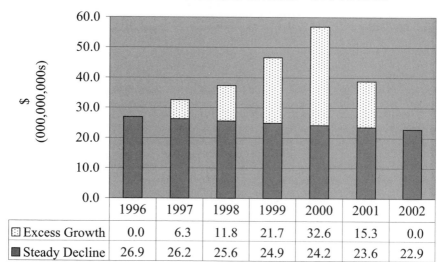

FIGURE 9-3.
LUCENT AND NORTEL COMBINED REVENUE—1996 TO 2002.

	1996	1997	1998	1999	2000	2001	2002
▣ Excess Growth	0.0	6.3	11.8	21.7	32.6	15.3	0.0
▪ Steady Decline	26.9	26.2	25.6	24.9	24.2	23.6	22.9

peak of the market, the carriers had the steady revenue of existing custom-ers to fall back on. The equipment providers did not.

Steady-state revenue for the equipment makers is unlikely to exceed pre-boom levels as carriers become more efficient in their newly competitive markets. That being said, post-telebomb sales were depressed below steady-state levels by the excess equipment sold in the late 1990s and still underuti-lized in 2003. Particularly when the industry was in its early recovery, cash was tight so the carriers made do with what they had on hand where pos-sible.

If revenue for the equipment providers had declined steadily from 1996 levels through 2002 rather than reaching high levels and dropping precipi-tously, the changes in the industry would have been much more manage-able for the equipment manufacturers. That, of course, was not the way the market developed. Figure 9-3 shows what that steady decline might have looked like. Counting the revenue above a steady decline rate is a reason-able way to estimate the equipment spend that was a result of the incremen-tal investment in new business opportunities. Using that methodology and Nortel and Lucent as a proxy for the industry, equipment providers re-ceived $88 billion (shown in Figure 9-3) out of the $220 billion in incre-mental spending by the industry during the telecommunications boom. Another way to say it is that $88 billion, or roughly a third of the $262 billion in revenue earned by the equipment manufacturers during the boom and bust, was bubble spend.

The equipment providers received a lot of the capital spent during the boom but had to deal with a more significant downside once the boom was over. Not only did their revenue decline more precipitously than the carriers' once the industry's growth spurt was over but the equipment providers saw steep increases in accounts payable from bankrupt CLECs. During better times, the equipment vendors offered financing to many of the startups that bought their equipment. As it turned out, offering financing to companies with no cash flow proved to be disastrous as these carriers started to file for bankruptcy protection.

The equipment manufacturers learned the same hard lesson as the Arthur Andersen accounting firm: Friends don't let friends drive drunk. Facilitating your client's aggressive business practices without any safeguards carries high, uncontrollable risks.

CORNING'S TELECOMMUNICATIONS ROLLER COASTER

Lucent and Nortel weren't the only equipment manufacturers that saw sharp declines in their business during the telebomb. Corning, one of the largest manufacturers of fiber-optic cable, saw even steeper declines in revenue when network construction abruptly stopped in 2001.

Corning has been in business since 1851. Throughout its history, it has been known for the manufacture and sales of many innovative products. It is most widely known for its cooking and other consumer products. It is perhaps most infamous for its interest in Dow Corning, a maker of silicone breast implants that was driven into bankruptcy by product liability lawsuits in the early 1990s.

With the increase in demand for precision glass products for the new optical transmission systems in the 1980s, Corning began manufacturing fiber-optic cable for the telecommunications industry. During the 1990s, Corning sold off its laboratory service business and its consumer products business to focus on fiber-optic cable and other high-tech products.

In 1994, Corning's telecommunications industry revenue was less than half of the company's overall revenue. Once the second race began in earnest in 1998, though, sales of Corning's fiber-optic products took off. Corning's telecommunications industry sales increased 150 percent between 1998 and 2000, from $2.1 billion to $5.2 billion. In both 2000 and 2001, sales of products to the telecommunications industry were 75 percent of Corning's overall sales. At the peak, Corning bought several other optical fiber businesses, concentrating the industry and increasing Corning's market share.[5]

The industry downturn that began in 2000 hit Corning hard. Demand for optical fiber dropped dramatically over a short time. From $5.2 billion in 2000, Corning's communications industry sales fell to $4.5 billion in 2001, and then to $1.6 billion in 2002. Its 2003 communications industry sales, at about $1.4 billion, represented a 72 percent decline from its peak in 2000. In 2003 and again in 2004, Corning's telecommunications revenue was less than 50 percent of corporate revenue, almost identical to its comparable figures for 1994.

Such dramatic shifts in any company's business cause problems. Corning announced a restructuring program in 2001 that included closing seven manufacturing facilities, laying off 12,000 workers, and a write-off of nearly $1 billion. By 2003, the company was cash flow positive again and would have been profitable if not for a nontelecommunications-related litigation settlement.

Employees

A great deal has been written about the number of jobs that have been lost in the industry as a result of the telebomb. According to statistics published by the FCC, industry employment peaked at 1.2 million jobs in 2001.[6] From that peak, 162,000 jobs were lost by early 2003. This job loss amounted to 14 percent of the industry's workers. It also represented between 5 percent and 10 percent of the total job losses during the 2000 to 2002 recession.

That magnitude of job loss has hurt the economy, but it is interesting to point out that post-telebomb industry employment is still higher than it was in 1998 (at the beginning of the hiring boom) and higher than it was between 1983 (immediately before AT&T's first divestiture) and 1998. The job loss from the telebomb compares to a loss of 188,400 jobs from the industry restructuring after the divestiture of the RBOCs from AT&T and the introduction of a competitive long-distance business in 1984.

Although the job losses of the past few years have been painful, industry employment in 2003 was 133,000 more than it was in 1995, before the Telecommunications Act was passed. Although many companies have failed, the net effect of the boom and bomb periods has been a contribution of more jobs to the U.S. economy. Important in the addition of jobs has been the migration of jobs from the landline side of the industry to the wireless companies.

Differentiating between those employed for speculative investment purposes and those who were hired for other reasons is a subjective matter, but it is reasonable to assume that most of the investment during the boom was aimed at creating new or expanded businesses. Those new business activities employed additional people to operate the businesses.

If the jobs created were the result of investment during the boom, it is also reasonable to make the case that the job losses during the telebomb (as well as those at the dead dot-coms) were more the result of the overinvest-ment of the 1990s than of any particular economic policy begun during George W. Bush's administration. Significant investments were made. Some paid off; others did not.

If the capital spending generated new businesses (which added employ-ees) at a steady rate during the boom, then the number of jobs above that steady rate could be considered to be the incremental employment that was a result of the boom. Figure 9-4 shows total industry employment during the telebomb period. Within total employment, the areas labeled "steady growth" show straight line growth from industry employment in 1996 to employment in 2003. Employment levels above that line are an estimate of boom-related hiring.

By looking at growth above the steady-growth rate, the amount of the boom investment that was spent on labor can be estimated. Adding the number of employees above the straight line rate for each year yields nearly 672,000 employee years. During the boom years, it became increasingly difficult to find telecommunications-knowledgeable workers. Thus, the prices paid to attract workers accelerated. For the purposes of this high-level estimate, it is reasonable to use $100,000 per year as an estimate for salary and benefits. By way of reference, engineers with skills in highly

FIGURE 9-4.
TELECOMMUNICATIONS INDUSTRY EMPLOYMENT, 1996 TO 2003.

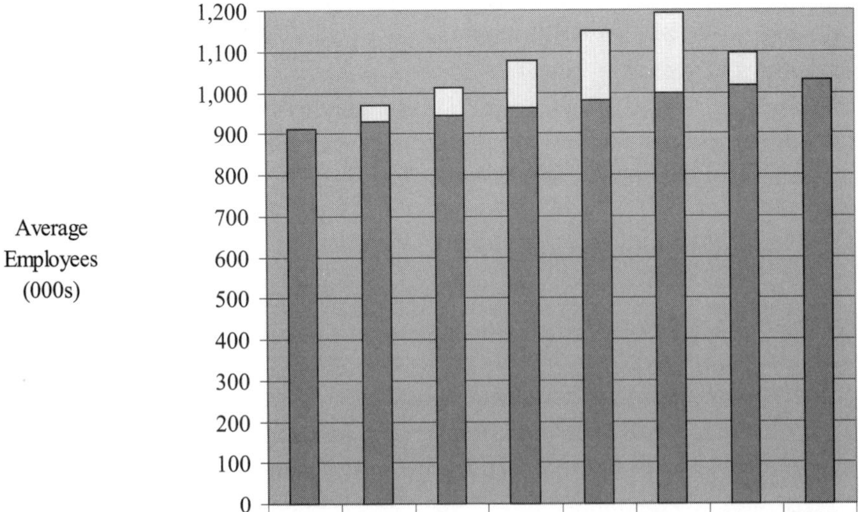

Average Employees (000s)

	1996	1997	1998	1999	2000	2001	2002	2003
☐ Excess Growth		42.7	67.3	115.9	170.2	196.7	79.1	
■ Steady Growth	911	928.3	945.5	962.8	980	997.3	1014.6	1032

sought-after telecommunications disciplines at the time could attract salary and benefit packages of more than $150,000. The boom years also coincided with the hype surrounding the year 2000 problem facing computer systems. This issue also created demand for computer programmers, driving up their salaries as well. Given those data points, an average of $100,000 overall is conservative.

Multiplying 672,000 employee years by $100,000 yields an estimate of $67 billion spent on employee compensation as part of the creation of new businesses during the boom. Of course not all this compensation was capitalized but, particularly for the more aggressive companies, most of it was.

Construction Companies

The construction companies that built the networks during the second race received contracts worth billions of dollars. Since most of the large construction companies in the United States are privately held, it is hard to determine what they gained during the boom years. One exception is Peter Kiewit Sons, Inc. Because of its common parentage with Level 3, Kiewit was able to win contracts to perform a significant portion of Level 3's network build. During Level 3's heavy building period from 1999 through 2001, Kiewit gained more than $2.8 billion in revenue from Level 3 representing 23 percent of Level 3's $12 billion in capital spending during those years.

While most of the capital spending of the time was not for heavy construction, two specific segments of the industry were heavy constructors: the second racers and the CLEC builders, such as McLeod ($2 billion), XO ($4.5 billion), and e.spire ($1 billion).

The second racers collectively spent about $40 billion (including Level 3, Qwest, Williams, GST, 360networks, and others). The CLEC builders as a group spent about $20 billion. If these companies spent, on average, 20 percent of the $60 billion capital spending on construction services, that would total $12 billion.

The CLEC resellers spent very little on construction. Their focus was on selling someone else's assets rather than building their own. The RBOCs spent comparatively less on heavy construction because they were, in most cases, adding network in existing buildings and rights-of-way rather than green field areas. But it is reasonable to estimate that they spent another $5 billion on heavy construction services outside their own organizations.

The cable companies built in their existing rights-of-way, but did entire replacements of large portions of their networks. Thus, it is reasonable to estimate that they spent 10 percent of their nearly $90 billion capital spend during the boom on construction services: a total of $9 billion.

The wireless providers also went through significant network builds in the late 1990s. The wireless carriers didn't have to trench fiber over long routes to connect their networks, so it is reasonable to assume that they spent less than 20 percent of their capital on heavy construction. If they spent 10 percent of their nearly $80 billion in network builds on construction services, another $8 billion went to construction companies. A cursory look at the revenue of the major cell tower construction and management companies (American Tower, Crown Castle International, and LCC International) supports an estimate of $8 billion.

The total estimate from all these groups is $34 billion: more than 15 percent of the industry's incremental spend during the boom and bomb years.

Investment Banks

The investment banks made money coming and going during the boom times. The carriers that raised money paid the investment banks typically 1 to 3 percent of the total amount raised. At the high end of the range, 3 percent of the $220 billion bubble spend is $6.6 billion, not bad for an industry that took little risk in the process. In addition, the investment bankers also received fees from the investors who bought the stocks and bonds sold to raise the funds.

Following the money shows that more than half the bubble investment was spent on equipment and the labor required to build the new networks and services established during both the boom and the bomb. But what goes up must come down. The telecom equipment market crashed harder than any other industry related to telecommunications. Industry employment also decreased as the investment boom ended. The construction companies and investment banks have moved on to greener pastures. For the investment banks, the greener pastures have included advising bankrupt or near-bankrupt carriers on how to best monetize the remaining assets purchased with money raised by other investment banks.

NOTES

1. "The State of Local Competition 2003," ALTS, April 2003, p. 7.
2. e.spire's company reports to the SEC on Form 10-K.
3. XO's company reports to the SEC.
4. "Executives on Trial," *Wall Street Journal* online, October 3, 2003; Phyllis Plitch, "Rigas-Style Guaranteed Loans on Their Way Out," Dow Jones News Service, July 8, 2003.
5. Corning's company reports to the SEC.
6. "Trends in Telephone Service," Industry Analysis and Technology Division, Wireline Competition Bureau, FCC, August 2003, p. 5-3.

CHAPTER 10

WHO WON?

The telebomb affected companies throughout the industry, both large and small. Although many survived, many more failed. In general the large, established carriers made it through without being forced to file for bankruptcy, with WorldCom being the notable exception. A few of the new entrants survived, but there is more to success than merely existing.

The telecommunications industry still has major issues to work out before another stasis is reached. New competitive boundaries have not been staked out, and critical regulatory issues such as access reform and unbundling rules have yet to be decided. But even with skeptical financial markets and indecisive regulators, there are companies in the industry that managed their markets and finances well and came out of the crash better able to react to regulatory or competitive changes than those who are living close to the edge.

As the telebomb has eased into a recovery, it is more apparent who came out of the telebomb best prepared for the future. This chapter explores two ways to define success throughout the telebomb era:

1. *Investment Performance.* Which stocks actually made money during this period?

2. *Financially Strong Carriers.* Which industry segments adapted best to the new environment and are positioned to prosper in the early twenty-first century?

INVESTMENT PERFORMANCE

Stock price is perhaps the easiest way to quantify a company's performance. Buyers and sellers change the price of securities

---

1880
1890
1900
1910
1920
1930
1940
1950
1960
1970
1980
1981
1982
1983
1984
1985
1986
1987
1988
1989
1990
1991
1992
1993
1994
1995
1996
1997
1998
1999
2000
2001
2002
2003
2004
2005
FUTURE

MONOPOLY
DIVESTITURE
STABILITY
BOOM
BOMB
RECOVERY?

every day in reaction to any new information. Dividing the wheat from the chaff in the telecommunications industry from an investor's perspective is straightforward because of the widely varying performance over different periods including both the boom and the telebomb.

As the dust cleared from the telebomb, many executives in the telecommunications industry took steps to clean up their financial act. After the first year of the recovery, some looked poised for success when their future existence previously had been in doubt. However, the stock market didn't always reward companies with solid or improving financial performance during the dot-com era. Investor psychology was more akin to herd mentality during the boom and bomb than it was like a reasoned approach to investing.

Dr. Alexander Elder, a psychiatrist and a professional trader, describes analyzing the stock market as an exercise in mass psychology.[1] The masses in the market in the late 1990s were rooting for the dot-coms and for the telecommunications companies that were seen as critical enablers of the fundamental fallacy, which was described in Chapter 4. Once the bubble burst, the same investors participated in a not-so-orderly exit from the crowded theater that the stock market had become. As shown in Chapter 9, investments by the industry first saw a steady increase followed by a steady, but steep decrease. The stock market followed a more extreme pattern of boom and bust during the same period.

This chapter analyzes twenty-six publicly held companies that offered carrier services in the United States during the boom and bust. The companies included in the analysis are shown in Table 10-1. Because the analysis is focused on determining the winners, stocks of companies that went out of business through merger, acquisition, or bankruptcy are not included. Also omitted are some small public carriers. This study focuses on how the stocks of the carriers performed in each of three overlapping periods:

1. *From the Beginning.* Throughout the boom, bust, and recovery from the beginning of 1996 through 2003.

2. *Down the Mountain.* From the peak of the market in March 2000 through 2003.

3. *On the Rebound.* From the trough in the market in the fourth quarter of 2002 through the first full year of the recovery.

From the Beginning—1996 to 2003

Thirteen of the twenty-six stocks were publicly traded throughout the analysis period. (The other thirteen were either spun out or went through an

TABLE 10-1.
STOCKS ANALYZED ALONG WITH THEIR MAJOR BUSINESS SEGMENTS.

	Cable	ILEC	Long-Distance	CLEC/DLEC	Mobile	International
Alltel		X	X		X	
AT&T			X	X		X
AT&T Wireless Services					X	
BellSouth		X	X		X	
CenturyTel		X	X			
Charter Communications	X					
Cincinnati Bell		X	X			
Citizens Communications		X	X	X		
Comcast	X			X		
Cox Communications	X			X		
DSL.net				X		
Equant						X
Level 3 Communications			X	X		
Nextel Communications					X	
Pac-West Telecomm				X		
Qwest Communications International		X	X			
Savvis Communications				X		X
SBC Communications		X	X		X	
Sprint (FON Group)		X	X			
Sprint PCS					X	
Talk America Holdings			X	X		
Telephone & Data Systems (TDS)		X	X	X	X	
Time Warner	X			X		
Trinsic				X		
US LEC				X		
Verizon Communications		X	X		X	

IPO after 1996.) Surprisingly enough, given the turbulence of the times, twelve of the thirteen had positive total returns (stock appreciation plus dividends) over the eight-year period. (For the analysis, stock dividends were converted to cash as soon as possible once received so as to focus on continuing operations. Stock dividends were distributed by Sprint [360 Communications and Sprint PCS], Cincinnati Bell [Convergys], and AT&T [Lucent, NCR, AT&T Wireless, and AT&T Broadband].)

Table 10-2 shows the total returns of all thirteen stocks that survived the boom and the telebomb. (Analysis is based on quarter-end prices from shortly before the Telecommunications Act was passed (end of 4Q95) through the first full year of the recovery (end of 4Q03). The numbers shown in Table 10-2 are total returns, not annual returns.)

Comcast was an example of the growth mantra of the dot-com era, doubling its subscriber count three times in ten years. It was rewarded handsomely during the run-up of stock prices, almost quintupling its stock price at the top of the market. Comcast continued to grow its business even past the peak of the market. It picked up AT&T Broadband about the same time the stock market was at its lowest point, getting a 20 percent discount from what AT&T paid for the same franchises (but still overpaying).

Cox Communications saw the same treatment as Comcast, but Cox was more prudent in its acquisitions. That caution cost it some speculative favor during the boom but may turn out to be its savior in the end.

Among the carriers that made it through the period, Nextel's stock saw the biggest speculative bubble. Nextel grew from a small, specialized mobile carrier to a national presence with its unique (at the time) offering of wide-area walkie-talkie functionality. While each of the thirteen companies had some sort of exposure to the cellular marketplace during the telebomb, Nextel was the only one of the thirteen that was a pure-play mobile company. During the time when everyone thought that mobile phone penetration

TABLE 10-2.
TOTAL RETURNS FOR SELECTED STOCKS, 1996 TO 2003.

COMPANY	TOTAL RETURN 1996 TO 2003
Comcast	303%
Nextel Communications	280%
CenturyTel	142%
Sprint (FON group only)	98%
Alltel	92%
Cox Communications	77%
Telephone & Data Systems (TDS)	68%
Cincinnati Bell	62%
BellSouth	58%
Verizon	41%
SBC	19%
Citizens Communications	13%
AT&T	−21%

rates would grow at double-digit rates every year, Nextel was a must-have stock. Helping Nextel during the speculative bubble were the persistent rumors that it was an acquisition candidate.

Following Comcast and Nextel in the total return rankings were the stocks of the large independent local carriers. CenturyTel and Alltel produced healthy returns throughout the telebomb, providing both stock price appreciation and current income in the form of dividends. Their conservative approaches made them the tortoises versus the cable and CLEC hares in the marketplace. The only independent ILEC to have a near-death experience was Cincinnati Bell, which, during the boom, looked more like a CLEC or a second racer than a stable, local company. It engaged in several merger-and-acquisition transactions and even stopped paying dividends in 2000 to focus on growth.

Citizens also executed a broad expansion strategy that made it look for a time more like a CLEC. The hangover of that expansion was reflected in the $4.7 billion of debt on its balance sheet in 2003, nearly twice its revenue that year.

During the period of this analysis, Sprint (the largest of the independent local carriers after GTE merged with Bell Atlantic) was aggressive only in building out its PCS business. The rocky performance of the wireless business was reflected in Sprint's tracking stock for the PCS business, not in the FON group stock, which represented the rest of the company (the local and long-distance business). Sprint created the PCS stock in November 1998, as a way to track separately the performance of Sprint's mobile business, since it was a new business requiring much investment and producing little in the way of profits. Once the PCS business matured, the tracking stock was folded back into the rest of Sprint in April 2004.

Telephone & Data Systems (TDS) and Citizens Communications lagged within the group of stable independents. TDS's problems were mostly due to the poor performance of its United States Cellular subsidiary (itself a publicly traded company). U.S. Cellular simply couldn't execute on its opportunity to build a wireless brand. With mostly second- and third-tier cities, it was the eighth-largest wireless carrier in the United States in 2003, stuck well behind the six big national providers (plus Alltel), and could not distinguish itself.

Among the RBOCs, BellSouth was the clear leader. It saw enough stock price appreciation to outperform Verizon, even though Verizon paid much larger dividends. SBC barely came out of the telebomb in positive territory. BellSouth had higher returns than any of the other RBOCs and it was the only RBOC that didn't engage in a large merger transaction.

During this period, investors were generally better off buying RBOC bonds than common stock. A 6 percent coupon bond bought at par and held through the eight-year period returned more to an investor (a 48 percent total return) than any RBOC stock except BellSouth. The bondholders also endured much less volatility.

Taken as a group, the performance of the ILECs provides more evidence that their mergers had no financial benefit. Of the nine stocks in the group that include significant ILEC components, three of the four that were the most active in the merger-and-acquisition market (Verizon, SBC, and Citizens) were the worst performers. Cincinnati Bell would have joined them at the bottom of the pile if not for the gain on the Convergys spinout.

The lone carrier posting negative returns throughout the period, AT&T, also went through significant merger-and-acquisition activities. In fact, AT&T's returns would have been worse were it not for the value of its many stock distributions. An investor who held 1,000 shares of AT&T on January 1, 1996, and stayed with AT&T through the eight years received $37,690 worth of stock dividends over the period. Looking solely at stock performance, AT&T was by far the worst performer through this period, losing 90 percent of its value.

Back in the days of the Bell system, AT&T was considered a slow and steady dividend-paying investment. Its stock was of sufficient quality that it was appropriate to be held by "widows and orphans," presumably those most in need of steady returns and little risk. That impression held for some time after AT&T's first divestiture when the RBOCs left the fold. By the time of its third divestiture, though, AT&T became a risky stock.

Throughout this book, mergers and acquisitions have been a large factor in the analysis of the companies and market segments in the industry. In the end, did the merger activity translate into market value for investors? For the cable companies: yes. For the Bells: no. The total return performance of the RBOC's stocks stands in further contrast to Comcast's and Cox's performance, given that the two cable companies do not pay dividends and three of the four RBOC stocks (plus AT&T) do. The Bells' dividends were a large part of their total returns.

The conclusion to be drawn from this sharp difference in the performance of two industry subsegments that engaged in significant merger-and-acquisition activity is that acquisitions make sense when growth opportunities exist that scale can catalyze. When growth opportunities don't exist or don't materialize, the excess baggage taken on in the merger process becomes too much of a weight, and the stock of the merged company falls flat. This does not imply that the cable companies are out of the woods yet. The debt lurking on their balance sheets will constrain their ability to grow for some time.

Down the Mountain—2000 to 2003

No carrier stock was spared the effects of the stock market crash. At the end of 2003, none of the twenty-six carrier stocks analyzed returned more than its price at the end of the first quarter of 2000 in either capital gains or total returns. Some fared markedly better than others, though. Interestingly, even though this analysis includes only companies that made it through the boom and bomb, the tenth best performer of the twenty-six stocks (Nextel) lost 62 percent of its market value during the period. Total returns for the top ten stocks in this analysis are shown in Table 10-3.

Looking solely at stock performance, the large, stable independent telcos outperformed the bulk of the industry. Admittedly, these stocks were not bid up as high in the frenzy of the late 1990s, but they held their value best in the group. In addition, almost all these stocks paid dividends.

The RBOCs were all in the top ten with the exception of Qwest. Both Comcast and Cox also made it into the top ten. The cable business in general was able to continue on its growth path, even given the general economic conditions. Cable revenue growth averaged 7 percent to 10 percent per subscriber, even accelerating during the downturn.

No CLECs were in the top ten. Talk America was the closest to breaking into that group. It lost 76 percent of its market value during the period when most of the CLECs lost 80 percent or more. The CLECs were tripped up in many ways because of the immaturity of their business models. Talk America at least had the remnants of a long-distance resale business to generate cash flow when the capital markets closed for the season.

TABLE 10-3.
TOTAL RETURNS, TOP 10 SELECTED STOCKS, 2000 TO 2003.

COMPANY	TOTAL RETURN 2000 TO 2003
CenturyTel	−10%
Alltel	−18%
Comcast	−21%
Citizens Communications	−24%
SBC Communications	−28%
Cox Communications	−29%
Verizon	−32.5%
BellSouth	−32.9%
Telephone & Data Systems (TDS)	−42%
Nextel Communications	−62%

This is not to say that long distance was a good place to be. Notably absent in the top ten are any of the long-distance companies, because of the results of the second race. AT&T, Qwest, and Level 3 all lost more than 90 percent of their stocks' value during the crash. They joined five other of the twenty-six carriers in losing more than 90 percent of their value during the period. Sprint, even with its steady local business, missed the top ten because of the effect of the price wars on the long-distance side of its business.

Timing Is Everything

If holding stocks was a risky game during the decline of the long-distance carriers, the best way to invest in the telecommunications market during the bubble was to be an early investor and get out before the crash. Two examples of early investors who timed the market well are Philip Anschutz at Qwest and Gary Winnick at Global Crossing. Anschutz and Winnick sold a large percentage of their holdings in their companies' stock at or near the top of the market.

Qwest's principal owner, Anschutz Company, led by founder Philip Anschutz, took away $1.7 billion from a timely sale of Qwest stock. Virtually all of that was accomplished as the result of a $3.5 billion sale of stock by Qwest to BellSouth in April 1999. The sale consisted of Qwest selling new shares to BellSouth for $1.9 billion and Anschutz Company selling some of its shares of Qwest stock for $1.6 billion.[2] At the end of 2003, BellSouth's $3.5 billion investment was worth about $350 million, a 90 percent decline.

Similarly, Pacific Capital Group, headed by Gary Winnick (former associate of Michael Milken, the junk bond king) walked away with a hefty profit from the sale of Global Crossing stock. Winnick was the chair of the board of Global Crossing. Pacific Capital sold almost 95 million shares of Global Crossing stock in 1999. During the year, the stock sold between a high of $64.25 and a low of $18.94. At the low end of that range, Pacific Capital's proceeds were worth about $2 billion.

For every Anschutz and Winnick, however, there has been a Clark McLeod and a Paul Allen. McLeodUSA and Charter (Allen's cable company) both made billion-dollar bets on the future of the network and couldn't deliver.

On the Rebound—2002 to 2003

Another way to evaluate investment performance is to assess who has done well since the stock market hit bottom in late 2002. The largest gains seen during the early recovery generally accrued to those who were battered most on their way down the mountain. Many carriers were not going concerns at the trough, but the ones that were resuscitated fared well. Each of the top ten stocks during this period lost at least 60 percent of its value between the end of the first quarter of 2000 and the end of the third quarter of 2002. (Analysis period runs from the end of 4Q02 through the end of 4Q03.) Total returns for the top ten stocks during this period are shown in Table 10-4.

While no CLECs led in stock performance during the storm, the stocks of these newer carriers experienced significant percentage gains as the clouds cleared. These stocks fell farther than those of the mainline carriers during the depths of the telebomb, so even small dollar gains became large percentage gains. The CLEC stocks fell so far, in fact, that many were considered penny stocks.

Even so, for the investor who maintained a strong stomach after the losses of the 2000 to 2002 period, the CLECs and other small carriers offered significant opportunities.

Where all twenty-six of the carriers in the study group had negative returns from the top of the market through 2003, twenty-two of the twenty-six had positive total returns coming out of the recession (for the full year, 2003). Only Alltel, Verizon, AT&T, and Qwest had negative total returns in 2003.

Two extreme cases of post-bomb gains were Pac-West Telecomm and Savvis Communications. Pac-West's stock bottomed out at 21 cents per share on October 9, 2002. It lost more than 99.5 percent of its peak market value, and yet survived.

TABLE 10-4.
TOTAL RETURNS, TOP 10 SELECTED STOCKS, 2000 TO 2003.

COMPANY	TOTAL RETURN 2002 TO 2003
Pac-West Telecomm	284%
Savvis	275%
US LEC	250%
Charter Communications	241%
Trinsic (formerly Z-Tel Technologies)	149%
Nextel Communications	143%
Equant	126%
Talk America	106%
Cincinnati Bell	44%
AT&T Wireless	41%

Savvis is a data network provider with a deep niche providing private ISP services to the financial services industry. Savvis was in financial trouble through 2002 because it was saddled with debt from a former parent company, Bridge Information Systems, which went bankrupt. Savvis's stock hit a low of 28 cents on September 24, 2002. After that, Savvis went through a financial restructuring and a generally easier time for small carriers in the market. It recovered and traded as high as $1.88 per share less than nine months later.

In addition to the CLECs, the wireless players did well in the initial recovery. Like the cable companies, the wireless carriers were debt laden, but they continued to show revenue growth throughout the period.

Equant, the only primarily international carrier not to file bankruptcy during the crash, made it into the top ten. Like the new entrants, however, its performance during the rebound was more likely a result of how badly beaten the stock was during the crash.

The gains of 2003 didn't last long for the CLECs. The CLECs gave back many of their rebound gains in early 2004 as the federal courts again ruled against the FCC and its guidelines for how RBOC services would be sold to the CLECs. This was the third major defeat for the FCC and a particularly tough loss for the CLECs because the court specifically called out the FCC's pricing guidelines for UNEs. These rules mandated low prices that, the RBOCs claimed, caused the RBOCs to lose money. The potential of much higher costs for financially strapped CLECs, as well as the uncertainty of when the pricing issues would be resolved, caused many CLEC stocks to drop in early 2004. Another effect of the changing regulations was that the CLECs and their investors were reminded again that the FCC was unable to develop UNE resale rules that could withstand any scrutiny, making the business environment less stable and, therefore, the CLEC stocks more risky.

The dependence of most CLECs on the ability to lease cheap UNEs from the incumbents was recognized by the market. But the change in pricing rules also brought out the differences between those CLECs that built a business to withstand changes in its cost structure and those that were living on the edge and unable to adjust.

In that sense, the CLECs were a microcosm of the industry. As the clouds parted from the telebomb years, the carriers that were best prepared to capitalize on new opportunities were able to grow. Since each segment of the industry was forced to compete against the others in the post-telebomb world, it is interesting to take a look at how the residents of each of the former walled gardens adapted to the bigger, more competitive market.

FINANCIALLY STRONG CARRIERS

Even before the telebomb made capital dollars hard to find, carriers competed more with pricing/packaging and customer service than with new products. One characteristic of the many CLECs and second racers was that each deployed the same services and network equipment as its direct competitors, including the incumbents. At a time of undifferentiated technology, the importance of financial strength to compete for customers was magnified. In other words, if a given company's product offerings were the same as those offered by any other company, consumers would tend to buy the product with the lower price or some measure of better customer service.

Before the telecommunications industry was thrown open to all comers, each of the walled gardens had its own financial rubrics. As the industry segments coalesce, though, there will be less tolerance for what may have been the norm but is now maladaptive. "Everybody's doing it" will no longer be an acceptable excuse. Increasingly, companies with different financial histories will be competing directly to provide similar sets of services to the same customer.

To determine the segments and companies best suited to a changing future, each segment and its members are evaluated based on the following four financial measures:

1. Revenue growth

2. Operating income

3. Long-term debt

4. Intangible assets

Each segment was rated as positive, negative, or neutral based on how it performed relative to the other segments. There were not many cases where the companies within the segments differ materially. Most of those that did were within the CLEC segment, because the CLECs were created to break down barriers within the industry, not to conform to old ways of doing business.

Revenue Growth

Revenue is traditionally called the *top line number* because it is the starting point of the income statement. Growth in that top line number increases the availability of dollars for current profits. Table 10-5 shows how the different segments of the industry have fared relative to each other.

The wireless carriers and CLECs grew revenue through the market downturn by adding subscribers even though their revenue per subscriber had flattened out (CLECs) or fallen (wireless).

Since 1996, the CLECs have grown to $13.6 billion in annual revenue, most of it taken from the incumbents.[3] The CLEC's revenue grew, even through the economic downturn. The growth rates would be called incredible, if it weren't for the high initial expectations. The unrealistic expectations stemmed mostly from the dot-com times in which the CLECs' business plans were created and funded. However, the expectations were also a natural reaction to being up against the RBOCs. It takes a bold plan to be credible when competing against some of the largest companies on the planet.

The incumbents had more than 99 percent market share through 1996. A natural result of the CLEC gains has been flat-to-falling revenue for the landline business of the ILECs.

The cable companies also grew revenue beyond the effects of their many mergers. Unlike the wireless carriers and CLECs, the cable companies grew revenue per subscriber by raising rates and offering new services while their internal subscriber growth rates remained flat. This growth has been expensive for the cable companies, however.

The long-distance business, mired in destructive competition because of the second race and RBOC entry into the market, has seen dramatic revenue declines.

Operating Income

Revenue tallies the total dollars brought in through sales. Operating income represents the dollars left over after the expenses of running the business are deducted from revenue. These profits from operations generate cash

TABLE 10-5.
RELATIVE REVENUE GROWTH BY INDUSTRY SEGMENT.

REVENUE GROWTH	
Cable	+
Wireless	+
CLEC	+
Local	0
Long-Distance	−

that can be used to expand the business, pay dividends, or service debt. Operating income is one of the clearest and most consistent indicators of the core financial health of a company. Table 10-6 shows how the different segments of the industry have fared relative to each other in maintaining operating income through the boom and bust.

The ILECs maintained their consistent income generation, even through a time of flat-to-declining revenue. Not counting Qwest, the RBOCs have been able to maintain businesses that collectively produce $20 billion in operating income annually. That amount of profit can sustain their business models for some time. The trick for the incumbents will be to maintain their competitive balance and profitability as they continue to lose market share.

The wireless companies have also begun to produce positive operating income. Their income trend has been positive for some time, but a lot of growth was required to show positive returns on the huge investments of the 1990s. The trend is now established and, barring any new rounds of destructive competition, the wireless companies should continue to show increases in profitability.

The cable companies are still struggling to manage their growth. Although the mergers have slowed to a trickle and the huge build outs begun in the late 1990s are essentially done, margins have not returned to historical levels for the most aggressive cable companies. Before the merger frenzy, operating margins were commonly 20 to 25 percent of revenue. Only Time Warner Cable is still in that range. The others are in the 10 percent to 15 percent range. Only when operating margins increase can the huge debt loads taken on to finance the expansion be significantly reduced.

The CLECs are also in the position of trying to grow into their initial investments. Few of them are profitable, even with reduced debt loads from bankruptcies. Nevertheless, the trend was for smaller losses, and more of them were becoming profitable. The changes pending final UNE resale rules will have a large part in determining the ultimate success of the CLECs.

TABLE 10-6.
RELATIVE OPERATING INCOME BY INDUSTRY SEGMENT.

OPERATING INCOME	
Cable	0
Wireless	+
CLEC	0
Local	+
Long-Distance	−

The long-distance business has yet to find any bottom for pricing, so it is hard to manage profitability.

Long-Term Debt

One item that gets deducted after calculating operating income is interest payments on the indebtedness incurred to finance the company. Many companies profiled in this book took on too much debt too fast, contributing to their downfall. Table 10-7 shows how the different segments of the industry have fared relative to each other in managing their debt.

At the end of 2003 the former Big 3 long-distance companies, as a group, had less debt ($24.5 billion) than Comcast ($27 billion). Collectively, the Big 3 had more than three times the revenue of Comcast in 2003. The Big 3's debt is less because of WorldCom's bankruptcy, but still stands in sharp contrast to that carried by others in the industry.

Before divestiture, the Bells' debt levels were managed to about 45 percent of revenue. Only SBC has stayed true to that old rule. Qwest is the most obvious exception because of the Classic Qwest train wreck that the former USWest business is propping up. Verizon is also exceeding the traditional debt level in part because GTE carried more debt than the RBOCs. Another plausible explanation for increased debt levels among the RBOCs in 2003 was the record low interest rates of the period compared with the high dividend yields that the RBOC stocks carry.

Some CLECs carry low debt (Trinsic and Talk America, for example) whereas others are still left with their hangover from the high-yield bond parties of the late 1990s. Generally, though, the worst of the debt junkies have already been put into rehab.

The wireless companies carried significant debt because of their seemingly endless network builds. After the initial construction came the digital conversions and then the move to add data services to their networks. The companies are just now seeing returns on those networks, so the mountain of debt still looks big.

TABLE 10-7.
RELATIVE LONG-TERM DEBT BY INDUSTRY SEGMENT.

LONG-TERM DEBT	
Cable	–
Wireless	–
CLEC	0
Local	0
Long-Distance	+

By far the most debt-hungry segment of the market has been the cable business. The five largest cable companies based on the number of subscribers—Comcast, Time Warner, Charter Communications, Cox, and Adelphia Communications—were carrying more than $75 billion in debt in late 2003. Of that figure, $16 billion belonged to Adelphia Communications, which was likely to shed much of the debt in bankruptcy. Collectively, the top five cable companies have 80 percent of the debt level of the RBOCs but only 28 percent as much revenue.

Intangible Assets

An indicator that too much was paid for acquisitions is the amount of intangibles on the acquirer's balance sheet. Writing Off Intangibles 101 is the first class corporations take upon enrollment at the financial fat farm. Goodwill represents the difference between the price paid for an asset, usually another business, and any otherwise identifiable value of the purchased asset. Large amounts of goodwill were booked because of acquisitions during the dot-com bubble. The prices paid for companies well exceeded the value of their tangible assets. The excess price paid was booked to goodwill. Table 10-8 shows how the different segments of the industry have managed intangible assets relative to each other.

The presence of goodwill is not in and of itself a bad thing, but it is an indicator that too much was paid for an asset. It can also cause sensational news when it is written off, as happened when Time Warner wrote down $54 billion of its investment in America Online in the first quarter of 2002. Staying away from intangibles is a sign of conservative financial management.

The ILECs—with the exception of Verizon—stayed away from overuse of this type of accounting. In combining Vodafone's U.S. operations into Verizon Wireless, Verizon booked $31 billion of intangible assets. The goodwill booked in that transaction exceeds the sum of all the other intan-

TABLE 10-8.
RELATIVE INTANGIBLE ASSET LOAD BY INDUSTRY SEGMENT.

INTANGIBLE ASSETS	
Cable	–
Wireless	0
CLEC	0
Local	0
Long-Distance	0

gible assets of the RBOCs, including the intangibles held by both Bell Atlantic and GTE before their merger.

The former Big 3 long-distance companies carry few intangibles, mostly because they have made efforts to clean up their balance sheets. AT&T was carrying more than $70 billion of goodwill and other intangibles before its third divestiture and the related recapitalization of the company. It lost $65 billion of intangibles through that process. WorldCom took similar charges during its stay in bankruptcy, having carried as much as $50 billion in goodwill at one point. Sprint didn't pursue significant acquisition transactions, so it never had to deal with this problem.

The CLECs have also stayed away from this particular gimmick, although it may be due more to their inability to complete acquisitions since the dot-com meltdown than anything else.

The cable industry has completed more merger transactions than any other industry segment. Unlike the RBOC mergers, the cable industry consolidation was very competitive and, at the top of the market, unreasonably expensive. Prices for cable franchises were bid up more during the bubble than those of any other telecommunications properties in the United States. The top five cable companies were carrying nearly $200 billion of intangibles toward the end of 2003.[4] These five carriers have more intangible assets than the rest of the domestic carriers combined.

The wireless industry segment has also seen some consolidation, but the deals have mostly been small and, therefore, goodwill has stayed under control. With many national brands competing against one another, though, consolidation became more likely once mergers and acquisitions come back into favor. That consolidation began when AT&T Wireless sold itself to Cingular in 2004 and Sprint and Nextel announced a similar deal.

The Bottom Line

Table 10-9 summarizes the relative financial strength of the different segments within the industry. Looking at the four key financial metrics, the ILECs and the remaining CLECs adapted best to the new world they faced at the end of 2003. They each had strengths and no significant financial disadvantages. They had challenges but are in a better position to deal with the problems as they arise. Each of the other segments has at least one skeleton lurking in its closet that, with the wrong combination of events, could prove disastrous.

Through 2003 the CLECs were driving pricing in the local phone market. They started the $50-per-month-all-you-can-call packages, for example. However, the balance of power between the ILECs and the CLECs

TABLE 10-9.
RELATIVE FINANCIAL STRENGTH BY INDUSTRY SEGMENT.

	REVENUE GROWTH	OPERATING INCOME	LONG-TERM DEBT	INTANGIBLE ASSETS
Cable	+	0	−	−
Wireless	+	+	−	0
CLEC	+	0	0	0
Local	0	+	0	0
Long-Distance	−	−	+	0

changed in 2004 when the FCC's pricing rules were struck down. Over time, the change will mean cost increases for the CLECs that could cause another round of financial stress. Only time will tell.

The ILECs made it through the telebomb with a clean bill of financial health. Even Cincinnati Bell, after a series of near-disastrous acquisitions, is profitable and has begun to clean up its balance sheet. With the exception of Qwest, the ILECs still have the financial wherewithal to invest in the next bright, shiny object that comes along. While the RBOCs' mergers cannot be defended based on improved financial performance, they are defensible on the grounds that, in an era of instability, the RBOCs circled the wagons and maintained their presence while still throwing off nearly $10 billion per year in cash as dividends to shareholders. Remember, size matters. The RBOCs' markets are beginning to erode, though, leading them to the point where they will soon have to make tough choices. Chapter 12 discusses what the RBOCs need to do to stay successful.

The telebomb period has been particularly Darwinian for the CLECs in that only the strongest have survived (two-thirds of the erstwhile competitors have gone out of business). Although some have survived the telebomb years and appear poised to thrive, it is too soon to say whether any of them will be long-term winners. Merely surviving the telebomb earned them kudos, even more than the established carriers, but not the right to claim any future success.

Each of the surviving CLECs picked a path that fits in with a particular niche in the industry. Unlike the companies that grew up in one of the walled gardens, the CLECs were cast out into a Wild West marketplace and had to find their own way to survive. Several of the surviving CLECs have sound fundamentals. However, these are small companies compared with the other companies in the industry. The CLECs are unlikely ever to grow to be the size of the RBOCs. And, even among the survivors, the competitive battles are likely to leave some scars, bring additional consolidation, and cause additional bankruptcies.

The wireless companies have built solid businesses but need to get the network builds behind them and grow their revenue base so that they are better able to cover the large amounts of debt they carry. Further consolidation, although likely among the wireless carriers, will not improve fundamentals directly, but it will allow the wireless segment of the industry to better maintain pricing discipline. With those prospects, the wireless business seems well situated.

The long-distance business will be rocky for companies that are still carrying the cost of a national network build. WorldCom and the new Wil-Tel Communications Group have been through bankruptcy. Qwest only barely avoided it by becoming an integrated carrier. Level 3 was teetering.

With the wireless companies poised for continued growth while the long-distance business continues to search for the bottom of the pricing quicksand, it seems odd that AT&T would have let AT&T Wireless go in its third divestiture. AT&T Broadband was a boat anchor, given the prices paid for its franchises. Liberty Media was never in AT&T's plans and its chair, John Malone, was not welcome as AT&T's largest individual shareholder. Nevertheless, if AT&T had held on to the wireless business a bit longer, it could have become a welcome counter to the sliding revenue and profitability of long distance. Sprint clearly benefited from holding on to the PCS business.

The cable companies are at the biggest risk, particularly those that borrowed significant amounts of money to finance their expansion. Their debt service requires continued revenue increases. In an increasingly competitive market, this is a risky proposition. This is a particular problem if the RBOCs finally put together a competitive threat for traditional cable services. History is against the Bells' putting together such a credible threat quickly, but they are the companies best outfitted with the technical and financial skill to do it. The cable companies don't have much room to maneuver.

> *"It ain't what you don't know that gets you into trouble.*
> *It's what you know for sure that just ain't so."*
> —MARK TWAIN, AMERICAN WRITER

Outside of Sprint's two big bets, fiber-optic networks in the 1980s and PCS in the 1990s, the company took its Midwestern conservatism seriously.

Sprint was a middling performer throughout the telebomb period. Sprint's FON group stock performed well, as a diversified investment should. However, the Sprint PCS business was still looking for firm footing in the competitive wireless business.

The finances of Sprint's executives were much more aggressive, though.

Two of its top executives, William Esrey and Ronald LeMay, used tax shelters promoted by Sprint's outside auditor, Ernst & Young. The shelters were used to avoid tax on the exercise of stock options granted to the executives. The shelters depended on a controversial reading of the tax code that became a target for the IRS in its search for abusive tax avoidance techniques.

Once the use of these shelters by Esrey and LeMay became public, Sprint dismissed the executives rather than have them work with the company's auditors, whose bad advice they took. In addition to Esrey and LeMay, Ernst & Young also lost its appointment as Sprint's auditor in 2003, after having audited the company since 1966.

In an ironic twist to the corporate scandals that followed the stock bubble of the late 1990s, the same type of tax shelter that took down Esrey and LeMay was proposed to Enron executives by Enron's auditor, Arthur Andersen. However, the Enron executives turned the transaction down as being too risky.[5]

NOTES

1. Alexander Elder, *Trading for a Living* (Hoboken, NJ: Wiley, 1993), p. 82.
2. Qwest Communications International, Form 10-K405, 1999.
3. "Trends in Telephone Service," Industry Analysis Division, Wireline Competition Division, FCC, August 2003, p. 8-9.
4. Intangibles from company filings with the SEC. Intangibles include franchise fees. Total includes all of Time Warner because it doesn't report intangibles by segment.
5. "IRS Targets Tax Shelter for Stock-Options Income," *Wall Street Journal*, July 2, 2003.

CHAPTER 11

LIKELY FUTURE WINNERS AND LOSERS

The first ten chapters of *Telebomb* tell the story of what happened within the telecommunications industry during turbulent times. As the industry begins to right itself, a look into the near future is in order to assess how the industry is likely to fare. Accordingly, from this point on, the book looks forward and, thus, contains the author's conjecture.

The question of which companies will thrive and which ones face troubled futures is clearly a subjective one. While financial strength is an objective measure that can be used to assess future strength, other factors such as competitive dynamics, continued regulatory uncertainty, and technology development will also drive future changes.

Three categories of potential winners are explored:

1. *Specialized Carriers.* The general category of CLEC will morph into a group of specialized carriers that will focus on subsegments of the telecommunications market.

2. *Consumer Broadband Providers.* Although use of the Internet does not double every ninety days (if it ever did), it will still continue to grow for the foreseeable future. More use means more demand, and more demand means one thing to the vast majority of Americans: broadband.

3. *Companies That Successfully Negotiate Bankruptcy.* Reorganizing under bankruptcy protection can give a carrier a fresh start in the market. Those that take the opportunity to revise their strategy and focus on profitable markets can use the experience to their benefit.

MONOPOLY

1880
1890
1900
1910
1920
1930
1940
1950
1960
1970

DIVESTITURE

1980
1981
1982
1983
1984
1985
1986
1987

STABILITY

1988
1989
1990
1991
1992
1993
1994
1995

BOOM

1996
1997
1998
1999

BOMB

2000
2001
2002

RECOVERY?

2003
2004
2005
FUTURE

Three types of potential losers will be analyzed:

1. *Long-Distance-Only Carriers.* The long-distance business was one of the unintentional anachronisms created by the Telecommunications Act of 1996 and the telebomb. In 2004, pricing in the long-haul market was still searching for a bottom. Companies that rely mostly on this segment of the market will disappear.

2. *Overleveraged Cable Companies.* Most bankrupt companies profiled in this book went into bankruptcy because they couldn't pay the interest on their debt. Many cable companies in the industry are still carrying around too much debt. Any adverse change in the operating or lending environment within the industry will likely cause more trips to the financial fat farm.

3. *Telecommunications Equipment Providers.* The hangover from the boom will haunt this subsector of the telecommunications market for some time. Spending was at such high levels during the boom that immense amounts of equipment were bought and never put to good use. Some equipment providers are likely to recover and thrive earlier, while some have a long way to go.

There is one common thread running through all these potential winners and losers that cannot be ignored by carriers who want to join the winners and avoid being one of the losers. It is a trend toward general-purpose networks rather than networks designed for a single application, such as analog voice or video.

The bankrupt carriers and others that left the industry in recent years flooded the market with cheap telecommunications assets left over from their aborted network builds. These assets extend beyond transmission systems to fiber networks and specialized buildings and other structures. Most of the oversupplied equipment is available on the secondary markets at very low prices because the carriers that ordered the equipment want to monetize it by selling it rather than by placing it in the network to provide service to customers. This oversupply of telecommunications equipment spells trouble for the future of the equipment manufacturers.

The oversupply meant that, beginning in 2003, competing carriers could cobble together a modern network at low cost with pieces left over from the boom days. By definition, the carriers that pursue this strategy must have a network plan that is flexible enough to accommodate the available supply of used equipment and dark fiber. This leads to the newer carriers having similar networks based on the same technologies. In the modern network, that means fiber-optic networks that support the Internet proto-col. These IP-based networks are the common denominator of all future networks in the United States as well as worldwide. If an increasing number of carriers have the same type of network, purchased at low cost, and band-width is plentiful, then these new carriers will need to compete on some other basis.

LIKELY WINNERS

Along with opportunities created by cheap, leftover network assets, the sub-stantive changes wrought by the telebomb have created openings for carri-ers that can think differently about the industry.

Specialized Carriers

Historically, telecom companies chose the scope of their business to fit within one (or more) of the walled gardens defined by the FCC and the Communications Act of 1934. Now free from these bureaucratic defini-tions, carriers have more freedom to define the boundaries of what they can offer. Often in the case of new carriers, this freedom means a focus on one or a few customer segments that may not be served well by the tradi-tional incumbents in the industry. For example, existing carriers limited to specific geographic areas (for example, the RBOCs and cable companies) have a difficult time competing for business customers with locations out-side the traditional carrier's geography. For specialized carriers, the drive to a more customer-oriented scope of services generally means creating unique product features or bundles of services designed to appeal to specific customer segments. These packages are sold against the blanket offerings of the incumbents.

There are a handful of successful carriers that were able to focus on niche markets well throughout the boom and the telebomb. The successful CLECs noted in Chapters 7 and 10 are examples of companies that grew by providing services to narrow market segments. Companies such as Trinsic (consumer) and US LEC (business) built product bundles around specific customer segments and sold well into those markets. These innovative of-ferings may not have matched the product breadth of the RBOCs but met unique requirements of certain segments of the market.

Another specific example of the emergence of the specialized carrier is evident in how the former Big 3 long-distance carriers are competing in the new environment. As discussed later in this chapter, the long-distance business in the future will at best be a commodity and at worst disappear altogether. The emergence of all-you-can-call, any distance pricing plans points toward the latter case, a complete eradication of long-distance service as a separate product category. The former Big 3 reacted to this trend by becoming the top national carriers for large business customers. They are taking advantage of the RBOCs' limited geography by positioning themselves as the only carriers with truly national reach.

Still other carriers are likely to focus on the international market. With bandwidth on many transoceanic routes now as cheap as domestic routes, it is easy to see one or more new carriers (or formerly bankrupt international carriers) choosing a focus on newly globalizing companies, offering packages of services to ease the transition to multinational operations.

In an improving economy, the specialized carriers will broaden their offerings, attacking different subsegments of the market. They will grow in different directions in the search for profitable markets. In another manifestation of the trend toward more specialized carriers, the term *CLEC*, always difficult to define, will become even less meaningful when describing competitive carriers as a class.

The base transmission technology offered, even by the specialized carriers, will be similar to that of the incumbents and other competitors. The Internet (a general-purpose network) will be used increasingly as a delivery network for these new, innovative services. The difference will lie in packaging, pricing, and features of the products, not the underlying transmission technology. General-purpose networks, as discussed previously, provide the opportunity for the lowest cost, an important precursor to success in an increasingly competitive business. Without a clear advantage in network transmission technology, the successful specialized carriers will focus their investment in unique technology on areas of high impact, meaning those that provide differentiation from their competition.

The focus of the specialized carriers on cheap, existing network technology with unique overlays will parallel that of the long-distance market of the late 1980s and early 1990s. After every carrier had access to modern fiber optics, the focus of competition in the long-distance industry moved to pricing and packaging (remember MCI's Friends and Family package). In the telecommunications market of 2005, the number of competitors is still high and the economics are still undefined, but the same technology deployment rules will apply.

The biggest wild card for the trend toward specialized carriers is the inability of the FCC to set stable rules that govern the resale market.

Will the RBOCs allow the specialized carriers to take these niches without a fight? The simple technological answer is that the RBOCs can do nothing to prevent it. The more complex answer is that the incumbents actually have good reasons to stay in their current business. As shown in Chapter 10, the incumbent local carriers were the tortoises during the dot-com era compared with the dot-com hares. The incumbents won the race and can claim bragging rights (for the time being) for that accomplishment.

Because the traditional local business is so stable, it is hard to develop a culture within the RBOCs where risks are rewarded and innovation comes to the forefront. The CLECs have almost no interest in the status quo. They exist to innovate and will take bigger risks. They will take these risks in part because they have less to lose and in part because their investors are pushing for higher returns than RBOC investors. This will also have the effect of forcing the CLECs to persevere in the face of an intransigent Congress and FCC.

Also, remember that the RBOCs are not the only large incumbents. A cable company can be both the innovator and the incumbent. As innovators, they continue to develop and offer new communications services, such as cable modem and cable telephony. However, as incumbents, they must be aware that digital satellite video providers are offering more innovative services in the cable companies' traditional market of video programming.

Almost regardless of how the RBOCs decide to fight back, the impact of specialized carriers on RBOC market share will occur over a long period of time. Consider how long it has taken AT&T to lose market share. AT&T had an undifferentiated product in the consumer long-distance business for twenty years but still held 37 percent market share at the end of 2001, even in the face of mounting RBOC marketing following its long-distance entry. In addition, AT&T had no monopoly protection or natural geographic advantages.

In 1984, it was difficult to convince anyone more than forty years old that he or she needed a different phone company. For years after divestiture, many older Americans still thought of AT&T as *the* phone company and didn't differentiate it from their local RBOC. The fact that the RBOCs took the familiar bell logo with them and still use it today added to the confusion for many who were used to not caring about who provided their phone service as long as the phone continued to ring. Similarly, most Americans over forty years old in the post-telebomb era are unlikely to give up their landline phone and use a mobile phone exclusively.

DEATH KNELL FOR THE RBOCs?

Will the emergence of larger and stronger specialized carriers spell the end of the local telephony network for consumers? It is easy to construct a scenario in which it will no longer be economical to spend $1,000 to string a pair of copper wires with their constrained bandwidth into a single home. Wireless carriers can provide basic voice connectivity at a lower marginal cost. Pricing doesn't yet reflect these economics, but the trends are established.

This does not mean that the RBOCs will go away—far from it—but it does mean that they will be pushed to offer other services over their networks and/or move to different, more efficient network technologies. Moreover, a safety net is available to the RBOCs (and not the CLECs) in the form of their regulated rates for basic wholesale and retail services. The RBOCs have the ability to go to the public utility commissions in their various states and ask for increases to their regulated rates, if necessary. Competition is not yet so heavy that they have lost pricing power as completely as have the long-distance providers.

Even beyond the regulated safety nets, the incumbents' businesses have many advantages. These monopoly services provide consistent revenue and cash flow. Many of the same regulatory structures that guaranteed a return on capital invested for thirty- to forty-year periods still existed in 2004. The tremendous cash flow of the regulated local telephone business is made possible by those regulations.

Consumer Broadband Providers

Even through the dot-com bust, Internet traffic grew steadily. The companies that bet on this trend and went out of business ignored good business practices. Although it is not a law of nature that Internet traffic will continue to grow, the trend to increased usage is likely to persist for a long time.

With Internet traffic increasing and broadband available to most U.S. households, it is now a question of when, not if, broadband Internet will take over from dial-up services as the Internet access method of choice. One of the reasons for the dot-com meltdown was that the many services newly available over the Internet in the late 1990s required more bandwidth than was available to most users. Napster and other file-sharing services weren't widely used until universities made broadband Internet connections widely accessible on campuses (not just from the computer lab). Then broke teenagers had access to enough bandwidth to download all the music they wanted instead of buying the CDs.

By the end of 2003, broadband Internet access reached critical mass, being used by more than 20 percent of U.S. Internet users.[1] As more people begin using broadband, the increased bandwidth will have more uses created for it.

The idea that the Internet would become more useful as more people gained access to it was described succinctly by Robert Metcalfe, founder of 3Com Corporation. Metcalfe's Law states that the utility of a network can be expressed as the square of the number of connected users. The same principle applies not only to the mere existence of another Internet user but also the amount of bandwidth the user has. More bandwidth drives higher use and, thus, higher utility.

By 2001, the ILECs (DSL) and cable providers (cable modem) became the providers of choice for residential and small business broadband because they were the only carriers to offer reasonably priced, widely deployed broadband Internet services. They have this business locked up for the near future because no technology is on the horizon that can challenge the price points for this fully deployed technology. The problems are that DSL is unprofitable for the RBOCs, and neither technology approaches the ubiquity of dial-up Internet services—yet.

By way of historical analogy, the automobile was useful for local driving, but little else until the 1930s, when the national system of numbered routes was first introduced. This system gave drivers the ability to navigate easily between cities with little foreknowledge of the route. The U.S. route system encouraged more long-distance travel than ever before. However, it also exposed certain other weaknesses in the auto travel system in the United States, such as the lack of lodging and auto service, the lack of reliability and comfort of that generation of automobiles, and the need for a more robust national fuel distribution system.

Hotel and service station chains popped up around the country to offer a recognizable face to weary travelers looking to reduce the risk of any purchase made outside familiar territory. Holiday Inn, the first large hotel chain to focus on the auto traveler, traded on familiarity. Then, as automobiles became more reliable, the next step in the transportation network was made: the interstate highway system. This system, originally built during the 1960s and 1970s, extended the reach of the traveler from as little as a few hundred miles per day in densely populated areas to as much as a thousand miles a day for motivated travelers with more than one driver in the car.

These changes occurred over a long period of forty years. Changes in Internet usage habits will not take as long but will follow a similar pattern. Broadband Internet access is to dial-up what interstate highways are when compared to the U.S. routes. Dial-up Internet access will go the way of the U.S. routes, serving as local connectors and access methods of last resort, but enabling nothing more. Perhaps someday people will be nostalgic for AOL the way they are for old U.S. Route 66.

The second race radically lowered the price of long-distance services.

Democratizing the last piece of the telecommunications puzzle by making broadband connections available at reasonable prices is an important step for all Americans to receive the benefits of the Internet. In the United States, there are many areas of high unemployment and underemployment. Most of these areas are rural, such as the upper Midwest and Appalachia. These areas also can be characterized by rugged terrain. The terrain combined with sparse population makes the investment required for broadband access less attractive.

Broadband Internet subscribers are also candidates to buy add-on services such as telephony and high-end video services. The cable companies are in a better position to offer multiple services over their existing networks than the ILECs. Not only are the cable providers selling more cable modems than the ILECs are selling DSL, but cable modems have more potential bandwidth. Also, from a competitive standpoint, the cable companies are selling services that eat away at the RBOCs' core product (telephony) at a faster rate than the ILECs are doing the same to the cable companies' video services.

As proof of this, note that in 2003 both Comcast and Cox reported take rates on telephone service that were close to that of their cable modem services. Perhaps the RBOCs' dislike of the local resellers is a misplaced vestige of the competitive days of the late 1990s; the RBOCs should instead be looking at the cable providers more closely. Cable telephony is a greater threat to the ILECs than the resellers. At least with the resellers, the RBOCs get some revenue (from CLECs' UNE rentals) to cover their large fixed investments. Because the cable companies are essentially done with their major network upgrades, they have more bandwidth available into homes than the RBOCs and can offer new services at a lower marginal cost.

How did the cable companies come to their leadership position in broadband? The ISDN rollout of the late 1980s and the early 1990s can be blamed for the RBOCs' initial lack of enthusiasm for DSL. ISDN was supposed to be the future of telephone service. It offered multiline voice capabilities as well as dial-up data speeds many times faster than regular modems offered at the time. In a sign of the deep pockets of the ILEC industry at the time, the RBOCs collectively spent several billion dollars upgrading the electronics in the network and the operations support systems that manage the network to offer these services.

From a financial point of view, the huge capital investment in equipment and software was wasted. ISDN was only a marginal improvement from traditional analog phone lines. By the time ISDN was broadly available, regular modems were up to a third of the data speed of residential ISDN at no additional cost. ISDN's few advantages came at a high cost, and the service also came with hassles such as a long and complicated setup process and confusing, often incorrect bills. Whereas the phone companies like slow and steady growth, customers wanted more dramatic improvement in their phone service before putting up with such hassles. Potential customers stayed away in droves.

From an RBOC employee's point of view, DSL was seen as likely to cannibalize ISDN. While RBOC leadership got behind DSL in 1997, many RBOC employees didn't take DSL seriously until cable modems already had a lead. On top of many employees' lack of enthusiasm, the large bureaucracy at the Bells made the deployment of the technology cumbersome. Not only were many internal constituencies involved but also the threat of unbundling requirements made the RBOCs jump through many needless hoops to try to keep their DSL technology out of the hands of competitors. In the end, DSL services were generally offered through (yet another) separate subsidiary, resulting in additional complications.

While the FCC's inability to set the rules of the road for resale generally hurt the CLECs more than the incumbents, DSL is a case where the regulatory regime, or lack thereof, placed hurdles (like the separate subsidiary requirements) in front of the RBOCs that the cable companies didn't have. This was a contributing factor to the lag in ILEC DSL deployment, not a root cause of the competitive imbalance in and of itself.

When the FCC began tracking high-speed line penetration in 1999, there were 1 million more cable modem subscribers than DSL subscribers. At the end of 2003, that lead had grown to almost seven million lines.

More significantly, in the FCC category of advanced services lines, a higher-capacity category than high-speed lines, cable modems represented five times as many lines as DSL at the end of 2003.[2] (High-speed lines are defined as having a capability to transmit data more than 200 Kb/s in at least one direction. Advanced services lines must have 200 Kb/s capability in both directions.) In 2004, typical broadband data speed on upgraded cable networks was about four times the top DSL speeds available to consumers (3 Mb/s for cable versus 768 Kb/s for DSL).

The winner will realize that broadband is not about content. It is about getting access to all the content that is already out there. This is true for the vast majority of Internet users who don't need the Internet to be sanitized for their protection. The idea of carriers focusing on network development rather than content development is discussed in more detail in Chapter 12.

The benefit that attracted people to the Internet in the first place was that it offered access to many information services with only one network connection. Anyone who worked in an industry that could afford to be technology rich before the Internet understands that many of the services available over the Internet today were available before, but separate network connections had to be established (and paid for) as part of each service. A typical financial securities trading floor had to manage separate feeds for news, stock prices, bond prices, trade entry, and so forth. All that information is now available over one connection.

The ultimate winner of the broadband Internet access race will realize that, in this consumer market, price will eventually rule. Performance is important, but price will be the weapon used most often by new competitors. This means that providers need to be as lean as possible. The cost of content will not be sustainable for Internet access providers. Sorry, AOL. The RBOCs will have to clean up the corporate ownership and complicated processes required to build, install, and maintain DSL or, better yet, move to a different broadband technology. The cable companies need to work off their mountains of debt and get over their desire to be content companies. Their lead in Internet access is the best thing they have going for them.

Bankruptcy—The Ultimate Tax Dodge

Many companies have gone or will go through bankruptcy as a result of the telebomb and its aftermath. Billions of investor dollars have been lost at the financial fat farm. The companies that reorganized their finances have the ability to reenter the market with a new perspective and without the debt payments that saddled their old operations. Simply reorganizing under bankruptcy protection and losing debt will not guarantee success, though. The companies likely to succeed are the ones that come out with a customer base and sufficiently broad operational skills to compete in the new world of specialized telecommunications services. The companies that don't shed enough debt and the ones that never had a real business model in the first place are likely to become recidivists, returning to the fat farm or being scrapped like a 1972 Ford Pinto.

The companies that had successful operations at one time, such as MCI, are more likely to be able to stay afloat than companies such as McLeod-USA that never had a profitable operation or enough focus on one segment to make the company profitable in the long run. After Chapter 11, McLeod-USA was still unable to reach financial breakeven, much less meet its reduced debt obligations.

What is also likely is that the companies that come back from the fat farm rested and ready will alter the competitive dynamics of their corner of the industry. The reduction in required debt service will give the slimmer companies a competitive edge that will likely increase already strong downward pressure on prices. WorldCom's long-term debt accounts left bankruptcy $23 billion lighter. The interest on WorldCom's pre-bankruptcy debt amounted to more than $2 billion per year, nearly 10 percent of WorldCom's expected post-bankruptcy revenue. Taking away that interest payment leaves a lot of room for price decreases.

It is reasonable to speculate that the price reductions afforded by one company's bankruptcy may cause price wars that lead to other bankruptcies down the road. The only way out of such a price war is for a company to develop other ways to compete such as becoming a specialized carrier.

For the companies that don't successfully pass through bankruptcy, there have been willing buyers for the various assets put on the auction block. These assets are being used to build other carriers' networks. The question remains: What are those assets worth?

One characteristic of each of the groups of winners in the post-telebomb world is that they will adapt to the changes still going on in the industry and take advantage of those changes to provide better products and product packages as well as better customer service. The number of customers and the average spend per customer is not increasing at a rapid rate. The winners will be able to build market share at the expense of others in the industry. The potential losers described next are at risk of losing market share to the winners.

LIKELY FUTURE LOSERS

The telebomb created lasting changes in the landscape of the industry, both for better and for worse. The combination of unintended consequences and financial hangover from the 1990s alone has created some very large potholes in the road ahead. Participants in the industry can use the map in this section to help avoid a bumpy ride through the rest of the first decade of the twenty-first century.

Long-Distance-Only Carriers—Caught in the Act

Perhaps the biggest anachronism created by the Telecommunications Act of 1996 was the long-distance-only company. (The paging and fixed wireless businesses disappeared faster, but they were much smaller.) The death of the long-distance business is almost certainly another one of the unintended consequences of the act. In 1995, the writers of the act could not have predicted the deleterious effects of the second race. Among the second racers, only Qwest had begun its network build. But the combination of the act breaking down barriers between market segments and the second racers' immense investments combined to kill long-distance as a stand-alone business.

The Big 3 knew that the RBOCs were coming after their markets once the act was passed, but no one knew precisely how much of the market the local Bells would take away. Since the line between local and long-distance service was somewhat arbitrarily drawn in 1983 (the same distinction doesn't exist in most other countries' telecommunications markets), there were no equivalents in market development from other countries' telecommunications markets. Any estimates of RBOC market-share gains at the time were just guesses.

The combination of the second race and the entry of the RBOCs into the long-distance market made difficult going for the long-distance companies over the past few years. Couple the existing difficulties with the trend toward specialized carriers, and it is reasonable to assert that the long-distance carriers will disappear altogether as separate entities. Whereas middle-aged consumers are likely to stick with a system they know, many who remember what telephone service was like before AT&T's first divestiture are also likely to revert to the old Bell System mentality of having local and long-distance service from the same (RBOC) carrier. Younger consumers have little or no brand loyalty because they grew up with the continual marketing of mobile and long-distance services. They are used to switching carriers to get the next, best deal. That next deal is increasingly likely to bundle long-distance service in with the rest of the package.

Combine rapidly declining prices, no monopoly protection, and an increased tendency to bundle long-distance into packages, and the result is the commoditization of long-distance services. It is logical then that long distance will become part of other, integrated communications services, because it is unlikely to carry reasonable profits on its own. This is a twist on the convergence trend that was popular during the mid- to late 1990s. The former Big 3 will morph into something else. Among them, only Sprint is a diversified carrier today. As AT&T proved, the window of opportunity for carriers to milk the long-distance business for cash to invest in other businesses has already closed.

The former Big 3 long-distance carriers do have advantages, though. They have national networks, national brand recognition, and an ability to serve large corporations in their many locations better than the RBOCs or other geographically constrained companies. One niche they have explored and rejected is a full-service local offering (with local loop resold from the RBOCs) even though they became the biggest CLECs.

The long-distance resellers don't have advantages of scale like the former Big 3. Scale in this sense means customer scale; there is no more advantage to owning a large network, particularly if the network was funded with debt that is still on the carriers' balance sheet. The resellers will feel the pricing pinch and will be the first to go away. Expect a decline in their numbers for the first time since divestiture.

The second-race participants, to the extent that they don't merge with profitable businesses (Qwest) or find sugar daddies (Level 3, we thought), will be the next to go. In fact, many of them have already been through bankruptcy. Expect merger-and-acquisition activity as the market finds a bottom for the value of telecom assets and begins to drive the weaker competitors to that point.

Recent combining of voice skills and brand recognition of the Big 3 with the broadband networks of the cable companies is a combination that fits both well. The cable providers proved that telephony sells but were slow to roll it out because of their limited ability to bring in fresh investment capital. The long-distance carriers have a voice network in place and better access to fresh capital for implementation. If the combined services work out, look for merger activity in this space. The cable companies can provide the last-mile access that fixed wireless couldn't deliver.

Overleveraged Cable Companies—An Extended Hangover

Because of the debt load they carry, the cable companies are generally unable to invest. Any sustained economic slowdown or heavy investment by their competitors is likely to cause failures, particularly among the companies with already stressed books. As shown in Chapter 10, the financial practices of that segment of the industry may have been okay when everybody within his or her particular walled garden was doing it, but now that the cable companies have to compete with other companies that have better managed finances, those practices have been shown to be the risky maneuvers they are. The cable companies, particularly Comcast, were able to play the growth card well when it came to their stock prices. They continue to increase revenues but have not yet adequately addressed the problems created when they took on significant debt to make their acquisitions.

The cable companies have one significant advantage that may be their trump card in the end: They can deliver more bandwidth into homes than any current residential technology. The cable networks were expanded to offer many new services, but Internet access and telephone service are the only services that worked and provided significant new revenue as of 2004. Since the cable networks can carry telephone service into homes on their networks now, they are the only credible, landline threat to take residential telephony services completely away from the ILECs. The trick is to grow revenue and cut debt while returning to profitability.

One irony in this situation is that the RBOCs used to be the companies with the desirable high-quality network. In the early 1990s, many RBOC engineers made light of the potential of competition from the cable networks because of cable's reputation for high trouble rates and low picture quality. The cable networks were rebuilt beginning in the late 1990s with reliable fiber optics. The service reputation of the cable companies isn't much better now, but consumers are at least used to it. And now the cable companies can offer 3-Mb/s Internet access to residential users for $50 or less per month; the RBOCs cannot. Given the ability of the ILECs to compete and the trend toward wireless substitution for basic landline telephone service, it is unlikely that cable telephony will ever be the leading voice technology. However, it could reach up to 20 million customers over the next five years.

Another irony is that these same overleveraged cable companies were listed previously in this chapter as potential winners. The reality is that the cable companies are on the bubble and can go either way. Investors have much to gain with these companies but need to proceed with caution.

One of the risks that the cable companies face is that their success at selling broadband Internet connections may have armed their competition. While the cable companies look for ways to sell services that the ILECs sell today, such as telephony, companies such as Vonage are also offering telephony over broadband Internet connections (cable and DSL). This could limit the cable companies' growth in the telephony market. As is true of the RBOCs renting UNEs to CLECs, Vonage may increase demand for cable modem service (or, at least, higher-bandwidth, higher-quality service).

The ability to offer high-quality video over the Internet already exists for certain types of content. It is not hard to imagine a scenario where the RBOCs' traditional circuit-switched voice services move to packet-based networking. The cable companies' traditional video services could move to a packet-based network architecture as well. This will happen gradually, and more slowly than for voice, but cable networks have the bandwidth to make this change, unlike the ILECs, for whom the change requires significant investment.

Another wild card is the regulatory environment. While cable video regulations have been reasonably stable, the cable companies want to get into the voice business with all its built-in cross-subsidies. The federal regulation of voice services and the ultimate resolution of the differences in the tax and subsidy regulations between the Internet and the traditional network may change the attractiveness of the voice market for the cable companies as well as for any other new entrants. Regulatory uncertainty, if it persists, may cool the ardor of the cable companies to get into the voice business.

Look for the cable companies to start sacrificing video channels to add bandwidth to their Internet access services. As shown in Chapter 8, the cable companies have more local bandwidth than anyone else. As the next increment of revenue becomes harder to gain in the competitive market, the cable companies will need to make more bandwidth available to potential partners that are willing to cut the cable companies in on revenue from services that require higher bandwidth. Just as personal computers had to be replaced every two or three years in the 1990s because they needed faster chips and larger hard drives to run the next big application, the next big application on the Internet will require more bandwidth of local connections.

Since video is likely to be one of the applications that will need the additional bandwidth, it will be in the cable companies' best interest to work with video content providers to move their content over to the broadband IP network. If the cable companies miss the opportunity to move video over to their Internet networks, they risk being disintermediated entirely. In addition to the competitive advantage of keeping video on their networks, the cable companies may find that the incremental value of offering tiers of higher-bandwidth, higher-quality Internet connections is greater than the value of having the marginal video channel. How many cooking channels is the public really demanding?

In order to compete, even in their traditional markets, the cable companies will need to be open to new ways of using their immense bandwidth to structure and sell services. It may seem like they need to eat their own young to survive, and it may actually come to that if their interest payments don't decrease.

Equipment Providers—Bubble Boys

The equipment providers who supply telecommunications carriers were caught short and suffered most from the decline of telecom spending. The largest equipment providers are likely to survive if they aggressively cut costs. Lucent Technologies and Nortel Networks, the two largest providers of telecommunications transmission gear in the United States, both lost at least two-thirds of their revenue between 2000 and 2003. It is hard for any company to adjust to such a steep decrease in revenue, even if the companies stabilize between $8 billion and $10 billion in annual revenue, as Lucent and Nortel should.

Many of the smaller equipment manufacturers from the 1990s are already gone. Many others are not likely to survive in their current form. A significant number of them were only able to grow in the 1990s because of the excess capital being flung around the industry. The next generation of network technology will be deployed much more deliberately in large part because of the scars carried by the investors who lived through the tele-bomb period. Building entire new networks will be an extremely unpopular investment vehicle.

The economics of the equipment side of the industry changed permanently because of the new investment philosophies on the carrier side. Back in the monopoly days, AT&T's Bell Labs used to be the innovation engine for the entire industry (back when AT&T was, in essence, the whole industry). However, of course, Bell Labs was bankrolled by a monopoly. As the industry opened up, smaller companies became the innovation engine, as in most high-tech industries. Several of those companies are either direct descendents of the Bell System (such as Avaya, Agere, and Paradyne) or direct beneficiaries of its technology (such as Terabeam, now part of YDI Wireless). These companies became innovators and took on greater risks. Few of them, though, were prepared for the telebomb.

Chapter 9 described the steep increases and decreases that the equipment providers saw during the boom and bomb. A look into the future of the equipment sector of the industry requires discrimination between the subsegments of the equipment market. As telecommunications construction economics change yet again in the early twenty-first century, a look at the network, layer by layer, is necessary to identify which manufacturers have a chance to recover and when.

In general, the first segment of the equipment industry to rebound will be the makers of customer premises equipment. Customers still move. Broadband Internet usage is still on the rise. VoIP is becoming an accepted application on the Internet. Spending for broadband access and Internet services drives the need for more sophisticated networking in homes and offices.

As Internet use continues to increase, the size and sophistication of routers and related Internet protocol–based gear will also need to increase. The demand equipment in this sector stabilized in 2003 and should rebound once the oversupply of used equipment made available as a result of the dot-com bust is absorbed by the market.

Lower-layer transmission equipment is likely to be stalled for a longer period. A more fundamental shift is that customers are moving away from protocols such as frame relay and asynchronous transfer mode in favor of Ethernet. This will cause an adjustment as these technologies sink into the core of the network or shrink from use altogether. Ethernet for local access networks was once a poor substitute for the point-to-point, Frame Relay, and ATM networks of the major carriers. But as security technologies improve and bandwidth prices drop, Ethernet is becoming the standard for future network implementations. It is supported on virtually all cable modem and DSL installations.

The last segment of the equipment business to recover will be the makers of fiber-optic cable and the equipment used to light it. So much fiber was placed in the ground in the late 1990s that it is unlikely that any large fiber builds will take place in the next ten to twenty years. Remember that the Big 3 long-distance companies essentially stopped adding to their long-haul fiber networks *before* the second race began. They were able to increase capacity by simply upgrading their existing transmission equipment to take advantage of advances in optical networking, such as dense wave-division multiplexing.

Corning, profiled in Chapter 9, is a good example of a company that faces a slow climb out of the telebomb because its main communications product, optical fiber, will not be in high demand.

When the carriers were able to maintain some pricing discipline, they could use technology to attain a lower cost position and gradually lower prices. Once pricing discipline was lost, however, the incentive to continue the gradual implementation of new optical transmission technology was also lost. Now carriers will upgrade only when absolutely required. Most intercity routes have enough dark (unused) fiber strands in place to feed the network for many years to come.

WHERE THINGS STAND

The turmoil in the telecommunications industry is typical of recently deregulated industries. The business models of the incumbents have changed permanently. In either case, the reality is that new carriers can achieve scale more quickly through the cheap assets available on the market. Innovative carriers will be aligning with their customers rather than along traditional industry lines. The new carriers will build general-purpose networks that allow them to change more rapidly to meet the market for their services. That will cause the incumbents grief as they adjust. Nevertheless, the incumbents will adjust, because they have deep pockets, clever executives, and at least a few protected markets left (at least for the time being).

Unlike the newly deregulated airline industry of the late 1970s and early 1980s, most of the telecommunications industry incumbents are unlikely to fail for reasons other than their own fraud (see WorldCom). There are no Easterns or Braniffs in the telecommunications industry. So while bankruptcy has become all too common in the industry, the resulting cheap assets will likely be used to spawn new killer applications as the Internet develops and adapts to broadband access as the norm. The cheap assets will not be used to kill the RBOCs; most of the cheap assets are in, or come from, the long-haul market. The RBOCs (and the cable companies, for that matter) still have a lock on local, landline networks.

However, were the discarded assets bought cheaply enough? Companies that paid 10 cents on the dollar for some telecom assets are likely to find out that they paid too much.

360networks, one of the later participants in the second race, built cross-country and international fiber routes and, as most international carriers did at the time, filed bankruptcy, in June 2001. One of its fiber routes spanned the North Atlantic Ocean, running near the point of the *Andrea Gail*'s final demise as depicted in Sebastian Junger's book *The Perfect Storm* and the later movie.

As part of 360networks's bankruptcy proceedings, the $850 million North Atlantic route was purchased by investor Kenneth Peterson, Jr., for $18 million. The fiber system, operated by Peterson's firm, Hibernia Atlantic, offers service between North America and Ireland.[3] Hibernia is not yet a going concern, nor is its success guaranteed given that the route is saturated. The question is: Were the assets bought cheaply enough to weather the storm? It may come to pass that two cents on the dollar was too much to pay.

NOTES

1. Broadband usage is extrapolated from "Trends in Telephone Service," Industry Analysis and Technology Division, Wireline Competition Bureau, FCC, August 2003, pp. 2-3 and 16-3.
2. Data from "Trends in Telephone Service," Industry Analysis and Technology Division, Wireline Competition Bureau, FCC, August 2003, p. 2-3.
3. Dennis K. Berman, "Telecom Investors Envision Potential in Failed Networks," *Wall Street Journal,* August 14, 2003.

CHAPTER 12

A LOOK BACK AND A LOOK FORWARD

"Prophesy is a good line of business, but it is full of risks."
—MARK TWAIN, AMERICAN WRITER

This chapter discusses in detail several longer-term directions that the telecommunications industry can or must take to ensure that it continues to lead U.S. high-technology industries and provide investors with profitable returns. The goal of these prescriptions is to develop a fair, competitive marketplace for all carriers, current and future. In that environment, all carriers would be free to use their best technology and abilities to serve customers in all segments and to generate healthy revenues.

Before we gaze too deeply into the crystal ball, though, it is worth a look at the single biggest influence of the past twenty years to see how it changed the market, for better and for worse.

Long after the dot-com boom, the Telecommunications Act of 1996 should be remembered as one of the main contributory events that opened the investment sluices and flooded the market with bandwidth; capital; new entrants; and ultimately, more than one hundred bankruptcies. The Telecommunications Act enabled the creation of business plans containing limitless wealth. By throwing the market open to all competitors, an industry with already large revenues and potential for much more became accessible to anyone with a new idea and investment capital. The act gave legitimacy to business plans that otherwise would not have seen the light of day. The changes in the industry, and thus the business plans, were government sanctioned, it seemed. It was, officially, a wide-open market and the FCC would

	Year
	1880
	1890
	1900
	1910
	1920
MONOPOLY	1930
	1940
	1950
	1960
	1970
	1980
	1981
	1982
	1983
DIVESTITURE	1984
	1985
	1986
	1987
	1988
	1989
	1990
STABILITY	1991
	1992
	1993
	1994
	1995
	1996
	1997
BOOM	1998
	1999
	2000
BOMB	2001
	2002
	2003
RECOVERY?	2004
	2005

FUTURE

ensure that competitors were given every advantage. That was the logic at the time but, of course, it didn't work out exactly that way.

Congress left most of the important decisions and implementation details regarding the Telecommunications Act to the FCC and gave the agency wide latitude to determine the best course. In granting the FCC freedom to interpret the intent of the act, Congress also left the public (that is, telco lawyers) wide room to interpret as well. Every advantage granted by the FCC to one part of the industry was litigated by another. Delays in implementing the new rules almost always favored the incumbents. Even if the rules were neutral, the incumbents had steady cash flow to fund their businesses. The competitors had only a short window of opportunity to get their businesses up and running before their investment capital ran out. And after the market peak in 2000, there was no going back to the well for more capital. Justice delayed, in fact, meant death for the less well-capitalized new entrants.

Although Congress wanted the markets to decide who the winners and losers would be, in many ways, the survivors were the ones with resources to move the fight to the judicial branch. It is unknown how many of the 133,000 net jobs added to the industry since 1996 are attorneys.

It is likely that the Internet would have changed things on its own or, more likely, caused a later telecom act if the Telecommunications Act had not happened. However, the changes in the telecommunications end of the Internet industry would have come about more slowly. For example, among the second racers, Qwest was the only one that committed to a national build before the act became law. WilTel could have built at a more measured pace. Moreover, Level 3 might not have happened at all.

WAS THE TELECOMMUNICATIONS ACT OF 1996 A SUCCESS?

Based on the subtitle of the Telecommunications Act, the goals of the bill were to:

- Promote competition
- Reduce regulation
- Reduce prices
- Increase service quality
- Encourage rapid deployment of new technology

At this point, with a few years of experience seeing the act's effect on the marketplace, the author's opinion of its effectiveness on each goal is as follows:

Promote Competition—Grade: B

Hundreds of new entrants came into the market and changed the competitive landscape. Although many of them left the market almost as quickly as they arrived, the CLEC market is alive and taking retail market share from the ILECs. If the market settles down to a dozen or so regional-to-national carriers providing a variety of services in competition with the traditional incumbents, the competitive goals of the act can be considered a success.

In this competitive environment, though, only the cable companies and CLECs serving certain business districts are actually building networks to compete with the RBOCs. The rest of the competition isn't building new networks to offer services; it is renting the lines of the local ILEC or using an existing broadband Internet connection. Less than a quarter of the CLEC lines in service at the end of 2003 were provisioned entirely on CLEC-owned facilities. If the act had set off investment in new network technologies, facilities-based competition would have followed. So far, it hasn't.

The effects of the telebomb are not the only reason that investment in the competitive carrier space is down. Investment has also been affected by the fact that there is no stable regulation that can be depended on to give an investor assurances that at least the competitive rules of the road will remain the same for a reasonable period of time. As stated before, the act was too vague to be of use by the FCC, which means that potential competing carriers had to guess what the rules would look like in the end. Guessing wrong often led to failure. That is too high a price for a business and its employees to pay for the inconclusiveness of the FCC.

Reduce Regulation—Grade: B

The Telecommunications Act was effective at breaking down the regulatory boundaries that defined the walled gardens within the industry. It opened the existing telecommunications market segments to all comers. More prevalent than new competitors, though, were existing companies from one segment of the industry that began to compete in other industry segments. The fact that the former Big 3 long-distance companies became the biggest CLECs is evidence that the newly opened markets were more easily attacked by carriers in adjacent segments of the industry than by start-ups or companies from other industries.

The euphoria of the late 1990s has subsided, but the rules governing competition are still undefined, and the traditional segments are still defended by capable competitors. The old boundaries are gone, and the new boundaries created by competitors in the market are not stable because the FCC and the federal courts keep playing tennis with the FCC's rules. This has happened in part because the rules resulting from the Telecommunications Act are too undefined to be of value in structuring any new business. This will have the long-term effect of restricting capital flows to green field entrants (companies entering the market for the first time). But the goal, as stated in the act, was to reduce regulation, not to build it back where necessary to promote long-term growth.

One of the chief reasons that little new technology was deployed during the boom to compete with the RBOCs was that no network architecture could be counted on to last through the next regulatory pronouncement or its court challenges. The FCC's inability to define a stable set of UNEs and the rules governing their provisioning and maintenance has created unnecessary uncertainty in the market. Ever-changing regulation is just as bad as poor regulation.

New investment in transmission technology is generally depreciated over three to ten years. If the regulatory environment is likely to have a material adverse change within that time period, large capital expenditures are likely to be challenged by investors and, potentially, not made.

Stability can be attained should the FCC ever complete a set of UNE rules that will pass judicial muster. This is an extremely difficult task given the vagueness of the act, but it must happen if a level playing field is to be created. Fortunately, if a set of rules can be defined—and allowed to stand—that list is likely to be around for a while. Only a list that stays in place for at least five years can be depended on so that companies can invest with some assurance that any advantage they gain will not be regulated away.

Reduce Prices—Grade: C

The opening of the long-distance market to the RBOCs was supposed to increase competition and bring prices down in that market. In fact, the second race did more to reduce prices than anything the FCC or Congress did. The second race began before the Telecommunications Act was passed; it was just spun into the stratosphere by the act and the dot-com mania. In fact, it is not hard to construct scenarios whereby if the RBOCs had gained long-distance permission earlier they could have financed more competitive builds leading to even more destructive competition.

Outside long distance, prices became more competitive in all markets, whether or not the Telecommunications Act addressed them. In the local market, competition took longer to take root, but the existence of multiple companies offering similarly priced packages to local subscribers indicates that competitive pricing is now at work, even if the underlying regulatory work and network economics are still in turmoil. Another move that has helped consumers is the move to all-in-one packages of local services, thus avoiding many of the myriad pricing elements that exist for all aspects of local service. Easier to understand bills are of value to consumers.

When the federal courts defeated the FCC's UNE pricing rules in early 2004, though, this grade dropped from *B* to *C*. Not only has the FCC been unable to put forth stable rules but the pricing methodology that was most favorable to the competitors was not supportable in the face of the legal muscle that the RBOCs could muster.

Increase Service Quality—Grade: C

Service quality, as perceived by the customer, has two components. First, does the service work? Second, when it doesn't work, is it fixed quickly and competently?

Does service work any better today than it did before the act was passed? Most of the investment in the marketplace has been put toward building new services and networks rather than making old ones work more reliably. The U.S. telephone network in the days of the ubiquitous Bell System was considered to be gold plated—that is, it had very high reliability. After AT&T's first divestiture, some of the plating wore off the telephone network as the companies found their new footing in a more competitive industry, but the reliability of the network was improved through implementation of new technologies such as fiber optics. With no new technologies in the immediate future for the network, and competition driving costs out of the business, it is hard to see the network becoming more reliable. On the other hand, competition will punish carriers that don't meet minimum standards.

For the second part of the service quality equation, competition caused the carriers to focus on customer issues more than ever before. The start-ups felt bumps in the road but spurred all in the industry to try harder. Based on perceived experience with old and new carriers, the industry still has a way to go. However, perception of increased utility through the roll-out of new services and choices among existing service providers will increase customers' perception of control and, thus, satisfaction.

Encourage Rapid Deployment of New Technology—Grade: F

Most people have the same number of wires entering their home now as they did ten years ago. Some have fewer, having disconnected a second phone line in favor of broadband Internet access that comes in over the same connection as cable TV. Many now have wireless phones, some even using them in place of a landline phone. But the Telecommunications Act was essentially silent on the mobile industry. The digital conversion of the network had already begun before the act was passed.

No lasting technological developments were introduced or deployed at any scale as a result of the act. Because of that fact, it is fair to claim that this book is as much about the use of business strategy and finance to compete for customers and capital investment as it is about technology, even though the telecommunications industry is one of the most technology-intense industries in our economy. The determiners of success, particularly after the capital spigot was closed in 2000, were business decisions and the ability to implement them, not who had the best technology.

The CLECs that compete with the former monopoly carriers use the same technology (in fact the exact same lines) that the ILECs use. The cable companies that compete with the ILECs use technology that, while highly refined over the past ten years, bears a strong resemblance to the architecture that was in place at the birth of community-access television systems in the late 1940s.

In discussing the impact of the act on technology deployment, it is important to differentiate between transmission technology and the services, or applications, that are accessed using the network. Internet connections apply telecommunications transmission technology to connect the user to the World Wide Web. Once connected, the user can view Web sites, purchase goods, complete financial transactions, and so forth. What users do once they are connected to the Web is partake of available services provided by organizations separate from the Internet connectivity provider. And what users do on the Internet has almost nothing to do with who provides the network connection beyond the constraints set by the connection speed.

The great power of the Internet is its ability to use one connection, regardless of who provides it, to gain access to many services. In the old, pre-Internet days, each service generally needed a separate network connection. To get video programming, a user needed to pay for connection to a cable provider. To get access to the public switched telephone network, a user had to rent a telephone line (or take a roll of coins to a pay phone).

But increasingly, voice and video are just applications that ride on the network. We are used to thinking of voice services and the telephone network as one and the same. However, this perception has been changing ever since long-distance services were made competitive. With competitive long-distance service, one local phone connection could connect a subscriber to any of hundreds of long-distance service providers (including the "I Don't Care" long-distance service described in Chapter 1).

The pulling apart of voice services from the network has taken another step forward through creation of the CLECs. Now local voice services can be provided by a separate company. In the case of Internet telephony, the user doesn't even need the traditional phone company to provide the physical connection anymore.

The technology used to create services on the Web has changed significantly since the Telecommunications Act was passed, but Internet services were, in general, neither helped nor limited by the act. Outside of two particular services available over the Internet (voice and video), such services (which exploded in both number and variety over the last decade) are not within the jurisdiction of the FCC at all. The Telecommunications Act created no lasting deployment of new transmission systems technology, or pipes, used to connect people to their network of choice.

Final Grade

What was easy to tear down was torn down. The walls separating local, long-distance, and cable fell, but no coherent, stable regulation has replaced them. The FCC was given so little to work with that it is unable to make major regulatory decisions without facing massive litigation. The UNE orders alone caused more money to be spent on legal fees than the cost of bringing modern fiber-to-the-premises network technology to a midsized city. The act contained too many blanks to be filled in later. The many competitors in the industry each had their own ideas on how to fill in the blanks and litigated any proposed FCC rules they didn't like. The letter of the act could support many different interpretations of any given passage.

The federal government's regulation of the telecommunications industry gets a 2.0 GPA, or a C. In the end, the biggest impact of Congress on the industry was not a result of what it did but, rather, a result of what it did not do.

LONG-TERM PRESCRIPTIONS FOR THE INDUSTRY

The telecommunications industry isn't going to get much help from Washington. The individual state public utility commissions will continue to bear the burden of making sure that phones still ring and consumers aren't abused. State regulators are not only closer to the details of the situation, but the states and their localities have billions of dollars in tax revenue at stake in the outcome of the regulatory morass that the federal government has created.

Without effective adult supervision from the FCC, what actions can carriers and regulators take to make themselves and the industry healthy? Some fundamental shifts are in process within the industry; recognizing those changes and being prepared to take advantage of them are the first steps.

Being aware of the trends can also help users of telecommunications services choose the right carriers and services. Many customers faced disruptions during the telebomb, particularly when one of the many new carriers went out of business. Understanding the long-term needs of the industry gives prospective buyers another yardstick to measure a potential supplier to see if the potential supplier is headed in the right direction. Likewise, investors can avoid a carrier's stock if the company is not preparing for the coming competitive environment while it takes care of today's customers.

Now that the investment cycle in the telecommunications industry has come full circle, it is time to look at the lessons we can learn from both the boom and the telebomb. The following three long-term ideas are based on the author's attempt to learn the lessons of history and apply them to likely future scenarios. The prescriptions are as follows:

1. *Content vs. Pipes.* The telecommunications industry is littered with the failures of ventures that tried to marry content (data, video, etc.) with the networks that deliver the content. The Internet ended the purpose-built network business for the last time. It's time for the rest of the industry to focus instead on building the best networks they can.

2. *Efficient Wholesaler.* The RBOCs, like AT&T in the mid-1980s, were dragged into the competitive arena. They spent eight years developing their support of the CLECs to the point where they could all win approval to offer long distance. However, in this competitive environment, the CLECs should be considered another customer that brings revenue to help cover the high fixed cost of the network.

3. *Regulatory Reform.* Access rules need to be changed. Interconnect rules need to be set and stable. Moreover, the USF needs to be overhauled, starting with a new definition of universal service.

Content vs. Pipes

The Telecommunications Act gave no help supporting new telecommunications technologies even though the services available over the Internet were proliferating at an amazing rate. In fact, an argument can be made that the services proliferated *because* there was little federal regulation. (Any effort to place taxes on the Internet should be seriously scrutinized as to how it would affect the growth engine that the Internet has become.)

The creation of services (*content* as it is known in the industry) is a very different business from building and maintaining networks. Content is creative (right brain); networks are technical (left brain).

The two businesses, content and network, are typically found in separate companies because the scale and investment decisions required to be successful in these businesses are so different. Much was made of the possibilities of joining content and networks during the dot-com boom. These pronouncements were made without understanding the power of the Internet to disintermediate content distributors. Disintermediation happens when links fall out of a value (or distribution) chain. When a manufacturer sells goods directly to consumers over the Internet instead of relying on retailers, the retailers have been cut out of the distribution chain, or disintermediated. Many poor business decisions were made based on the mistaken idea that having content and network under one corporate umbrella would generate synergies. The Excite/@Home and AOL/Time Warner mergers were examples. So were the video content ventures sponsored by the ILECs: TeleTV and Americast.

The pipe providers (cable, ILEC, and facilities-based CLECs) must realize that the fundamental defensible position they have in the industry is to provide the best pipes they can and let the content developers drive demand for increasing bandwidth (more pipe). For sure, content uses features that are provided by the network and always "ride on top of" the transport pipes in that they can only go where the network reaches. Nevertheless, supporting content and creating content are two different businesses.

The separation advocated here between content and pipes is that carriers are wasting their time if they try to gain value from an environment (content creation) they know nothing about. If a carrier provides value-added features like decreased latency or guaranteed quality of service, features that are only possible if the network provides them, then the carrier should be compensated for that above normal use of its resources. But for any carrier to claim that it understands a content creator's material well enough to charge differentially based on what is in one data packet versus another is folly. Carriers have neither the knowledge of the content business to make such a judgment nor the ability to waste time and money in today's competitive environment trying such a scheme.

If services such as telemedicine are ever going to take off, the users of the telemedicine services will have to be sure that the privacy of the network is guaranteed. If the carriers are opening individual packets of data to look for valuable content, that network will not be seen as secure. Telemedicine, like telecommuting, was made possible by cheap transport and broadband access. Telemedicine had an additional requirement, which was the availability of low-cost software to securely transmit, store, and retrieve medical images and other information. That software was beginning to hit the market in 2004, pushed forward by new medical information security requirements that made physical records a security risk. Look for many more telemedicine applications to be launched throughout the first decade of the twenty-first century.

The ILECs have an additional defensible position that is now or will soon be decoupled from their networks: voice telephony. Voice as an application is being freed from the purpose-built pipes of the ILEC network, which creates great opportunities for those who are good at voice. However, voice is also a different sort of application from most services, because of the interconnectedness required to make it work. Another way to look at this is to apply Metcalfe's Law to the voice network. The utility of the network is measurable by the number of voice customers it supports. The ILECs still counted 151,837,752 voice lines at the end of 2003.

The cable companies' traditional service, video content delivery, will change like the RBOCs' voice service. Metcalfe's Law doesn't apply to traditional cable service. The Internet is not yet robust enough to carry quantities of video, but it is only a matter of time before it is capable of delivering high-quality, long-form (half- to two-hour) programs. The cable companies are caught square in the middle of what is known as the innovator's dilemma.[1] They are trying to roll out higher-value digital video services that have high margins but ever lower take rates among subscribers. Meanwhile, more and more video content is available over the Internet. Internet video is still a poor substitute for high-definition television, but the price is generally right.

However, the cable companies will still have their broadband pipes into tens of millions of homes across America. The bandwidth advantage that they have, for now, is their most lasting advantage. Better to sell based on that advantage than sit on the traditional cable video service too long.

Efficient Wholesaler

In the 1990s, the RBOCs spent billions of dollars upgrading their networks' capacity to add second lines for Internet access. These assets produced revenue for up to ten years, but they are now dead weight because the extra capacity was primarily copper (not upgradeable fiber), which is becoming an anachronism. Copper network facilities are designed (technically and financially) to last thirty to forty years. If part of the network stops producing revenue now, the RBOC will still have three-fourths of its useful life left to depreciate. If the assets become truly stranded, they will have to be written off.

The RBOCs also face the innovator's dilemma, sticking to what they know and losing market share to newly developed products. Twenty percent of the households in the United States have broadband Internet access. More than half of the individuals in the United States have cell phones. Both of these technologies have the potential to substitute for traditional telephony.

To avoid letting the business melt away, the incumbent connectivity providers must stake out territory they can defend while making sure they make the most of their legacy businesses. This means building an access network that can be used for any application, anytime (even anywhere). The Internet, at its heart a collection of interconnected general-purpose networks, is the transport network of the future.

Efficient wholesaler means that the combination of low cost and adequate service offered by a carrier should be strong enough that every company that offers services over that network will be in a low cost position and will be able to add its own services on top to create a value proposition to its customers. Lowest cost means both lowest total cost and lowest marginal cost. The carriers should also look at what low cost means from the perspective of the CLECs and other service and content developers. Low cost is not just about rental rates for UNEs but the whole picture of what it costs to provide a service. What services can the ILECs (or cable companies) provide that lowers the CLECs' cost?

Voice is just another application that can ride on about any modern (that is, broadband) network. But voice still produces plenty of revenue. The data network is the transport network of the future for all applications: voice, data, images, and video. The old voice-only revenue models will fade away (again over a long period of time).

It is a given that more voice and data traffic will move to wireless networks. But wireless networks, particularly for data, will not replace wireline networks in any now-foreseeable scenario. Wireline networks are here to stay. Because of the investment and scale required, the battle for wireline connectivity to consumers will come down to two carriers: a cable company and a phone company. Even with tsunamis of investment capital flowing into the industry between 1996 and 2000, no technology was able to supplant the cable and phone providers in last-mile physical access to the majority of the homes in the United States.

Competition will be for providing services that customers demand once they have connectivity. No one else will pay to build pipes into all of the homes in America. (Connectivity to businesses is a different situation and is likely to stay competitive for both physical connectivity and services.)

It used to be a conundrum for consumers: When is there enough value in the collected applications on the network that it is worth paying to connect? That argument was solved by the Internet. Now, with one connection, a consumer can get access to many applications. The connection, or pipe, to the Internet has value. Once that bridge has been crossed, and it has for virtually all Americans, then the battle to sell services that ride over those connections can begin. The move to broadband will only send the change into hyperspace.

Providing services (other than voice) over the Internet will be done by content owners and creative media outlets. The margins available to content aggregators will be minimal. Money is there to be made by providing connectivity. It is the surest bet in making money from the Internet.

Embracing the CLECs

> *"To know your enemy, you must become your enemy.*
> *Keep your friends close and your enemies closer."*
> —SUN TZU, ANCIENT CHINESE GENERAL, FROM *THE ART OF WAR*

To win the battle for local connectivity, a carrier (cable, ILEC, and business bandwidth providers) must have the best, lowest-cost platform to deliver services to the home. The network must be built to handle the next new application that someone else creates to be delivered over the Internet. It has to have the fastest, broadest bandwidth, most congestion-free pipes available.

Until that time, the cable companies need to pay down their debt, and the phone companies need to make sure that their stranded asset problem doesn't become an epidemic. This means that anyone, including a CLEC, who wants to rent facilities should be welcome. The RBOCs have already made the infrastructure investments required to bring the CLECs along, so the marginal cost of having a CLEC on board is no more than any other type of customer. If a CLEC can persuade a customer not to untether with a feature or price plan that puts it on a UNE loop, then that keeps the revenue flowing and feeds the bear for a little while longer while the RBOCs put together a competitive network architecture. If the RBOCs don't provide the right services for the CLECs, the revenue-hungry cable companies just might. The defeat of the FCC's pricing rules for UNEs may turn out to be a hollow victory for the RBOCs if, by increasing wholesale prices, the RBOCs drive the CLECs away, exacerbating the RBOCs' stranded asset problems.

Can This Change Be Made?

If you take nothing else away from this book, remember that size matters. Moreover, the RBOCs are bigger than anyone else in the industry. There was a time when AT&T, and even Lucent (after the second divestiture of AT&T) by itself, claimed the scale of the RBOCs, but those days are past. The RBOCs have the resources to mount a change campaign of this magnitude. Unfortunately, they also have a history of short attention spans when it comes to new technology deployment.

The RBOCs need to learn two lessons from AT&T's history. The first is how to best manage down from 100 percent market share, as AT&T did quite successfully in the 1980s and 1990s. AT&T was the leader of the oligopoly and set the tone for the consistent managing down of prices over time. Then the second race ended the opportunity for leadership as the scramble to find revenue at any cost began.

The second lesson for the RBOCs to learn from AT&T is how *not* to invest in their future. AT&T took on immense amounts of debt while overpaying for the properties that became the AT&T Broadband cable network in the late 1990s. It depended on cash from the long-distance business to fund the expansion. Once the second race happened, there was no cash lying around to invest in cable networks, and the new vision of AT&T once again being the all-things-to-all-people phone company was unraveled at great expense to AT&T shareholders.

The RBOCs have a fast-closing window of opportunity to invest in the technology that will allow them to offer a broad range of services without expensive installation processes. DSL is not the model to follow because it is a money loser, the technology capabilities are too limited, and the processes required to operate it are too cumbersome. This is not a technology question but a business question: What network architecture will support the broadest range of services and offer the best ability to compete with the cable companies? It's a good bet that the answer has more fiber than copper in it.

If the RBOCs don't learn the lessons of history and make a bold move to rebuild their network, they may follow the passenger railroads of the 1940s and 1950s, sliding into oblivion, only to be rescued by a federal bailout program. Amtrak is one of the best ways to travel in the Northeast Corridor of the United States, but it is a heavily subsidized business that doesn't pay dividends to its shareholders.

The cable companies have already done the network build to provide additional bandwidth to support new services. However, they haven't shown any interest in accommodating new services by providing features that make the applications work better. Cable is vulnerable until it pays down its heavy debt load. To keep their companies alive, the cable companies need continuing revenue increases. The RBOCs can compete well with the cable companies by beating them to their next source of increased revenue.

Regulatory Reform

In addition to developing regulations that can withstand a judicial challenge, there are several specific items that need to be on the agenda of regulators when changes to the Telecommunications Act of 1996 are contemplated.

Access and Interconnect Reform

Access rates are higher-than-normal interconnect fees paid on interexchange traffic. Originally, access rates were designed to replace the subsidies paid by AT&T's Long Lines department to help keep basic local service affordable. One of the contributing factors to the demise of the long-distance-only carrier is that if regulations are left unchanged the long-distance carriers are likely to be the only ones left paying these rates. Said another way, if long-distance carriers are disadvantaged in the marketplace, why would any new carrier claim to be one? In the end, the access rate structures are anachronisms, just like the long-distance-only carriers.

Immediately after the divestiture of the RBOCs from AT&T, access charges amounted to about 50 cents for every dollar of revenue brought in by the long-distance companies. This percentage steadily declined to less than 30 percent before increasing as a result of falling retail prices for long-distance service. It is time to finish the job and junk the access rate structures for a more market-based interconnect system. This means that long-distance carriers shouldn't pay to both originate and terminate traffic.

It made economic sense to skim a percentage from long-distance traffic when even light users of the phone network spent more on long-distance service than local. Now that long-distance pricing seems to have no floor and local rates are relatively constant, it no longer makes sense to try to use access rates to fund the local network.

Many of the direct burdens of universal service were shifted to the consumer through higher subscriber line charges and other regulatory fees added to phone bills. Consumers in high-cost areas are likely to bear even more of the burden if states ever decide to de-average telephone rates.

Much was made during the WorldCom bankruptcy case about World-Com's attempts to move its traffic into lower-rate categories (onto the low-cost Internet) to avoid access charges. Elaborate schemes designed to circumvent the access pricing regime are as old as the competitive long-distance industry because the difference between access rates and any comparative, competitively priced service is so great as to invite the application of dollars and smart minds to see how the rates can be circumvented. This is the same company, after all, that hired the engineers who figured out that Americans couldn't spell the word *operator*.

Voice is now available over the traditional phone network; over the cable network; from a few facilities-based CLECs; and from a group of new companies such as Vonage, the stealth CLEC. With that much competition, voice is a commodity and likely will stay that way.

If voice service is (1) an application on the network and (2) a commodity, then basing interconnect rules on old access rates is inefficient. It is, in effect, a two-tiered system. And, in a competitive market, a two-tiered system isn't fair. It creates the wrong incentives when different carriers have to pay different interconnection rates based on outdated regulatory mechanisms left over from a voice-only world. Congress and the FCC must decide: Do they want an open, competitive market, or do they want regulated access rates like those that existed in the Bell System? We can't have both.

Bill and Keep

There are several viable alternatives to the current voice interconnect regimes. The one that is most attractive in a freely competitive market is modeled after the peering system in the Internet. The network interconnection points for Internet providers are called peering points. Where Internet carriers are of equal or near-equal size, they split the cost of interconnecting and use a "bill and keep" methodology, which is a recognition that the relative costs of the traffic being traded at the interconnect point are roughly the same. Therefore, it is not worth the cost of negotiating, measuring, billing, and collecting settlement charges. The two networks are connected, and the traffic flows. It is the equivalent of toll-free interstate highway interchanges. Where the carriers do not exchange equal amounts of traffic, charges are assessed based on gross traffic measurements, not on individual packets of data. These charges are negotiated in the free market.

The current access rate system is the near equivalent of a driver (in this case, the interconnecting carrier) having the choice of a toll highway (ILEC network) or a free highway (the Internet) that goes to all of the same places with the same speed limits and other characteristics. What the interconnect system needs is the ability for the free market to set the tolls through bilateral negotiation (as with peering arrangements) rather than an arbitrary toll. Of course, if highway tolls were actually assessed based on the quality of the service provided, the Pennsylvania Turnpike would be free. Drivers would get money back if they used the Breezewood interchange.

VoIP, the main challenger to the old voice network, is undoing one hundred years of voice-focused regulation. VoIP will have a bigger effect on the industry than the Telecommunications Act because it is happening whether or not the regulators get it right. Regulatory regimes move more slowly than markets or entrepreneurs. The proper role for the FCC is to set minimum and maximum charges for the interconnecting carriers to protect new entrants, with a bias toward bill and keep. Like the Federal Reserve Bank that moves interest rates to keep inflation and growth balanced in our economy, the FCC can perform a similar role in encouraging competition in certain geographic or otherwise-defined market segments by changing interconnect rules and rates with more latitude than it does now. To implement such a system would require much stronger legislation by Congress, strong enough to withstand the firestorm of litigation that would surely follow.

The result of how Congress and the FCC addresses these needed items will help set the course for the industry going forward. What is also likely, given the history of regulations since the Telecommunications Act was first implemented, is that the FCC will do nothing. Or take baby steps when the industry needs bold action.

Universal Service

Changes to the access pricing regime and other federal regulations must be done in concert with reform of the universal service mechanisms so that underserved populations aren't left out. The definition of universal service must be made flexible so that it can change over time as the amount of bandwidth available to or required by consumers increases.

One of the fundamental difficulties in regulating the telecommunications industry is the desire to have both competition and universal service. They can coexist, but the pressure of a competitive market has the potential to leave those stuck with the bill for universal service in a poor position vis-à-vis their competitors. Any change to access rates has to make sure that universal service, particularly as that concept expands to provide for Internet access, doesn't suffer.

There is nothing preventing carriers wishing to interconnect or purchase UNEs from paying a slightly higher rate to support universal service. Any increase in rates for this should be minimal, though, not the general support program that it is today unless it is focused on a national broadband policy that will prevent the digital divide from becoming a larger social issue.

A better solution, though, would be to scrap the myriad fees that are now charged under such names as Universal Service Fund Contribution, Federal Subscriber Line Charge, and the ever so generically titled Network Access Fee. A simple, straightforward percentage tax on telecommunications revenue (either at the corporate level or directly on consumer bills) makes more sense than per-minute and per-line charges in a changing environment where charges are no longer always assessed on a per-line or per-minute basis. This new regime would be charged on all network connectivity charges and related feature charges. It is the equivalent of a flat tax that affects those who buy services, regardless of how they used to be charged during the days of the Bell System. A modern taxation system for a modern network. Now if we can only get the UNE rules to be so simple.

FINAL WORDS

"That which does not kill us makes us stronger."
—FRIEDRICH NIETZSCHE, GERMAN PHILOSOPHER

The telecommunications network has changed in many ways since the divestiture of the RBOCs from AT&T in 1984. The intervening twenty-plus years have seen the RBOCs rise from being the Baby Bells to being larger individually than their former parent. The mobile phone has become as important as the landline phone to many people. Moreover, the Internet has survived the hype of the late 1990s to be the delivery method of choice for all manner of information services.

The companies that make up the industry have been through many gut-wrenching changes, particularly since the dot-com bubble burst. Those changes caused dislocation of customers, employees, and investors, the people who make the industry run. In the end, though, those still employed and invested in the industry can feel a true sense of accomplishment at surviving a set of bewildering markets. At the time, the capital markets were rewarding the most outlandish business plans, including those of companies that had no operational history and yet claimed they could be Bell beaters. Customers were just chasing lower prices; they expected the services to work and they often didn't. Those customers, once bitten, deserve to be twice shy, even as they are approached by the more stable, post-telebomb, carriers.

The investment cycle has come full circle, but the industry shakeout may not have. The increase in number and variety of services offered by carriers will challenge the existing local network providers. It will also increase demand and make more opportunities for competitors to enter. Competition will only increase as the former residents of the walled gardens make bolder forays into the other previously protected gardens.

Widely deployed broadband Internet connections will also cause new applications to be developed inexpensively and deployed for public consumption. One potential future model for the industry can be akin to the relationship between personal computer makers and software developers that existed for twenty years starting in the early 1980s. Every few months (right on schedule with Moore's Law), new and faster computers would hit the market. New software would then appear that used all the new horsepower and begged for more. We may soon be in a world where bandwidth can drive the relationship.

The winners of the broadband race will reap the benefits of having enabled a whole new generation of social and economic gains for the United States.

NOTE

1. Clayton M. Christensen, *The Innovator's Dilemma* (Cambridge: Harvard University Press, 1997).

APPENDIX A

GLOSSARY AND ACRONYM LIST

access circuits
Specific to the discussion in *Telebomb* about access pricing, access circuits are purchased by interexchange carriers to interconnect their networks with the ILECs. The fees carried by these circuits were originally set artificially high to subsidize local service.

ADSL
Asymmetric digital subscriber line (see DSL). One technology used by ILECs to deliver high-speed Internet connections to residential and small-business users. ADSL offers high download speed to the user and slower upload speed. Asymmetric services are best for residential use where more information is coming into the home (such as Web browsing) than is going to the Internet from the home.

AT&T
American Telephone and Telegraph Co., originally American Bell Telephone. The holding company for the Bell System companies. The subsidiaries and operating companies mentioned in *Telebomb*:
- AT&T Long Lines—The name for the division of AT&T that offered long-distance service before the first divestiture.
- AT&T Network Systems—Equipment manufacturing arm of AT&T, formerly Western Electric. Later to be named Lucent Technologies when it was spun out of AT&T in the second divestiture (1996).
- AT&T Global Information Systems—Originally (and later) called NCR. Purchased by AT&T in 1991 and spun out in the second divestiture (1996).

- AT&T Broadband—The company that held all of the cable properties bought between 1998 and 2000. Spun out to Comcast in the third divestiture.
- AT&T Wireless—The company that held McCaw Cellular and AT&T's other wireless properties, including PCS spectrum and the Project Angel technology discussed in Chapter 6. Also spun out in the third divestiture.
- The Bell Operating Companies. (See RBOC.)

BOC	See RBOC.
broadband access	Internet access at speeds faster than dial-up connections can offer. The FCC has defined two classes of broadband access. High-speed services offer at least 200 Kb/s of bandwidth in at least one direction (upload or download). Advanced services offer at least 200 Kb/s in both the upload and download directions.
CAP	Competitive access provider. Facilities-based local carriers generally used by long-distance carriers to bypass the ILEC networks and lower access charges.
CATV	Community access television. Commonly known as cable TV. Started in the late 1940s when people in rural areas were left out of the new television craze that was sweeping the country. Early CATV systems were no more than a powerful antenna designed to pull in television signals from distant cities and send the signals into individual homes using coaxial cable.
CLEC	Competitive (or competing) local exchange carrier. Any carrier that competes against an ILEC in a given area. Some carriers are both ILECs and CLECs. For example, Sprint offers local service as an ILEC to about 8 million local telephone lines in the United States. Outside its traditional ILEC territory it offers CLEC services both over facilities it owns and through the resale of RBOC facilities. (See DLEC.)
CMRS	Commercial mobile radio service. More general term for wireless service, includes CRS and PCS.

colocation	The ability for a CLEC to move its interconnection equipment into a Bell central office (network hub).
convergence	Theory, promoted heavily by the cable companies in the early 1990s, that many services could be offered over one network connection.
CRS	Commercial radiotelephone service. "Licensees use cellular radiotelephone service (commonly referred to as cellular) spectrum to provide a mobile telecommunications service for hire to the general public using cellular systems. Cellular licensees may operate using either analog or digital networks, or both. Cellular licensees that operate digital networks may also offer advanced two-way data services. The Commission and other wireless industry representatives often refer to these services as 'Mobile Telephone Services' and 'Mobile Data Services.'" Definition from http://wireless.fcc.gov/services/cellular.
dark fiber	Fiber strands placed in conduit within a network but not connected to any other network elements.
DBS	Direct broadcast satellite. Video programming services offered over GEO satellites. DirecTV and Dish Network are the most popular DBS services in North America.
dial-around service	Also known as 10-10 services. These services require the user to enter the digits 1-0-1 and then a four-digit number that usually starts with 0 in order to reach a different long-distance service from the one to which the line is presubscribed.
DLEC	Data local exchange carrier. A variant on the CLEC theme, DLECs generally offer only data services, such as DSL. (See CLEC.)
DOCSIS	Data over cable service interface specification. Developed by CableLabs, the cable industry research consortium. DOCSIS "defines interface requirements for cable modems involved in high-speed data distribution over cable television system networks." Definition from www.cablemodem.com.

DSL	Digital subscriber line. General term for data services that use the high-frequency portion of a local loop (above the voice frequencies) to offer data services. Variants include SDSL (Symmetric), ADSL (Asymmetric), IDSL (DSL over ISDN). (See ADSL.)
Ethernet	The most common local area network protocol, controls communication between individual computers, hubs, and routers. Now also used in metropolitan area networks.
facilities-based carrier	A telecommunications service provider that owns substantially all of the equipment and transmission media used to provide service.
FCC	Federal Communications Commission. "The Federal Communications Commission (FCC) is an independent United States government agency, directly responsible to Congress. The FCC was established by the Communications Act of 1934 and is charged with regulating interstate and international communications by radio, television, wire, satellite and cable. The FCC's jurisdiction covers the fifty states, the District of Columbia, and U.S. possessions." Definition from http://www.fcc.gov/aboutus.html.
fiber optics	Transmission medium that uses pulses or waves of light to transmit signals between stations on a circuit. Differentiated from copper wires that use electrical signals.
Gb/s	Gigabits per second. Used to indicate the line speed of a digital telecommunications circuit. One Gb/s equals 1,000,000,000 bits delivered for every second of continuous transmission. (See also Kb/s, Mb/s, and Tb/s.)
GEO	Geosynchronous earth orbit. Satellites in orbit 22,500 miles above the equator. At that altitude, the satellites orbit the earth at the same speed the earth rotates; thus, the satellites always appear to be in the same place relative to an antenna on Earth. (See also LEO.)

HFC	Hybrid fiber-coaxial. Network architecture used to replace traditional, all-coaxial cable networks. Uses a fiber-optic feeder cable to connect coaxial cable in neighborhoods (distribution cable) with regional head-end facilities.
hosting	The placement of data centers near Internet access points to house computer servers that are frequently accessed from the Internet.
ILEC	Incumbent local exchange carrier. Former monopoly providers of local telephony services. Each of the RBOCs is an ILEC. Within the category of ILECs, in addition to the RBOCs, are many independent phone companies. They are called independent because they were never part of the Bell System.
impairment standard	Used to define which network elements must be made available by ILECs to CLECs. CLECs in general must be unable to do business (impaired) without access to the network element in order for the ILEC to be required to offer it.
intangible assets	Also called goodwill. An accounting term used to present the difference between the price paid for an asset, usually another business, and any otherwise identifiable value of the purchased asset. (Definition from Chapter 10.)
integrated carrier	A carrier that offered service that fit into more than one of the "walled gardens." For example, nTelos is an integrated carrier offering traditional ILEC services as well as mobile, CLEC, and DLEC services.
interexchange carrier	A long-distance service provider.
IP	Internet protocol. Defines standards for data organization, routing, and services on the Internet and similar networks.
IRU	Indefeasible right to use. Prior to the second race, IRUs were the most common type of long-term contract used to lease bandwidth or fibers owned by another carrier. These transactions were particularly

popular in the undersea cable market (definition from Chapter 4).

ISDN	Integrated services digital network. Implemented by the RBOCs in the late 1980s and early 1990s, ISDN offered advanced voice features and higher data transmission rates than traditional voice lines.
ISP	Internet service provider. A carrier that offers connections to the Internet over either dial-up or leased lines.
junk bonds	Sold by borrowers that have less-than-perfect credit or no credit history. Junk bonds typically carry interest rates that are higher than those paid by more creditworthy borrowers. They were used to finance most of the excess network building by carriers beginning in the late 1990s.
Kb/s	Kilobits per second. Used to indicate the line speed of a digital telecommunications circuit. One Kb/s equals 1,000 bits delivered for every second of continuous transmission. (See also Gb/s, Mb/s, and Tb/s.)
KHz	Kilohertz. A measure of frequency equal to 1,000 cycles per second.
LATA	Local access and transport area. After AT&T's first divestiture, geographic boundaries were placed around local areas by state regulators to define the scope of the ILEC service area. Any call or circuit that originated and terminated within a LATA was handled by the ILEC. Any circuit or call that crossed a LATA boundary was handled by a long-distance carrier.
LEO	Low-earth orbit. Satellites flying up to 1,000 miles above the earth. LEO satellites solved some of the delay and echo problems inherent in GEO satellite transmission but still proved too expensive to be commercially viable. (See also GEO.)
line sharing	Also called frequency unbundling. A capability in which the high-frequency portion of a telephone line can be used to support DLEC DSL service while the

voice (lower-frequency) portion of the line supports ILEC telephony service.

LMDS

Local multipoint distribution service. Frequency used for fixed-wireless-data transmission. The FCC's rules allow for two-way data transmission in the LMDS frequency bands. The LMDS spectrum was auctioned by the FCC in 1998.

market capitalization

Current price of a company's shares times the total number of shares outstanding.

Mb/s

Megabits per second. Used to indicate the line speed of a digital telecommunications circuit. One Mb/s equals 1,000,000 bits delivered for every second of continuous transmission. (See also Gb/s, Kb/s, and Tb/s.)

Metcalfe's Law

First expressed by Robert Metcalfe, founder of 3Com. States that the utility of a network can be expressed as the square of the number of connected users. In other words, as more people are connected to a network, it becomes significantly more valuable.

MFJ

Modified Final Judgment. Also called the AT&T consent decree. The final order of Judge Harold Greene governing AT&T's first divestiture and the post-divestiture relationship among the RBOCs and AT&T. The MFJ regulation of the former Bell system was replaced with the Telecommunications Act of 1996.

MHz

Megahertz. A measure of frequency equal to 1,000,000 cycles per second.

MMDS

Multichannel, multipoint distribution service. Fixed wireless service originally used to transmit analog video signals. The FCC's rules now allow for two-way data transmission in the MMDS frequency bands.

Moore's Law

As stated by Gordon Moore of Intel, asserts that the price performance of computer processors doubles every eighteen months. Thus, the same chip will fall in price by half in eighteen months or the same dollar amount will buy double the chip speed every eighteen months.

MSO

Multisystem operator. A cable company that owns or operates in more than one franchise area. Typically used to refer to the largest cable companies.

NSFnet

National Science Foundation network. Predecessor of today's Internet. The National Science Foundation took over the management of the nonmilitary side of ARPAnet in the late 1980s and operated the network for commercial, educational, and scientific purposes.

OC-n

Optical Carrier-n, where n indicates the number of optical subcarriers, each subcarrier capable of carrying one T-3 circuit. (See T-3.)

packet switching

Packet switches break digital signals into sections (packets) that are then transmitted with header information so that the receiving station can put them back together. The packets created from one circuit are interleaved with packets from other circuits to make more efficient use of the bandwidth available between points on the network.

packet voice

(See VoIP.)

PCS

Personal communication service. "Personal communications service (PCS) encompasses a wide variety of mobile, portable and ancillary communications services to individuals and businesses. The [FCC] broadly defined PCS as mobile and fixed communications offerings that serve individuals and businesses, and can be integrated with a variety of competing networks. The spectrum allocated to PCS is divided into three major categories: (1) broadband, (2) narrowband, and (3) unlicensed." Definition from http://wireless.fcc.gov/services/narrowband pcs/. PCS spectrum is generally referred to separately from traditional cellular spectrum, known as CRS.

Ponzi scheme

Named after Carlo (Charles) Ponzi. A scheme where investors are promised above market returns and are paid the returns using the capital of later investors rather than from investment earnings.

POTS

Plain old telephone service. Traditional analog voice telephony.

powerline networking	A technique for using electrical supply lines to and within a home to deliver data signals.
PSTN	Public switched telephone network. Generally, reference term for the voice networks of all the interconnected telephone companies in the world. Specifically used to refer to interconnection that allows a given voice network to offer call terminations to all validly dialed telephone numbers.
PTT	Post, telephone, and telegraph companies. Before 1980, in most countries outside the United States, there was one communications company owned by the government that served all local and domestic long-distance needs within the country. These national carriers (Telefónica de España in Spain, France Telecom for France, etc.) generally served the international market with two notable exceptions: Cable and Wireless in the United Kingdom and Kokusai Denshin Denwa in Japan were separate companies from the domestic PTTs, British Telecom in the United Kingdom and Nippon Telegraph and Telephone in Japan. Any carrier wanting PSTN connections into a country needed interconnect agreements with the PTT in that country.
R&D	Research and development.
RBOC	Regional Bell operating company. Prior to its first divestiture, AT&T was the majority owner of twenty-two local operating companies, typically known as the Bell operating companies, or BOCs. At divestiture, the BOCs were grouped into seven companies of roughly equal size. These seven companies were designed to be the providers of monopoly local service after divestiture while AT&T kept all of the other operations of the Bell system. Table A-1 shows the original BOCs with their assignment to one of the RBOCs.
reciprocal compensation	Payments made between local carriers to compensate one for terminating the other's calls.

TABLE A-1.
ASSIGNMENT OF PRE-DIVESTITURE BOCs TO POST-DIVESTITURE RBOCs.

RBOC	PACIFIC TELESIS	USWEST	SOUTHWESTERN BELL	AMERITECH	BELLSOUTH	BELL ATLANTIC	NYNEX
BOCs	Pacific Bell	Pacific Northwest Bell	Southwestern Bell	Wisconsin Bell	Southern Bell	Chesapeake & Potomac (C&P) Telephone	New York Telephone
	Nevada Bell	Mountain Bell		Illinois Bell	South Central Bell	C&P of Virginia	New England Bell
		Northwest Bell		Indiana Bell		C&P of Maryland	
				Michigan Bell		C&P of West Virginia	
				Ohio Bell		Bell of Pennsylvania	
						Diamond State Telephone	
						New Jersey Bell	

resellers	General term for carriers that use other companies' networks to provide service; not a facilities-based carrier.
roaming	The ability to use a mobile phone on another network in areas where the phone's mobile carrier does not have network.
SDH	Synchronous digital hierarchy. Standard protocol and signal format for fiber-optic systems outside the United States.
SG&A	Selling, general, and administrative expenses. Generally composed of overhead expenses borne by a corporation.
SONET	Synchronous optical NETwork. Standard protocol and signal format for fiber-optic systems within the United States.
spectrum	Bands of radio frequency allocated to a given use by the FCC.
T-1	Designates digital circuits that have a capacity of 1.544 Mb/s, also known as data speed one, or DS-1.

	T-1 circuits are capable of carrying twenty-four voice channels of 64 Kb/s each.
T-3	Designates digital circuits that have a capacity of 45 Mb/s, also known as data speed three, or DS-3. T-3 circuits are capable of carrying twenty-eight T-1 circuits.
take rate	The number of customers who subscribe to a service divided by the total number who have the service available to them.
Tb/s	Terabits per second. One Tb/s equals 1,000,000,000,000 bits delivered for every second of continuous transmission. (See also Gb/s, Kb/s, and Mb/s.)
TSR	Total service resale. TSR involves the rental by a CLEC of an entire local telephone service. The rented service is resold by a CLEC to an end customer. TSR is one of the ways ILECs were required to support CLECs. The other is with unbundled network elements. (See UNE.)
UNE	Unbundled network element. With UNEs, a CLEC can specify only which elements of the local loop it needs to provide a local service. Also called UNE-P for unbundled network element—platform. UNE is one of the ways ILECs were required to support CLECs. The other is with total service resale. (See TSR.)
USF	Universal service fund. Taxes on communications services fund this government-sponsored program of charges and cross-subsidies designed to make basic telecommunications services affordable to all who want the service.
VoIP	Voice over Internet protocol. Service involving transmitting voice signals over a packet data network, usually the Internet.

APPENDIX B

BANKRUPT TELECOMMUNICATIONS CARRIERS, 1988 TO 2003

COMPANY	INDUSTRY SEGMENT	DATE FILED
Classic Communications	Cable	11/13/2001
Century Communications Corp.	Cable	6/10/2002
Adelphia Communications Corp.	Cable	6/25/2002
James Cable Partners	Cable	6/26/2003
USN Communications Inc.	CLEC	2/18/1999
GST Telecommunications Inc.	CLEC	5/17/2000
American Metrocomm	CLEC	8/16/2000
ICG Communications	CLEC	11/14/2000
NorthPoint Communications Inc.	CLEC	1/16/2001
Vitts Networks Inc.	CLEC	2/7/2001
e.spire Communications Inc.	CLEC	3/22/2001
Winstar Communications Inc.	CLEC	4/18/2001
Teligent Communications LLC	CLEC	5/21/2001
2nd Century Communications	CLEC	6/1/2001
Rhythms NetConnections Inc.	CLEC	8/1/2001
VelocityHSI	CLEC	8/14/2001
Covad	CLEC	8/15/2001
NetVoice Technologies	CLEC	10/17/2001
Net2000 Communications Inc.	CLEC	11/16/2001
DTI Holdings	CLEC	12/31/2001
Network Plus Corp.	CLEC	2/4/2002
YipesCommunications	CLEC	3/21/2002
Mpower	CLEC	4/8/2002
Convergent Communications Inc.	CLEC	4/19/2002
Advanced Telcom Group	CLEC	5/2/2002
Metromedia Fiber Network	CLEC	5/20/2002
XO Communications Inc.	CLEC	6/17/2002
Neon Communications Inc.	CLEC	6/25/2002

Log On America	CLEC	7/12/2002
CTC Communications Group Inc.	CLEC	10/3/2002
Supra Telecommunications	CLEC	10/23/2002
Allegiance Telecom Inc.	CLEC	5/14/2003
CAI Wireless	Fixed wireless	7/30/1998
Heartland Wireless Communications Inc.	Fixed wireless	12/4/1998
Wireless One Inc.	Fixed wireless	2/11/1999
Advanced Radio Telecom Corp.	Fixed wireless	4/20/2001
BroadLink Wireless Inc.	Fixed wireless	6/25/2002
Swiftcomm Inc.	Fixed wireless	5/2/2003
OpTel Inc.	Integrated	10/28/1999
McLeodUSA Inc	Integrated	1/30/2002
Logix Communications Enterprises Inc.	Integrated	2/28/2002
Western Integrated Networks	Integrated	3/11/2002
ITC-DeltaCom	Integrated	6/25/2002
Birch Telecom	Integrated	7/29/2002
nTelos Inc.	Integrated	3/4/2003
Telegroup Inc.	International	2/10/1999
Pacific Gateway Exchange Inc.	International	12/29/2000
Star Telecommunications Inc.	International	3/13/2001
RSL Communications Ltd.	International	3/19/2001
Ursus Telecom Corp.	International	4/6/2001
World Access Inc.	International	4/24/2001
Telscape International Inc.	International	4/27/2001
Viatel Inc.	International	5/2/2001
GRG Inc.	International	8/7/2001
Pensat Inc.	International	10/9/2001
Startec Global Communications Corp.	International	12/14/2001
FLAG Telecom Holdings Ltd.	International	4/12/2002
Teleglobe Holdings (US) Corp.	International	5/15/2002
Asia Global Crossing Ltd.	International	11/18/2002
ATSI Communications Inc.	International	2/4/2003
PSINet Inc.	ISP	5/31/2001
Internet Commerce and Communications	ISP	7/31/2001
Wavve Telecommunications	ISP	8/15/2001
@Home Corporation	ISP	9/29/2001
Ardent Communications	ISP	10/10/2001
LogicSouth Corp.	ISP	1/7/2002
Globix	ISP	3/1/2002

Genuity	ISP	11/27/2002
Focal Communications Corp.	ISP	12/19/2002
FASTNET Corp	ISP	6/10/2003
ALC Communications	Long-distance	6/29/1992
Value-Added	Long-distance	10/10/1995
In-flight Phone Corp.	Long-distance	1/24/1997
Total World Telecommunications Inc.	Long-distance	7/23/1997
Midcom Communications Inc.	Long-distance	11/7/1997
SA Telecommunications Inc.	Long-distance	11/19/1997
EqualNet Corp.	Long-distance	9/10/1998
UStel Inc.	Long-distance	3/10/1999
Incomnet Inc.	Long-distance	9/2/1999
EqualNet Communications Corp.	Long-distance	8/9/2000
Pathnet Telecommunications	Long-distance	4/2/2001
eGlobe Inc.	Long-distance	4/18/2001
360networks Inc.	Long-distance	6/28/2001
Dialpad Communications Inc.	Long-distance	12/19/2001
Global Crossing	Long-distance	1/28/2002
Williams Communications Group Inc.	Long-distance	4/22/2002
Velocita	Long-distance	5/30/2002
WorldCom Inc.	Long-distance	7/21/2002
Touch America Holdings Inc.	Long-distance	6/19/2003
MobileMedia Corp.	Paging	1/30/1997
Paging Network Inc.	Paging	7/24/2000
Weblink Wireless Inc.	Paging	5/23/2001
Arch Wireless	Paging	12/6/2001
Metrocall	Paging	6/3/2002
StarBand	Satellite—GEO	5/31/2002
Loral Space & Communications Ltd.	Satellite—GEO	7/15/2003
Globalstar Telecommunications Ltd.	Satellite—LEO	9/14/1998
Iridium LLC	Satellite—LEO	8/13/1999
ICO Global Communications (Holdings) Ltd.	Satellite—LEO	8/27/1999
Orbcomm Global LP	Satellite—LEO	9/15/2000
Globalstar LP	Satellite—LEO	2/15/2002
NextWave Personal Communications Inc.	Wireless	6/8/1998
Geotek Communications Inc.	Wireless	6/29/1998
iPCS Inc.	Wireless	2/23/2003
Leap Wireless International Inc.	Wireless	4/13/2003
Horizon PCS Inc.	Wireless	8/15/2003

INDEX